European Distance and E-Learning Network Annual Conference (EDEN 2015)

Expanding Learning Scenarios – Opening Out the Educational Landscape

Barcelona, Spain
9 – 12 June 2015

Editors:

Antonio Moreira Teixeira
Andras Szucs
Ildiko Mazar

ISBN: 978-1-5108-5021-7

Printed from e-media with permission by:

Curran Associates, Inc.
57 Morehouse Lane
Red Hook, NY 12571

Some format issues inherent in the e-media version may also appear in this print version.

Printed by Curran Associates, Inc. (2018)

European Distance and E-Learning Network (EDEN)
Budapest University of Technology & Economics
H-1111 Budapest, Egry J. u.1.
Hungary

Phone: +36 1 463 1628
Fax: +36 1 463 1858

secretariat@eden-online.org

Additional copies of this publication are available from:

Curran Associates, Inc.
57 Morehouse Lane
Red Hook, NY 12571 USA
Phone: 845-758-0400
Fax: 845-758-2633
Email: curran@proceedings.com
Web: www.proceedings.com

EDEN 2015 ANNUAL Conference

Expanding Learning Scenarios

Opening Out the Educational Landscape

EDEN 2015 Annual Conference

Barcelona, Spain

9-12 June 2015

BOOK OF ABSTRACTS

Including the Collection of "Synergy" Synopses

Edited by

António Moreira Teixeira, András Szűcs and Ildikó Mázár
on behalf of the European Distance and E-Learning Network

European Distance and E-Learning Network, 2015

EDEN 2015 Annual Conference
Barcelona, Spain

Published by the European Distance and E-Learning Network

Editors:

António Moreira Teixeira
András Szűcs
Ildikó Mázár

Editorial co-ordination:

Anna Wagner

EDEN Secretariat, c/o Budapest University of Technology and Economics
H-1111 Budapest, Egry J. u. 1, Hungary
Tel: (36) 1 463 1628, 463 2537
E-mail: secretariat@eden-online.org
http://www.eden-online.org

Supported by the
Erasmus+ Programme of
the European Union

Conference organised in collaboration with

Universitat Oberta de Catalunya

Introduction – Expanded learning scenarios: What Society Would Expect – What Digital Pedagogy can Offer?

The landscape of learning has changed substantially over the past few years. The ever-improving performance of mobile devices and the development of networking infrastructure continue to increase the appeal of new powerful educational tools. The rapid spread of technologies, reflected in their untameable demand and use, the momentous development of research as well as practices inevitably transform the information society – mostly outside of institutional settings and often along unexpected pathways.

The increased amount, improved quality and open accessibility of digital learning content are furthering rapid transformation of user habits and the social impact of new technologies in education. The re-interpretation of the terms 'openness' and 'resource management' have altered socio-economic and cultural aspects considerably. New educational business models and stakeholder alliances emerge, supported by fresh social and economic demands, scale, and clusters of interest.

All of this places new challenges on the educational system. The education and training sector needs to improve its efficiency by scaling up innovative solutions to better meet the current requirements of society. Research and innovative projects often deal with systematic data analysis, smart observations and validation. New functions and interactions between learners, teachers, researchers and managers emerge and shape the processes more than ever before.

How can the progressive and innovative academic and professional international community contribute in 2015 to a better understanding of the above expansion of the educational landscape? The traditional classroom is no longer an ideal place for education. We are living in a time when a collaborative learning culture blends with an ever more hybrid technological environment. There are great opportunities for, and availabilities of, modern solutions. Meanwhile, we are missing achievements in the burning issues of employment, corporate co-operations, anticipating and preparing for the jobs of the future, and strengthening vocational and in-company learning.

For Europe, as the focus of the new educational programme Erasmus+ indicates, priorities include serious enhancement of mobility in the education and training sector. This implies an impact for the increased and better use of ICTs (virtual mobility), which is a challenge for the field of learning innovation.

Conference themes help to understand and exploit the stimulating progress in the field, like: Multiculturality in the classroom – Intersection between higher education and MOOCs – Users as creators and curators of learning resources – Sharing open activities between higher educational institutions – Sustainable business models for openness in education – Learning analytics from learners' perspective – Data-driven learning personalisation – Empowering learners: Promoting self assessment and reflection – Tools for crowd participation and peer support – Scaling up pedagogies for crowd learning – Changing leadership models and practices – Challenges of diversity to learning and teaching.

The Conference Host and Partner is the Universitat Oberta de Catalunya (UOC), a truly innovative institution. Rooted in Catalonia and open to the world, the world's first online university is sensitive to the diversity of the global environment and committed to empowering development and social change through education. UOC at the Conference celebrates its 20th Anniversary with special sessions, reflecting on the contemporary challenges in our field.

András Szűcs
Secretary General

António Moreira Teixeira
EDEN President

Acknowledgement and thanks are given to the Programme and Evaluation Committee

António Moreira Teixeira, EDEN President, Open University, Lisbon, Portugal
Josep Planell, Universitat Oberta de Catalunya, Spain

Diana Andone, Politehnica University of Timisoara, Romania

Julia Minguillon Alfonso, Universitat Oberta de Catalunya – UOC, Spain

Christine Appel, Universitat Oberta de Catalunya – UOC, Spain

Deborah Arnold, University of Burgundy, France

Ari-Matti Auvinen, HCI Productions Ltd., Finland

Ulrich Bernath, Ulrich Bernath Foundation for Research in ODL, Germany

Lisa Marie Blaschke, Carl von Ossietzky University of Oldenburg, Germany

Mark Brown, Dublin City University, Ireland

Alan Bruce, Universal Learning Systems, Ireland

Cristobal Cobo, University of Oxford, UK

Grainne Conole, Bath Spa University, UK

Helga Dorner, Central European University, Hungary

Josep M. Duart, Chief Editor, RUSC, Universitat Oberta de Catalunya – UOC, Spain

Thomas Fischer, MENON Network EEIG, Belgium

Anne Gaskell, St Edmund's College Cambridge, United Kingdom

Inés Gil-Jaurena, Editor for Open Praxis, Universidad Nacional de Educación a Distancia, Spain

Lurdes Guardia, Universitat Oberta de Catalunya - UOC, Spain

Mehmet Kesim, Anadolu University, Turkey

Ene Koitla, Estonian Information Technology Foundation, Estonia

Sandra Kucina Softic, University of Zagreb, Croatia

Gila Kurtz, The Center for Academic Studies Or Yehuda, Israel

Michael Grahame Moore, The Pennsylvania State University, USA

Rory McGreal, Athabasca University, Canada

Som Naidu, The University of Melbourne, Australia

Fabio Nascimbeni, MENON Network, Belgium

Don Olcott, Universtiy of Maryland University College, USA

Ebba Ossiannilsson, Lund University, Sweden

Antonella Poce, University Roma III, Italy

Serge Ravet, ADPIOS, France

Albert Sangra, Universitat Oberta de Catalunya – UOC, Spain

Christian-Andreas Schumann, University of Applied Sciences Zwickau, Germany

Alfredo Soeiro, University of Porto, Portugal

Sofoklis Sotiriou, Ellinogermaniki Agogi, Greece

Andras Szucs, Secretary General, EDEN, UK

Alan Tait, The Open University, UK

TABLE OF CONTENTS

LEARNING THEORY, POLICY, GOVERNANCE AND THE IMPLEMENTATION PRACTICE

Applying Biggs Constructive Alignment to Online Interdisciplinary Education ... 1
Lina Xue, Gaëlle Le Bot, Wim Van Petegem, Astrid Van Wieringen, KU Leuven, Belgium

Micro-Innovations and Stakeholders Engagement as Drivers for Systemic Change in ICT-Supported Learning ... 2
Fabio Nascimbeni, Edison Spina, Universidade de Sao Paulo, Brazil

Visuality as a Tool for Expanding Learning ... 3
András Benedek, Budapest University of Technology and Economics, Hungary

In Search of Leadership: Innovative Approaches to Building Adaptive Learning Communities ... 4
Don Olcott, Jr., Charles Sturt University, Australia, Lisa Marie Blaschke, Carl von Ossietzky University of Oldenburg, Germany

Learners – Not Systems – Are the Value Creators ... 5
Ari-Matti Auvinen, HCI Productions Oy, Finland

Digital Learning in Irish Higher Education: Integrating Strategic and Leadership Perspectives into a Roadmap for Digital Capacity ... 6
Jim Devine, DEVINE Policy | Projects | Innovation, Terry Maguire, National Forum for the Enhancement of Teaching and Learning in Higher Education, Ireland

Strategies of Technology Usage in Lifelong Learning Programs ... 7
Helge Fischer, Matthias Heinz, Thomas Koehler, Dresden University of Technology, Germany

The Impact of an Ethics of Care on the Iron Triangle in ODL ... 8
Paul Prinsloo, University of South Africa, South Africa

Pedagogy as a Techné: Meaningful ICT Integration in Formal Learning Scenarios ... 9
Ana Mouta, Ana Paulino, João Ferreira, Filipe Couto, JP-inspiring knowledge, Portugal

E-Learning via Synchronous Communication- Experiences from a Learning Study Course in Higher Education ... 10
Eva Edman Stålbrandt, Kajsa Falkner, Stockholm University, Sweden

Coherence of Accelerated Transformations and Expanded Learning Scenarios ... 11
Christian-Andreas Schumann, Claudia Tittmann, Helge Gerischer, Anne Götze, West Saxon University of Zwickau, Germany, Feng Xiao, Tongji Universty Shanghai, China, Jana Weber, Technische Universittät Berlin, Germany

Digital, Material and Networked: Some Emerging Themes for Set Education ... 12
Sarah Davies, Elaine Thomas, Steve Walker, The Open University, United Kingdom

Online Digital Games and Education for Sustainable Development: A Controversial Relationship? ... 13
Antonia Boniati, Georgia Liarakou, Costas Tsolakidis, University of the Aegean, Costas Gavrilakis, University of Ioannina, Greece

MOOCS: ENRICHING AND CONSOLIDATING THE EXPERIENCE

The Online Learners in MOOC Social Environments ... 14
Udi Shimony, Anat Cohen, Rafi Nachmias, Tal Soffer, Tel Aviv University, Israel

Building Better MOOCs: Using Design Patterns for Massive Open Online Course Development ... 15
Steven Warburton, University of Surrey, United Kingdom; Yishay Mor, PAU Education, Spain

The Boot Camp Module in Massive Open Online Courses: Experiences in Two European Initiatives ... 16
Diana Morais, Maria João Leal, Maria João Spilker, Lina Morgado, Universidade Aberta, Portugal

A Peer-Mentoring Approach for the Continuous Professional Development of Educators in a MOOC Setting 17
Muriel Garreta, Universitat Oberta de Catalunya, Spain, Gemma Aguado, Consultant, Spain, Yishay Mor, Consultant, United Kingdom, Carles Fernandez, Consultant, Spain, Katerina Riviou, Ellinogermaniki Agogi, Greece

Courses of the Bavarian Virtual University Facing MOOCs 18
Regine Prem, Christina Stötzel, Bavarian Virtual University, Germany

What to Do About MOOCs? Beyond the Fear of Missing Out 19
Mark Brown, Eamon Costello, Mairéad Nic Giolla Mhichíl, Colette Kirwan, Dublin City University, Enda Donlon, Mater Dei Institute of Education, Ireland

Gamifying Massive Open Online Courses with ELGG: An Experimental Strategy Designed for the ECO Project 20
Antonio Garcia-Cabot, Eva Garcia-Lopez, University of Alcala, Spain, António Moreira Teixeira, Universidade Aberta & University of Lisbon, Portugal, Luis de-Marcos, University of Alcala, Spain, José Mota, LEaD, Portugal

OpenSNH – Developing an OER Open Repository Towards mOOC 21
Mats Brenner, University of Gävle, J. Ola Lindberg, Mid Sweden University, Sweden

Extending MOOC Capabilities with Dedicated Networks: The e-Portfolio Training Case 22
Marcelo Maina, Loudes Guàrdia and Ivan Alsina, Univesitat Oberta de Catalunya, Spain

The Potential and the Challenges of the Open Web in the Doctoral Journey: The Goal Orientations of Italian and UK PhD Students 23
Antonella Esposito, University of Milan, Italy, Albert Sangrà, Marcelo Maina, Open University of Catalonia, Spain

LEARNING DATA AND ANALYTICS

Evaluating Weekly Predictions of At-Risk Students at The Open University: Results and Issues 24
Drahomira Herrmannova, Martin Hlosta, The Open University, United Kingdom, Jakub Kuzilek, Zdenek Zdrahal, The Open University, United Kingdom, and CIIRC, Czech Technical University, Czech Republic

Student Vulnerability and Agency in Networked, Digital Learning 25
Paul Prinsloo, University of South Africa, South Africa, Sharon Slade, The Open University, United Kingdom

Stemming the Flow: Improving Retention for Distance Learning Students 26
Sharon Slade, The Open University, United Kingdom, Paul Prinsloo, University of South Africa, South Africa

Contribution of Normative Stakeholder Theory to an Educational Data Warehousing Project 27
Gábor Kismihók, Dávid Szörényi, University of Amsterdam, Netherlands

Learning Analytics of a MOOC with a Terminal Efficiency of 22.35% 28
Lorena Yadira Alemán de la Garza, Tecnológico de Monterrey, Mexico, Teresa Sancho Vinuesa, Universitat Oberta de Catalunya, Spain, Marcela Georgina Gómez Zermeño, Tecnológico de Monterrey, Mexico

Web-Based Analysis of Student Activity for Predicting Dropout 29
Anat Cohen, Tel Aviv University, Israel

Win, Win, Win: An Assessment System that Works for Students, Staff and the Academy 30
Danny Carroll, UNSW Business School, Australia

EVALUATION AND ASSESSMENT

10 Key Criteria to Manage and Sustain e-Feedback in Written Assignments 31
Teresa Guasch, Anna Espasa, M. Rosa Mayordomo, Open University of Catalonia, Spain

360º E-Assessment: An Online Collaborative Process in the Scenario of the Open University of Catalonia (UOC) 32
Montse Guitert, Teresa Romeu, Marc Romero, Universitat Oberta de Catalunya, Spain

Open Badges, a New Standard in the Expanding Learning Landscape 33
Eric Rousselle, Discendum Oy, Finland

Measuring a Critical Impact on Technology in Education: A Tool for OERs Evaluation 34
Antonella Poce, Francesco Agrusti, Università Roma TRE, Italy

Realizing the Potential of Competency-Based Learning and Badges 35
Deborah Everhart, Georgetown University and Blackboard, United States of America

PDPIE Framework: Online Course Development Quality Cycle 36
Afsaneh Sharif, University of British Columbia, Canada, Merce Gisbert, Universitat Rovira I Virgil, Spain

A Quality Scorecard for the Administration of Online Learning Programs in Higher Education 37
Kaye Shelton, Lamar University and Online Learning Consortium, United States of America

How Assessment Technology can Develop to Address the Current Challenges of Academic Integrity 38
William Dorman, Kryterion Inc., Rick Shearer, Penn State University, United States of America

LEARNING FOR AND AT THE WORKPLACE

Using MOOCs to Train the Next Generation of Web Entrepreneurs: Challenges and Opportunities 39
Eulalia Canals, Universitat Oberta de Catalunya, Spain, Yishay Mor, P.A.U. Education, United Kingdom

Competences and Skills for 21st Century Digital Media Professionals 40
Mathy Vanbuel, ATiT, Frauke Hein, ATiT, K.U.Leuven, Belgium

The 'Boomerang Effect': How Outsourcing Impacts on the Workload of Academics 41
Thomas Hülsmann, Britta Zawada, UNISA, South Africa

Teaching 21st Century Entrepreneurial Competences Using a Problem Based Approach 42
Ingrid le Roux, University of Pretoria, South Africa

Designing Applications to Support Mobile Work Based Learning in the Construction Industry 43
Graham Attwell, Pontydysgu, United Kingdom, Joanna Burchert, Bremen University, Germany, Raymond Elferink, Raycom, Netherlands, Gilbert Peffer, CINME, Spain

Building and Maintaining Operational Skills During Complex Change – A World Bank Group Staff Learning Case Study44
Darlene Christopher, East Asia Region, Jennifer Ross Gildee, Europe & Central Asia Region, Jeanette Murry, South Asia Region, World Bank

ICT ENHANCED LEARNING METHODOLOGY

Teachers' CPD Programme in Fostering Competences – Communities of Practice Support Mechanisms 45
Katerina Riviou, Sofoklis Sotiriou, Ellinogermaniki Agogi, Lamprini Kolovou, Antonis Ramfos, Intrasoft International, Greece

Inclusion's Final Frontier: Universal Design for Learning – ICT and Innovation in Transformative Education 46
Alan Bruce, Universal Learning Systems, Ireland

Distance Education in European Higher Education Institutions: Analysing Mechanisms for Increasing Participation of Adult Learners 47
Angela Owusu-Boampong, UNESCO Institute for Lifelong Learning, Germany, Carl Holmberg, ICDE, Sweden, Monique Udnæs, ICDE, Norway

Video-Based Learning in Higher Education: The Flipped or the Hands-On Classroom? 48
Laia Albó, Davinia Hernández-Leo, Jaume Barcelo, Luis Sanabria-Russo, Universitat Pompeu Fabra, Spain

Mastering the Blend: Students' Value of Classroom and Online Components in a Blended Accounting Course 49
Lynette Nagel, Louwtjie Venter, University of Pretoria, South Africa

Evaluating the Quality of Students Actions in a Distance Learning Programming Language Academic Discipline 50
Elizabeth S. Carvalho, Adérito F. Marcos, Universidade Aberta, Portugal

LEARNER NEEDS AND PERCEPTIONS

The Urban Game MobiGeo: Students Perceptions on Potential and Constraints of an Mobile Outdoor Education 51
Liliana Vieira, Clara Coutinho, Minho University, Portugal

Types of Participants' Behaviors in a Massive Open Online Course 52
Tali Kahan, Tal Soffer, Rafi Nachmias, Tel Aviv University, Israel

An Approach to Digital Learners in a Catalonian Public Face-To-Face University 53
Eliana E. Gallardo-Echenique, Luis Marqués-Molías, Universitat Rovira i Virgili, Spain, Mark Bullen, University of British Columbia, Canada

Learners' Behaviours and Autonomy in Livemocha and Busuu Online Communities 54
Maria Luisa Malerba, Open University of Catalonia, Spain

Mobile Technologies and Changing Learner Characteristics and Preferences: Teachers' Perceptions........ 55
Kwok-Wing Lai, Lee Smith, University of Otago, New Zealand

Flipped Learning: The Gateway to Learner Autonomy 56
Amany Atef, Hamdan Bin Mohammed Smart University, United Arab Emirates

Empowering Students by Co-Designing Expanded Learning Scenarios 57
Iolanda Garcia, Elena Barberà and Ingrid Noguera, Universitat Oberta de Catalunya, Spain

Making It Mobile: Changing Approaches to Clinical Learning Environments 58
Daniel Puntis, Laura Delgaty, Jennifer Hoban, Newcastle University, United Kingdom

Medical Students' Perceptions of Social Media (Sample of Hacettepe University)........ 59
Baris Sezer, Sukriye Ece Abay, Hacettepe University, Nezaket Bilge Basusta, Mersin University, Turkey

Pedagogical Models Student Voices: Innovative for Course Design 60
June Breivik, The Norwegian Business School BI, Norway

Lecture vs Webinar: Engagement and Distraction in Distance Learning Adult Teachers 61
M. E. Cigognini, INDIRE, G. Paoletti, R. Fattorini, M. Boscarol, University of Trieste, Italy

Teacher's Technology Use and Attitude Towards e-Learning in Higher Education 62
Sandra Kučina Softić, University of Zagreb, Croatia

Expanding Blended Learning Scenarios: How to Empower Adult Learners to Persist? 63
Ellen Van Twembeke, Katie Goeman, Luc De Grez, Jan Elen, KU Leuven, Belgium

User Perceptions on Relevance of a Learning Management System: An Evaluation of Behavioral Intention and Usage of SciPro System at University of Rwanda........ 64
Jean Claude Byungura, Henrik Hansson, Thashmee Kharunaratne, Stockholm University, Sweden.

SOCIAL MEDIA, DIGITAL COLLABORATIVE LEARNING

Exploring Causal Relationships among Teaching, Cognitive and Social Presence in International Collaborative Seminars: Initial Findings Using the Community of Inquiry Survey........ 65
Helga Dorner, Central European University, Hungary

Towards a Collaborative Space for Learning Digital Systems 66
David Baneres, Open University of Catalonia, Spain

Creating the Digital University: Open, Collaborative Models for Strategic Pedagogic and Technical 67
Sheila MacNeill, Glasgow Caledonian University, Keith Smyth, University of the Highlands and Island, Bill Johnston, University of Strathclyde, United Kingdom

Telepresence with iPads: Learning and Collaboration in Lower Secondary Schools 68
Bente Meyer, Aalborg University, Denmark

Creative Collaboration in Online Computer-Supported Collaborative Learning 69
Margarida Romero, Université Laval, Canada, Elena Barberà, Universitat Oberta de Catalunya, Spain

MOOCs Underutilise Video, Self-Assessment, Teacher Guidance 70
Jack Koumi, Educational Media Production Training, United Kingdom

Added Values and Challenges Social Media Represent in the Hybridisation of Teacher Training 71
Anders Grov Nilsen, Aslaug Grov Almås, Stord/Haugesund University College, Norway

The Correct Use and the Dangers of Misuse of Social Networks and Different Websites within/outside the Classroom72
Gyula Hegyi, Hungary

Open Source Learning Streams in Social Media in Year 11 Math Teaching 73
Thomas Kjærgaard, Elsebeth Korsgaard Sorensen, Aalborg University, Denmark

What do students say about eportfolios: utilizing social media to expand learning scenarios 74
Lori L. Hager, University of Oregon, United States of America

Digital Identity and Personal Learning Networks (PLN) in a PhD Researchers Community 75
Nuno Ricardo Oliveira, Lina Morgado, Universidade Aberta, Portugal

DIGITAL LEARNING CASES IN INTERNATIONAL DIMENSION

ICT Integration in Education: The Greek and Spain Perspectives Amidst an Economic Crisis 76
Munir Abbasi, Georgios Xydopoulos, Masoud Fakhimi, Lampros Stergioulas, Maria Fragkaki, University of Surrey, United Kingdom, Luis Anido, Manuel Fernandez, University of Vigo, Spain, Panayiota Vassilopoulou, University of Liverpool, United Kingdom

Boldic – Open Learning Resources Online 77
Ulf Sandström, Swedish Association Distance Education, Ebba Ossiannilsson , Lund University, Sweden, Torhild Slåtto, Flexible Education Norway, Norway

OER, Open Access and Scholarship in Portuguese Higher Education 78
Paula Cardoso, Lina Morgado, António Teixeira, Universidade Aberta, Portugal

The Implementation of ICT in Secondary Schools in Catalonia 79
Jordi Serarols, Albert Sangrà, Nati Cabrera, Universitat Oberta de Catalunya, Spain

Unlocking the Potential of Public Libraries in Supporting Teaching and Learning in Open and Distance Learning in Makerere University 80
Harriet Nabushawo Mutambo, Makerere University, Uganda, Jessica Norah Aguti, Commonwealth of Learning, Canada, Mark Winterbottom, University of Cambridge, United Kingdom

Higher Education in Brasil: Academy and Operation, a Challenge or a Paradox? 81
Susane Garrido, Universidade Tuiuti do Paraná, Brasil

DISTANCE AND E-LEARNING: SOCIO-ECONOMIC AND CULTURAL ASPECTS

Ilbes: an Innovative ICT-Enabled Intergenerational Learning Approach Implemented Across EU 82
Gabriel Rissola, D-O-T Research and Consulting, Andrea Diaz Mattei, University of Barcelona & D-O-T Research and Consulting, Spain

Technology as a Vehicle for Inclusion of Learners with Attention Deficits in Mainstream Schools 83
Hanne Voldborg & Elsebeth K. Sorensen, Aalborg University, Denmark

Educommunication Practices: How to Plan and Implement Communication Management Processes for Educational Projects Mediated by Communication Technologies 84
Luci Ferraz de Mello, Universidade de São Paulo, Brazil, Universal Learning Systems, Ireland

The Influence of the Sex Variable on how Participants in a MOOC Perceive Emotions 85
Urtza Garay Ruiz, Inmaculada Maiz Olazabalaga, Carlos Castaño Garrido, Universidad del País Vasco, Spain

"I am Different from Other Women in the World" The Experiences of Saudi Arabian Women Studying Online in International Master Programmes 86
Anna Szilagyi, Laureate Online Education, Netherlands

INSTITUTIONAL DEVELOPMENT STRATEGIES AND PRACTICE

A Case Study of Polysynchronous Learning in University Bioscience Education 87
Barney Dalgarno, Lucy Webster, Charles Sturt University, Australia

Defining a Pedagogical Model: The TU Delft Online Learning Experience 88
Nelson Jorge, Sofia Dopper, Willem van Valkenburg, Delft University of Technology, The Netherlands

Augmented Reality in Online Educational Contexts: The UOC Case Study 89
Ivan Alsina-Jurnet, Lourdes Guàrdia-Ortiz, Universitat Oberta de Catalunya, Spain

Bazaar: Informal Language Learning and Exchange at Market Places 90
Thomas Fischer, Walter F. Kugemann, Ulrike Mangwa, New Technologies and Learning in Europe, Germany; Corinna Bartoletti, Elena Zecchetto, Borgorete, Italy; Julide Inozu, Cem Can, Cukurova University, Turkey; Roy Smith, The MRS Consultancy, United Kingdom; Raffaela Pascucci, Claudio Crispoltoni, Commune di Perugia, Italy; José Luiz Fernandes, E-VIA / Palco de Sombras, Portugal; Tatiana Velitchkova, DIA-SPORT Association, Bulgaria

Online Training of Trainers from the Open University, Portugal 91
Susana Henriques, Jose Antonio Moreira, Maria de Fatime Goulão, Daniela Melare Vieira Barros, Universidade Aberta, Portugal

Embedding Digital Competences in the Curriculum a Case Study on Student-Experience of an Online Technology-Enhanced, Activity-Based Learning Design 92
George Evangelinos, Debbie Holley, Anglia Ruskin University, United Kingdom

POSTERS

Methods for e-Evaluation of Bulgarian Distance Students in Library and Information Sciences 93
Marina Encheva, State University of Library Studies and Information Technologies, Bulgaria

Teachers' it Training as an Important Element in Educational Process 94
Olga Grishina, Marina Melamud, Elena Sidorova, Plekhanov Russian University of Economics, Russia

Using Smartphones in Active Learning: Entrepreneurship Behavior Taught Differently 95
Isabella Chinelato Sacramento, Sandra Regina Holanda Mariano, Universidade Federal Fluminense, Brazil

Pericles or How to Assess and to Improve Quality in Higher Education 96
Anne Boyer Loria, Gerard Casanova, Azim Roussalany, Florence Ducreau, Université de Lorraine, France

The Manager is Blogging: Blog Making as a Teaching/Learning Method 97
Sidinei Rocha-de-Oliveira, Bibiana Volkmer, Universidade Federal do Rio Grande do Sul , Sandra R.H Mariano, Universidade Federal Fluminense, Brazil

Gamification of a Social Learning Network in a Virtual University: Implementation Proposal, an Academic Network 98
Fernando Bacelar, Lina Morgado, Universidade Aberta, Portugal

Student Owned e-Portfolio P3 (Portfolio – Process – Product) Empowering Students for Professional and Personal Development Using Systematic Reflection as a Pedagogical Method, in the Health Guidance Program, Luleå University of Technology 99
Martin Karlsson, Lotta Berglund, Institution of Health Science, Sweden

Learning to Learn Competency Development with Information and Communications Technology Use: Multiple Case Study at Secondary Schools 100
Balbina Rocosa, Albert Sangrà, Nati Cabrera, Universitat Oberta de Catalunya, Spain

Rapid Development of an Electronic Logbook to Satisfy Student Practicum on Placement in Audiology 101
Pearse Murphy, Athlone Institute of Technology, Ireland

Expanding the Environment of Adult Higher Education by Promoting Workplace/University Partnerships and the Use of Information and Communication Technologies and Social Media 102
Judith O. Brown, Pamela Luckett, Barry University School of Professional and Career Education, United States of America

Assuring Graduate Capabilities: A University-Wide Strategy to Exploit Technologies for Graduate Employability 103
Beverley Oliver, Deakin University, Australia

The European Career Development Programme: Supporting Higher Education Students to Acquire Professional Awareness and Career Management Skills 104
Gigliola Paviotti, Melius Srl, Gilda Rota, University of Padua, Italy

21st Century Citizen Skills: Digital Competences in Education. Cases in Catalonia 105
Azucena Vázquez Gutiérrez, Montse Guitert Catasús, Universitat Oberta de Catalunya, Spain

Developing Professional Identity in an Online Learning Environment: Perspectives of Peer Interaction 106
Line Helverskov Horn, Aalborg University, Denmark

Perceptions Regarding Student Workload for Lifelong Learning Skills in a Random Online Short Term Environment (ROSE) 107
Keren Levy, Elaine Hoter, David Burg, Ohalo College of Education, Israel

The Integration of Information Literacy Skills into the Curriculum 108
Luis Guadarrama, Marc Cels, Cindy Ives, Corinne Bosse, Athabasca University, Canada

Citizen Involvement via Smartphone a Development Project by Students in Public Administration 109
Jakob Djurhuus Albrechtsen, Linda Hauschildt Nielsen, University College Lillebaelt, Denmark

UISEL – Ubiquitous Information for Seniors Life through Mobile Devices 110
Licia Boccaletti, Serena D'Angelo, Anziani e Non Solo Soc. Coop., Italy; Pedro Cano, José Maria Roa, APFA, Spain; L'Ubica Gasilova, FPPS, Slovakia, Denisa Lombrea, Maria Toia, IREA, Romania; Carlos Carvalho, Claudia Azevedo, Virtual Campus, Portugal, Oldrich Stanek, Zivot90, Czech Republic

A Model for Building Trust in Online Environments 111
Elaine Hoter, Ohalo College of Education and the Mofet Institute, Israel

ICT for Lifelong Learning in Armenia and Georgia 112
Arusyak Abrahamyan, Harutyun Gzraryan, State Engineering University of Armenia, Armenia, Eva Szalma, European Distance and E-Learning Network, United Kingdom, Tamar Lominadze, Georgian Technical University, Georgia, Paata Gogishvili, St. Andrew the First-Called Georgian University, Georgia, Edita Gzoyan, Aram Mirzoyan, Institute for Informatics and Automation Problems, Armenia

The Application and Practice of Information Technology in Distance Education of Shanghai Open University 113
Hong Wang, Jianfeng Hong, Shanghai Open University, Shanghai, China

Cross-Border Collaborative e-Learning: The eSCART Group Work 114
M. Zolfo, C. Kiyan, L. Jiang, B. Ingelbeen, L. Lynen ,Institute of Tropical Medicine, Belgium

Educational Apps for High School Education at National Autonomous University of Mexico 115
León Martínez Jorge, Tapia Rangel Edith, National Autonomous University of Mexico, Mexico

Role of the Research in Educational Policies and Practices in Distance Education and e-Learning at High Education Level in Portugal 116
Angelina Costa, Lina Morgado, Universidade Aberta, Portugal

Languages for Specific Purposes – Language Centres for Cultural Heritage Preservation 117
Walter Zeller, astyle, linguistic competence, Austria, Evangelia Varella, Aristotle University of Thessaloniki, Greece

Edmondo: Immersive Teaching//Learning Experiences in Italy 118
Andrea Benassi, Letizia Cinganotto, INDIRE, Italy

Math Formula Edition in LMS, Present and Future 119
Ramon Eixarch, Albert Creus, Carles Aguiló, WIRIS team, Spain

Teacher Expending Pen: ICT Integration in Teacher Education Programs 120
Davoud Masoumi, University of Gävle; Maryam Bourbour, University of Gothenburg, Sweden

Expanding Learning Spaces in Higher Education – Understanding a HyFlex Model 121
Marie Leijon, Björn Lundgren, Malmo University, Sweden

Blended Learning Design – The Potentials and Pitfalls Designing Blended Learning Courses in a Professional Bachelor Context 122
Lise Lau Pedersen, University College Lillebaelt, Denmark

Designing and Developing Courses on Literacy and Computer Information Literacy Skills 123
Valeria Damiani, Francesco Agrusti, Università Roma Tre, Italy

International Virtual Mobilities for Opening up Education 124
Diana Andone, Politehnica University of Timisoara, Romania, Mark Frydenberg, Bentley University, United States of America

Flipped Classroom: Advantatges and Disadvantages of Application 125
Ramon Palau, Josep G. Rovira, Universitat Rovira i Virgili, F. Seritjol, Escola l'Agulla, X. Sune, Departament d'Ensenyament, Spain

Capacity Development for e-Learning – Educational Strategies at Mid Sweden Universities 126
Laura Brander, J. Ola Lindberg, Mid Sweden University, Sweden

Effective Learning Strategies: Making Sense of and with Learning by Means of $B^2R^2SDL^3$ and S2S* 127
Ignatius G.P. Gous, Univeristy of South Africa, South Africa

Competence Frameworks In Agriculture – PACT 128
Thomas Kretschmer, Christian M. Stracke, University of Duisburg-Essen, German, Cleo Sgouropoulou, Elisa Ninou, Technical Educational Institute of Athens, Greece, Carmen Müller, DLG-Academy, Germany

A Value Creation Framework for an Online Professional Learning Community 129
Gaëlle Le Bot, Lina Xue, Wim Van Petegem, Astrid Van Wieringen, KU Leuven, Belgium

Transforming, Expanding and Enriching Learning Scenarios with Cooperative Learning in Self-Paced Courses 130
Luis Guadarrama, Josh Evans, Cindy Ives, Corinne Bosse, Athabasca University, Canada

Distance Learning for Adult Learners – Needs and Considerations 131
Khalil Alsaadat, King Saud University Saudia Arabia

WORKSHOPS

Building a Leadership Culture 132
Bruce Chaloux, Southern Region Education Board, Lawrence C. Ragan, Penn State World Campus, United States of America, Brian Mulligan, Sligo Institute of Technology, Ireland

An Introduction to MOOC Design by the EMMA Team 133
Deborah Arnold, Université de Bourgogne, France, Sally Reynolds, ATiT, Belgium

Learning Analytics – What Data Could Tell if We Were Willing to Share Information. Exploring BenefitsaAnd Barriers to the Use of Analytics in Schools and Universities 134
Tore Hoel, Oslo and Akershus University College of Applied Sciences, Norway, Sally Reynolds, ATiT, Belgium, Dai Griffiths, CETIS, University of Bolton, United Kingdom

EMPOWERing Universities: The Transition of European Higher Education to New Modes of Teaching and Learning 135
George Ubachs, European Association of Distance Teaching Universities, the Netherlands

Towards Low-Cost Production of MOOCs 136
Brian Mulligan, Institute of Technology Sligo, Ireland, Miquel Duran, Silvia Simon, University of Girona, Spain, Jörn Loviscach, Fachhochschule Bielefeld, Germany, Gráinne Conole, Bath Spa University, United Kingdom

sMOOCs for All, All in sMOOCs: Discussing the Social Side of Massive Open Learning Experiences with the ECO Partnership 137
Divina Frau-Meigs, University Sorbonne Nouvelle, France

Lost in Transition? D-TRANSFORM as a Compass for the Use of ICT to Transform the Higher Education System ... 138
Paul Bacsich, Sero Consulting, United Kingdom

Cultural Gaps and Solutions for Education In International Settings 139
Thomas Richter, Thomas Kretschmer, University of Duisburg-Essen, Germany

"A Journey to the 'Open Discovery Space': Please Fasten your Seat Belts!" – Impact and Sustainability of Innovative e-Learning Portals – User Perspectives on Portals' Value Propositions 140
Lampros Stergioulas, Munir Abbasi, Georgios Xydopoulos, Maria Fragkaki, University of Surrey, United Kingdom, Marlies Bitter-Rijpkema, Open University of the Netherlands, The Netherlands, Alan Bruce, Universal Learning Systems, Ireland, Christian M. Stracke, University of Duisburg-Essen, Germany

Open Education and Internationalisation: Are You Up to the Challenge 141
Fabio Nascimbeni, Universidad Internacional de la Rioja, Brazil

Hands-On Collaboration for Open Education: Share Your Expertise and Ideas on Open Courses, Textbooks and Educational Software 142
Henri Pirkkalainen, University of Jyväskylä, Finland, Jan Pawlowski, Ruhr West University of Applied Sciences, Anne-Christin Tannhäuser, ESCP Europe Business School Berlin, Germany

Expanded Learning Scenarios of Best Practice in the United States 143
Sharon Goldstein, Berkeley College, Dale Gomez, Florida International University, Susan Aldridge, Drexel Online University, United States of America

Online, Open and Flexible Higher Education for the Future We Want: From Statements to Action: Policy Challenges – The European Voice 144
Gard Titlestad, International Council for Open and Distance Education, Maxim Jean-Louis, Contact North | Contact Nord, Canada

Educamps in Education: Enjoyable "Over-The-Shoulder Learning" to Show and Share ICT Practices 145
Sólveig Jakobsdóttir, University of Iceland, Iceland

DEMONSTRATIONS

Empowering Learners and Educators – Video Feedback to Written Assignments 146
Ann-Sofie Karlsson, Tobias Ruhtenberg, University of Borås, Sweden

Engineering Pedagogy at Universities in Chile – A Research and Further Education Project of TU Dresden and Universidad Autónoma De Chile 147
Steffen Kersten, Hartmut Simmert, Diego Gormaz, Technische Universität Dresden, Germany

The e-Hoop Learning Platform – An Innovative Approach to Expand Learning Experiences for Persons with Special Needs 148
Eleni Chatzidaki, Michalis Xenos, Lefteris Kozanidis, Hellenic Open University, Greece; Thomas Fischer, New Technologies and Learning in Europe, Germany; Aliki Economidou, Cyprus Neuroscience and Technology Institute, Cyprus

Pervasive Gamification with Augmented Reality and Remote Experiences 149
Paula Carolei, UNIFESP, Eliane Schlmmer, UNISINOS, Brazil

Remote Desktop Virtualization as a Means of Convergence of Student and Professional Workplaces 150
Oleksandr Melnychenko, Kherson National Technical University, Ukraine

Time to Assess Learning Outcomes in e-Learning – TALOE Web Tool ... 151
Sandra Kučina Softić, University of Zagreb, Croatia, Inés Gil-Jaurena, Universidad Nacional de Educación a Distancia, Spain, Alfredo Soeiro, Rita Falcão, Universidade do Porto, Portugal, Jüri Lõssenko, Information Technology Foundation for Education, Estonia

BOOK OF PROJECTS – COLLECTION OF "SYNERGY" SYNOPSES

VM-Pass ... 156
Implementing Recognition of Virtual Mobility and OER Learning through a Learning Passport

Panorama e-learning PT ... 158
Study on PT HEI e-Learning Governance and Practices 2015-2016

ECVET-STEP ... 159
ECVET for Strengthening Training to Employment Pathways

SADE ICDE ON ... 160
SADE ICDE Operational Network-Nordic and Baltic Countries

OERup! ... 161
OER Uptake in Adult Learning Institutions

ARMAZEG ... 162
Developing Tools for Lifelong Learning in the Transcaucasus Region: e-Learning

UAB System ... 163
Open education from distance learning of Brazil

UDLnet ... 165
Universal Design for Learning: A Framework for Addressing Learner Variability– UDLnet

LeHo ... 167
Learning at Home and the Hospital

Intergenerational Game Creation ... 169
Intergenerational Game Creation

EHLSSA ... 170
European Home Learning Service for Seniors Association

SenApp ... 171
Seniors Learning with APPs

PRONURSING ... 172

P4G ... 173
Play4Guidance: A European Business Game to Train and Guide Students and Young Unemployed on Entrepreneurial, Transversal and Mathematical Skills

EDUWORKS ... 175
Crossing Borders in the Comprehensive Investigation of Labour Market matching Processes: An EU-Wide, Trans-Disciplinary, Multilevel and Science-Practice-Bridging Training

RIPE NCC Academy ... 176
Réseaux IP Européens Network Coordination Centre Academy

CCD FLITE ... 178
Concurrent Design Framework for eLearning in IT Entrepreneurship

StartUP ... 180
Intelligent Training Needs Assessment and Open Educational Resources to Foster Entrepreneurship

iPro ... 181
The iProfessional

m-commerce ... 182
m-commerce

HOME ... 183
Higher Education Online: MOOCs the European Way

D-TRANSFORM ... 184
DigiTal Resources As a New Strategical Factor fOr a Renovation of Modernization in Higher Education

TALOE ... 185
Time to Assess Learning Outcomes in e-Learning

EDUOPEN ... 186
Federated Platform MOOCs

Flexible Toolbox Project ... 187
Student Success Toolbox for Flexible Learners: Supporting Transitions from Thinking about Study to the First Few Weeks

MMSQC ... 189
A Multi-Platform Mobile Learning System for More Qualified Courses in the ICT Era

BEU ... 191
Badge Europe!

eLene4work ... 192
Learning to Learn for New Digital Soft Skills for Employability

MERIT – Manufacturing Education and Research with Information Technology ... 193
Work-Integrated Learning and Technology Enhanced Competence Development for Experts in the Manufacturing Industry

ADOERUP ... 195
Adult Education and Open Educational Resources

OntoTechnology ... 196

ICARD ... 197
Individual CAReer Development

LACE ... 198
Learning Analytics Community Exchange

Digiskills – Network for the Enhancement of Digital Competence Skills ... 199
Sharing Best Practices in Teachers' Professional Development

SCORE2020 ... 201
Support Centres for Open education and MOOCS in different Regions of Europe 2020

SAILS ... 202
Strategies for Assessment of Inquiry Learning in Science

ODS ... 203
Open Discovery Space

Hands-On ICT ... 205
Hands-On ICT: Learn, Practice, Teach Creativity and ICT

INUITEL ... 206
Intelligent Tutoring Interface for Technology Enhanced Learning

CAMELOT ... 207
CreAting Machinima to Empower Live Online language Teaching and learning

JamToday ... 209
The European Game Jam Learning Hub

SharedOER ... 210
A Scoping Study on the Potential of Shared, Cross-Border OER and Syllabi in Europe

OEI2 ... 211
Open Educational Ideas and Innovations – Towards Open Idea and Innovations Sharing for Learning, Education and Training

OpenPROF ... 212
Open Professional Collaboration for Innovation

ECO ... 213
ECO Elearning Communication Open-Data

APPLYING BIGGS CONSTRUCTIVE ALIGNMENT TO ONLINE INTERDISCIPLINARY EDUCATION

Lina Xue, Gaëlle Le Bot, Wim Van Petegem, Astrid Van Wieringen, KU Leuven, Belgium

The FP7 project improving Children's Auditory Rehabilitation (iCARE) is an international and interdisciplinary consortium from academia, industry and socio-economic agencies. One of the objectives of iCARE is to provide interdisciplinary training to create a new generation of researchers capable of exploiting the synergies between different disciplines, for the ultimate aim of improving children's (4-12 years old) auditory rehabilitation. Online training appears as the main solution to accomplish iCARE interdisciplinary training. The main objective of the current study is to design an educational model which could facilitate effective online interdisciplinary training to iCARE researchers.

Due to the variety of interdisciplinary education contexts, there is not a widely accepted educational model yet. Critics of the interdisciplinary educational model design rise from the following aspects: i) Lack of theoretical support from learning and psychological background; ii) Poor instructional design such as lack of assessment methods or constructive alignment; iii) Lack of information to guide designing interventions. Learning the lessons from previous studies, we design the interdisciplinary education model for iCARE mainly based on Biggs' constructive alignment and we adjusted it into online interdisciplinary learning context.

The iCARE interdisciplinary educational model we propose is composed of four parts: learning needs analysis, curriculum objectives, teaching/learning activities (TLA) and assessment tasks. Curriculum objectives functioning as the central part of the model are used to be systematically aligned with the TLA and the assessment tasks. Two steps are introduced to guide TLA design. The first step is to select the appropriate online learning method; the second step is to complete the pre-, the main and the post-activity design. The three-step design is based on the studies of acquisition of intellectual skills and development of expertise. Then, the feedback of TLA goes back to the curriculum objectives to make necessary adjustment. Assessment tasks are also applied in online context. Three steps are listed to design the assessment tasks: selecting the appropriate online assessment type, developing grading criteria of desired learning outcomes and making sure the holistic grading reflect how well a given student's level of performance meets the desired objectives. The feedback of assessment tasks goes back as well to the curriculum objectives to make necessary adjustment.

This current study contributes to improving the knowledge of interdisciplinary education by providing an educational model with a strong theoretical background, and proposing guidelines for future interventions design in interdisciplinary education. We hope this study on a new learning scenario—online interdisciplinary education could contribute to the knowledge creation of the worlds of online learning.

MICRO-INNOVATIONS AND STAKEHOLDERS ENGAGEMENT AS DRIVERS FOR SYSTEMIC CHANGE IN ICT-SUPPORTED LEARNING

Fabio Nascimbeni, Edison Spina, Universidade de Sao Paulo, Brazil

The paper discusses the findings and the lessons learnt of two research projects that have worked to understand how to support mainstreaming and scalability of ICT for learning in Europe. These are the VISIR project, which explored how scouting grassroots micro-innovation practices can help to successfully mainstream the potential of ICT to contribute to change in education, and the HOTEL project, which worked on how to appropriately engage stakeholders in supporting innovation in the field of ICT for learning.

VISIR (www.visir-network.eu) has tackled the problem of mainstreaming of ICT-for-learning from a rather new standpoint, that is by focussing on *micro-innovation practices*: in a nutshell, innovative experience that are micro in terms of implementation scope, size of idea-generator, and degree of actual change, but that bear a very high impact potential. Similarly, the HOTEL project (www.hotel-project.eu) has designed and tested a mechanism to support innovations – and innovators – in the field of Technology Enhanced Learning (TEL) to move from the pilot and experimental phase to broader mainstream and adoption. In order to do this the project selected a set of innovators and innovations to be accompanied, for a period of time, through a series of interactions with experts, stakeholders' representatives and other critical colleagues who have concretely contributed to strengthen the success prospective of these innovations and contextually reflect on the proposed support in terms of content, process, outcomes and potential impact.

Building on the main findings of these projects as well as on other recent attempts to valorise innovation in education, the paper presents some ideas targeted to decision makers, researchers and practitioners, as possible starting points for future bottom-up efforts of innovation valorisation in the field of ICT-supported learning. We argue that active engagement of stakeholders and valorisation of grassroots micro innovation ideas should be two pillars of any innovation support strategy in the field of ICT-enhanced learning. If micro innovation support is a strategy that has been proving to work for example in the US, "inclusive strategies" would represent a unique feature of a European vision in support to innovation, as happens for example in the Living Labs concept.

VISUALITY AS A TOOL FOR EXPANDING LEARNING

András Benedek, Budapest University of Technology and Economics, Hungary

Visual learning – paradox or contradiction?

Influenced by ICTs, theorists of learning have recently recognised the role of networks while still relying on approaches like behaviourism, constructivism and cognitivism. This paper focuses on a contradiction related to visuality in learning, considered as critical and progressive element both in institutional and in broader context, Mass penetration of ICTs in the learning process have resulted significant increase of spontaneity; which is hard to make compatible with the visual contents of curricula designed and objectivised in algorithms that had been in turn designed in the framework of the national curricula.

The visual contents in traditional textbooks and online curricula, the latter also serving as an illustration of the actual status of the technical infrastructure, have not changed much in the past decades. Visual learning was already known in ancient societies and not only as a tool for daily communication or knowledge transfer. Parables created a virtual double dimension, where short, figurative speeches could convey the meaning of an idea by using a picture or metaphor of ordinary life. "Modern" curricula developed by the end of the 20th century have a linear structure and the prevailing dominance of verbal contents (80% on average) was changing only slowly, giving way to visual contents which were mostly composed by static pictures. Though online curricula and multimedia-based e-learning representations include more dynamic visual contents (flash, video), the "logic" of curricula design has not changed. Visual contents are still mostly considered as supplements to verbal (written and oral) messages.

Implementation of a new approach

The project "E-teaching Culture and Digital Content Development at the Budapest University of Technology and Economics (BME)" to be implemented in 2013-2015, aims at developing content, methodologies and services in support of competitiveness of higher education, structural changes of the Bologna Process and meeting the challenges of knowledge-based economies.

It is worth studying how to utilize the potential of networked learning, as such potentials are already perceived today, in the optimization of organic learning as demanded by individual learners and institutions. Our research proved that measurable learning activities show time-dependent features that correlate with the use of visual communication forms used in the study programs. In order to increase the volume of information transmitted, as an alternative to changing the curriculum design, may be to increase the amount of visual elements, together with the utilization of networked learning. According to our hypothesis, visual learning may provide opportunities to use parables that are able to improve the efficiency of learning, currently mostly based on traditional verbal communication thus often hindered by time constraints and information pressure.

IN SEARCH OF LEADERSHIP: INNOVATIVE APPROACHES TO BUILDING ADAPTIVE LEARNING COMMUNITIES

Don Olcott, Jr., Charles Sturt University, Australia, Lisa Marie Blaschke, Carl von Ossietzky University of Oldenburg, Germany

Learning is about making connections. This range of teaching-learning connections permeates the teaching and learning environment. We connect new knowledge to existing knowledge; we connect the digital world with the real world; we connect students to content, students to students, and students to teacher. We connect the classroom to the world, competencies to skills, individuals to groups, and groups to communities. And, most importantly, we connect technology to information – information to knowledge and knowledge to application in the real world. We connect students to life.

Adaptive Learning Communities (ALCs) look at digital learning through a broader lens than personal or digital learning environments and can be defined as:

The mobilization of digital technologies to transform schools through personal and community learning environments which serve as the catalyst for creating new relationships through a 'community for innovation' that connect all stakeholders to a common community action agenda.

ALCs extend previous research and theory about learning theory, PLEs, mobile technologies, and expanding real-virtual learning spaces to a broader community context. ALCs 'connect' all stakeholders in the community rather than just students and teachers. Parents, business leaders, community representatives, government agencies – the entire community is engaged in building one *mega-learning space* across the community for formal learning – but also for the collaborative linkages to address community development in all its guises. The elements of ALCs – or the 7Es – include:

- Engage;
- Experience;
- Empower;
- Effect;
- Emote;
- Evolve;
- Efficacy.

Combined together within the ALC, these elements have the potential to build powerful communities.

Digital transformation takes more than technology. It will require a rediscovery of **leadership** and putting innovation back in to the core of each leader. Building a community for innovation requires a synergy of the entire community – educators, government and ministry leaders, students, faculty, private providers, social service organizations, religious leaders, parents, and more. Indeed, what we should be developing with ALCs are ***communities for innovation*** that collectively embrace innovation in all its guises and creative capacities.

LEARNERS – NOT SYSTEMS – ARE THE VALUE CREATORS

Ari-Matti Auvinen, HCI Productions Oy, Finland

The high-quality course development process for eLearning has been often viewed as a value chain, which is tightly defined and structured, and covers various stages from needs analysis until evaluation. The value chain approach introduced originally by Michael Porter in the mid-1980s, and they value chain approach could nicely capture the essential elements in businesses based on manufacturing.

The economic benefits of the design, production and delivery of effective eLearning solutions have often been based on the ideas of effective manufacturing and its economic parameters, as one of the economic promises of eLearning has been to alter the economies of learning "from handicraft to mass production". The operational goal of the eLearning providers have been seen to be to streamline the actual eLearning course production process by using the well-tuned consecutive steps of needs analysis, course design, course delivery, course interaction, and assessment. The value has thus been understood to stem from efficient course provision and effective facilitation of various interactions.

However, another way of creating value is through co-creation, through interaction among faculty, learners and the larger society. Also value should be viewed from a new perspective - value should be measured only as direct learning outcomes, but also as participation and involvement of the learners, co-learners, teachers, and supporters. Some ten years ago the understanding of value creation took new, important steps, which are also essential in understanding the value creation mechanisms of eLearning courses. The new discourse of service-dominant logic (SDL) challenged the conventional thinking of value creation. Thus also the value creation happens differently – not by the effective production and provision mechanism only, but rather by the value creation within the interface of the producers and customers, and the market is becoming instead of a seller-buyer-market rather the environment for co-creation of value.

The understanding of value creation as a process as well as the understanding key actors of value creation has been developing during the last ten years, but so has also the understanding of learning been entering new areas. In contemporary environment, adult learners are highly self-directed, as learning does not only take place in institutions, but everywhere, during the course of one's whole life in a number of different episodes, in learning communities and social networks, using social software and individually compiled contents. The elementary trend in the changing learning approach is the active participation of the learners to their learning process in every stage.

One interesting trend is the growing importance of peer-produced eLearning content, which in practical terms shows the power of the co-creation of value. Not only are the learning individuals essential as learning content providers, but also the importance of the peer groups is growing. The modern eLearning environment also enables the learners to utilize available resources and visualize their competence e.g. by ePortfolios and collaborative project work. The eLearning environments provide usually such fora, where not only the users and the providers can meet, but also the users can meet with another.

Value co-creation in eLearning is a challenging approach. Value co-creation requires thorough planning, organization, implementation and continuous improvement. We are moving in eLearning – in particular, in courses of professional development - from closed learning environments towards open learning environments. The learners are able to identify, assess and utilize good learning resources and content from the wide provision on the Internet. Simultaneously the role of the faculty (including the teachers, tutors and learning supporters) in professional development is also changing, and their new key role is the facilitation of learning, knowledge creation, assessment and sharing.

At the heart of the new strategies for eLearning is the understanding of value creation: is value created by a well-planned and well-controlled educational provision or is value created with the users in continuous communication?

DIGITAL LEARNING IN IRISH HIGHER EDUCATION: INTEGRATING STRATEGIC AND LEADERSHIP PERSPECTIVES INTO A ROADMAP FOR DIGITAL CAPACITY

Jim Devine, DEVINE Policy | Projects | Innovation, Terry Maguire, National Forum for the Enhancement of Teaching and Learning in Higher Education, Ireland

Digital learning finds its way, as if by stealth, into the mainstream of higher education. As educators, however, we are aware of a persistence of traditional teaching and assessment practices. Taking innovative and potentially transformative pedagogical practices to scale is a well known but poorly addressed challenge. Bottom up approaches to digital learning, however, often give rise to an unsustainable multiplicity of practices across disciplines and faculties, usually layered on top of existing practices rather than replacing them. On the other hand, top down institutional initiatives, intended for mainstream adoption, are often seen by pedagogical innovators as driving conservative or constraining decisions about technologies, platforms and learning spaces. Addressing this bottom-up, top-down dilemma is today's key challenge for innovation and modernisation of higher education. Our paper looks at one facet of this challenge, and how the perceptions of those in academic leadership roles are informing discourse and strategy development for digital learning in Irish higher education. In particular it looks at how leaders' insights have contributed to the development by the (Irish) National Forum for the Enhancement of Teaching & Learning in Higher Education of a 'Roadmap for Enhancement in a Digital World 2015-2017', as a blueprint for the integration of digital learning and digital pedagogy consistently and at scale across the higher education sector as a whole.

Academics in senior/strategic roles can provide unique insights into the challenges of scale and sustainability of digital learning innovation. On the one hand, with their influence over strategic direction, budgets and the seed funding of innovative pilots, they can create an enabling environment. On the other hand, the imperative to manage scarce resources and to ensure that institutional reputation and quality remain demonstrably on a sound footing can make it difficult to choose between competing demands for up-scaling, mainstreaming or simply sustaining successful pilots. Staff in these roles embodies the bottom-up, top-down dilemma and the development of the Digital Capacity Roadmap provided an opportunity to discuss this with them on a one-to-one basis, using a semi-structured interview approach. The insights gained were then cross-referenced with institutional funding agreements introduced for the first time in 2014, 'Mission-Based Performance Compacts', covering the full range of HEI activities, including the environment for teaching and learning.

While many innovative digital learning projects and initiatives are evident in Irish HEIs, it has not been easy to assess their overall impact or to place them in the wider context of institutional strategic and leadership positions. By juxtaposing the interview process with staff in senior/strategic roles and the analysis of Compacts, it has been possible to gain a fruitful insight into how a range of innovative practices are viewed top-down. Taking as a model, Trowler's continuum from incrementalism (reform agenda) to reinvention (transformational agenda) a rich and complementary picture emerged of the day-to-day reality of fostering learning innovation in Irish HEIs. Dominant themes include strong support for academic staff CPD, for the professionalisation of the teaching role and for collaborative HE sector-level actions to deliver the required CPD. Much emphasis was placed on what was described as 'appropriate' integration of digital technologies, but there was agreement that current approaches are for the most part conservative *('doing the same in the old way but better')*. While learning innovation (digital) is taking place and bottom-up innovations are facilitated, there is little appetite as yet for strategic (top down) initiatives. There is broad agreement, however, that matters related to digital or online learning and digital capacity generally should be brought systematically into the mainstream of institutional quality assurance processes.

Ultimately, the view from staff in senior/strategic roles is optimistic, but with wide agreement that clarity is urgently needed about the overarching vision and goals for digital learning in higher education nationally. Informed, concerted effort is required to embed quality assured digital learning consistently and at scale within Irish HEIs and the recently published Roadmap provides the necessary strategic vision and focus in a manner that is grounded in actionable implementation items and guidelines about how to address them.

STRATEGIES OF TECHNOLOGY USAGE IN LIFELONG LEARNING PROGRAMS

Helge Fischer, Matthias Heinz, Thomas Koehler, Dresden University of Technology, Germany

Which technologies are used in academic continuing education programs? What are the strategic reasons for using these technologies? These questions are focused in the present paper. It will be shown why technologies are used in continuing educations programs (e.g. master programs, certificate courses). Therefore the findings of an online survey (n=173), which addressed the academic staff in Higher Education, will be discussed. Based on multivariate analysis three objectives for technology usage in this field could be identified: institution, participants and visibility. These objectives will be introduced in detail within the paper. Additionally will be analyzed how institutional affiliation and the position of the staff members or the educational program influence the use of internet technologies.

THE IMPACT OF AN ETHICS OF CARE ON THE IRON TRIANGLE IN ODL

Paul Prinsloo, University of South Africa, South Africa

There are claims that distance education and in particular open distance learning (ODL) are unique in providing broadened access to higher education at lower costs without compromising quality. While traditional face-to-face higher education is caught in the fixed vectors of quality, access and cost, the so-called 'iron triangle', distance education and in particular, *online* distance education promises to break the 'iron triangle.'

Much of the current discourse is centred on the notion of access and quality with little contemplation of the inter-dependencies between access, quality and cost in the light of often dismal student retention in distance education contexts. Amid increasing public and regulatory scrutiny, changing funding regimes, and increasingly underprepared student populations *and* faculty, ODL institutions spend more and more resources to improve student retention and success without compromising quality or 'closing' the revolving doors. While ODL's commitment to social justice in providing increased access is laudable, providing such access with little reasonable chance of success may actually constitute justice denied or deferred. Focusing just on justice is potentially insufficient and we should possibly move beyond frameworks of justice to frameworks of justice *and* care. The question arises then: *How scalable and cost-effective is an ethics of justice and care in ODL?*

This exploratory conceptual paper approaches the traditional vectors of access, cost and quality (the iron triangle) from the perspective of an ethics of justice and care. From the context of an ODL institution in a developing world context (the University of South Africa, Unisa), this paper questions the central claim of the iron triangle that high quality teaching and learning can be provided to an increasing number of students without raising the cost of provision or lowering quality. The paper briefly explores criticisms of the iron triangle before problematising its underpinning assumptions from the perspective of an ethics of justice and care.

PEDAGOGY AS A TECHNÉ: MEANINGFUL ICT INTEGRATION IN FORMAL LEARNING SCENARIOS

Ana Mouta, Ana Paulino, João Ferreira, Filipe Couto, JP-inspiring knowledge, Portugal

This paper presents a framework developed by JP-inspiring knowledge with different stakeholders that aims at the creation, preparation and evaluation of ICT integrative projects in formal learning scenarios.

This proposal served as a basis for master training on meaningful pedagogical strategies with ICT, in several countries: Angola, Bolivia, East Timor, El Salvador, Ivory Coast, Jordan, Peru, Portugal, and Puerto Rico.

Each of these training projects targeted different stakeholders: elements from Ministries of Education and Technologies, Pedagogic Specialists, Curricula Designers and Teachers. Its general structure was designed inside and outside classrooms, not only with teachers and students, but also with school directors, parents, educational advisers and ICT companies.

Here we present the main characteristics of this framework – the ik-Model – and the process through which it is being conceived as a relevant pedagogic transformational *medium*. ICTs are no more conceived and integrated as tools or resources in learning scenarios, but as contexts. This perspective challenges not only the way they may be thought inside those spaces, but also the way people look at their own role in those processes and environments.

Finally, we discuss how this approach – that is embedded in an anthropological perspective on pedagogy development – acts towards a reconfiguration of pedagogy as a *Techné* and how this requalifies teachers' momentum within most of the changing processes of actuality.

E-LEARNING VIA SYNCHRONOUS COMMUNICATION- EXPERIENCES FROM A LEARNING STUDY COURSE IN HIGHER EDUCATION

Eva Edman Stålbrandt, Kajsa Falkner, Stockholm University, Sweden

Introduction

At the department of Education at Stockholm University we offer a master program in didactic science. The participants are teachers with a teacher degree who would like to develop their work in school. The programme is half time studies and almost all the participants work full time at school. Since the autumn 2013 we offer the master programme as an e-learning programme. One reason is to offer teachers to combine education with work and another motive is to attract teachers from other parts of the country or abroad. Introducing distance education means creating major changes in how teaching and other resources are used. It challenges faculty staff to reflect on and improve the course design as well as exploiting digital technology in order to improve the students' learning processes. The overall aim of this project is to develop the learning environment within an e-learning course in relation to its content.

Course design and methodology

Learning/Lesson study is a 15 ECTs credit course within the master program in didactic science. The teaching materials were distributed via an open source LMS. Adobe Connect was used for synchronous audio- visible communication between participants peer-groups as well as university teachers - participants. Via the course design we tried to offer as many modes of communication as possible. Asynchronous and synchronous written communication was afforded in the LMS. Video lectures, different presentations, external links were also offered in the LMS as learning-resources. A critical and important mode of communication was the university teachers-participants' mode. In order to avoid solely asynchronous written feedback from university teachers to participants we organised seven web-based audio-visible seminars, which included all the participants led and structured by the university teachers. Every peer-group was represented in the web-seminar by a spokesperson – a different one at every seminar. Between the seminars managed by the university teachers, the peer-groups met in Adobe Connect, in their own "rooms" preparing the tasks for the web-based teacher-seminar. The tasks consisted of written protocols of the different proceedings and understandings of a learning study. The protocols were written by the participants together in the peer-groups and revised after reading three other peer-groups protocols. Another task in the middle of the course was to perform of a learning/lesson study together with several analyses. To make the performance and analysis possible for the peer-group, as they were physically spread geographically, the participants video-recorded the lessons and showed the film in Adobe Connect for those participants that could not attend physically during the lessons.

Results of the empirical study

Our experiences from the first e-format learning study course are more positive than we expected. The synchronous audio-visible discussions increased the focus of the content compared to our experiences from Campus-seminars. The e-learning format created possibilities for enhanced learning, however it required a strong engagement from the participants in the interaction with other peers and the course content. The result of the empirical study constitutes of three categories of description. In each category we present a critical feature expressed in our data related to the e-learning environment. The critical feature expresses what is crucial in the participants' experience of the learning study and how and where it appears in the learning environment.

Regarding our first critical feature we redesigned the synchronous audio-visible discussions into smaller groups. In this way each participant get larger possibilities to interact with the university teachers. Regarding, what we consider, our most important critical feature "to make difference between locating the issue to the educational activity or to the individual student" is still a challenge to overcome through future development regarding digital course design.

COHERENCE OF ACCELERATED TRANSFORMATIONS AND EXPANDED LEARNING SCENARIOS

Christian-Andreas Schumann, Claudia Tittmann, Helge Gerischer, Anne Götze, West Saxon University of Zwickau, Germany, Feng Xiao, Tongji Universty Shanghai, China, Jana Weber, Technische Universittät Berlin, Germany

The processes in all spheres of life of the society, particularly in innovation, knowledge transfer and the related teaching are dominated by permanent transformations. The organizations respond with new enhanced learning scenarios in order to control the acceleration of the transformations from the point of view of content, communication, and cooperation. The increasing knowledge of the management of transformation processes, however, leads to the situation that knowledge, including the appropriate educational systems and processes, can be converted and transferred even more quickly and efficiently. The question is which kinds of opportunities exist to control the acceleration by using appropriate methods and designing essential parts of the necessary educational systems.

Thus, the current situation is characterized by continuous innovation and resulting transformations leading in shorter time intervals to significant changes, i.e. leading to an acceleration of the processes of change. It is essential to react to the growing flood of requests with noticeable changes in the learning scenarios and the diversification of educational offers to meet the complex challenges adequately. Educational institutions have responded in the regional, national and global context by developing not only new kinds and methods of learning and teaching in special networks and alliances but also by focusing their activities increasingly on the user requirements based on new forms of collaborations

Nowadays, companies improve their innovation ability through optimization of organizational structure, business processes and functions. The foci are mainly harmonization of the innovation portfolio with the customer needs; development and retention of specialists, experts and professionals; consistency of innovation and management processes; use of new product- and service-oriented technologies and perspectives; slimming down of the organization in particular the processes in the product and service development. The necessary strategic direction of innovation projects requires the existence of a corporate strategy whose formulation is also linked to the availability of the necessary information, derived from the company itself (identifying strengths and weaknesses) and from the environment of the company (identification of opportunities and risks).

If this concept is applied to the field of education, major changes from the development of learning scenarios in unity of vision, business processes, information systems, technology, solutions, migrations and implementations through to change and requirement management and associated transformations will occur. This requires the enlargement of the learning scenarios in any case, too.

The often announced target-oriented and at the same time required individualized education is facilitated without binding exponentially increasing teaching resources. The developments in education show that all available options are used and combined to meet the immense challenges of knowledge exchange as prerequisites and part of social transformations. The scenarios technique is constantly being expanded and leads to expanded learning scenarios. There are extensive theoretical elaborations, educational approaches and models, and practical experience to the above mentioned examples. They are based on advanced learning scenarios in order to be able to efficiently control the acceleration of the transformations in education in particular and in society in general in regional, national and international manner.

The coherence of accelerated transformations and expended learning scenarios opens up new opportunities to meet the exponentially growing demands on educational institutions as result of the globalization, digitization, the dynamics of science and technology, the knowledge explosion resulting in an extreme acceleration of transformations. Learning scenarios provide new educational paths, methods as well as didactics and thus the mastery of knowledge transformations in different contexts.

DIGITAL, MATERIAL AND NETWORKED: SOME EMERGING THEMES FOR SET EDUCATION

Sarah Davies, Elaine Thomas, Steve Walker, The Open University, United Kingdom

Boundaries between the digital and material worlds are becoming blurred as the internet connects us to things as well as people and information. This is increasingly relevant to education as initiatives which significantly combine digital and material elements in networks are becoming a reality for Science, Engineering and Technology (SET) learning. SET subjects are primarily concerned either with understanding the material world (science) or with intervening in it to support human activity (engineering and technology), typically through experiments, observations, (physical) models and/or prototypes. In distance education, learning technologies tend to support discursive learning in through online, digital resources, such a text and images, audio-video recordings and communication systems. By 'material' we mean tangible, physical artefacts, such as a sensor or an astronomical telescope, from which 'real' world data can be gathered. We have used the term 'hybrid' to refer to networks of digital and material artefacts used in learning.

Educationally, the availability of such hybrid learning resources may present important opportunities. The term 'authentic learning' is widely used to refer to educational practices that connect what students learn in an educational setting with the kind of issues and problems encountered in professional or other practice. Outside educational settings, people learn from their mistakes and from having to solve problems; experimental work often entails dealing with complexity and uncertainty.

Our paper reports on the initial findings of a project to carry out a 'state of the art' review of literature to establish the key themes, opportunities and obstacles that are emerging from the development and use of these 'hybrid' systems in learning. We wanted to explore the extent to which this new domain of study is being reported in the literature and to identify work representative of this area. Our aim was to investigate the depth of research in this area by going beyond the technologically descriptive to focus on pedagogical and organisational issues raised in the literature.

To identify the state of current research in the area we carried out a systematic search of databases of Science, Engineering and Technology education literature. We found 808 papers relating to the hybrid learning initiatives we are interested in, of which the majority, 81%, involved the Engineering and Technology disciplines while 6.8% related to Science. The vast majority of papers referred to remote laboratories and most of these were concerned with describing the technologies involved. This suggests that current research is primarily concerned with pragmatic issues and the field is still developing. In order to explore issues emerging from the research, we carried out an in-depth text review of a particular subset of the papers found that focussed on pedagogical issues. The three main themes that emerged were: the importance of real data and authenticity in learning; the importance of a sense of presence (e.g. telepresence, social presence and/or immersion) and the locus of control in, and responsiveness of, a hybrid system.

Our exploration of 'hybrid' digital material networked learning literature suggests that this is still a developing field and there is not yet clearly defined shared terminology. We conclude that these new digital 'hybrid' pedagogies offer a lens with which to view both the more traditional material pedagogies, e.g. laboratory-based learning, and purely digital pedagogies, e.g. virtual labs. Finally, issues of authenticity, presence and control/responsiveness will be of increasing pedagogical importance to other 'hybrid' systems, such as those involving ubiquitous computing.

ONLINE DIGITAL GAMES AND EDUCATION FOR SUSTAINABLE DEVELOPMENT: A CONTROVERSIAL RELATIONSHIP?

Antonia Boniati, Georgia Liarakou, Costas Tsolakidis, University of the Aegean, Costas Gavrilakis, University of Ioannina, Greece

Introduction

Considering that sustainable development consists of three interrelated dimensions, namely environmental protection, economic efficiency and social justice, every kind of educational process that promotes or deals with messages and values consistent with these dimensions, potentially contributes to the vision of ESD. Online entertainment games constitute a noteworthy kind of informal education since their pedagogical role has been increasingly recognized. The present study examined three of the most popular games (Call of Duty, League of Legends, Minecraft) and specifically messages involved that are related to sustainable development, i.e. social, environmental and economic.

Methodology

15 high school students were selected. A purposive sampling approach was used so as all of them to be experienced on the three games. The sample consisted of 3 children of the 1st class, 5 of the 2nd and 7 of the 3rd class of high school. Individual interviews were conducted and qualitative content analysis was applied to interpret the data.

Results

The majority of the messages reported are associated more with the social rather than with the environmental and economic dimensions, even if some of them encompass more than one dimension. Teamwork, collaboration and solidarity are among the most evident messages/values promoted through different ways. Within this context, interaction, as a basic feature of online edutainment games, is evident across the three games, since the majority of players prefer to play with friends. These games promote socialization as well as mutual support, even with beginners, aiming at achieving a common goal. Such features and values are expected to guide children's attitudes in real life too. The values of life and equity also emerge implicitly or explicitly throughout these games. Children seem to be able to distinguish some negative perceptions, tasks and behaviors (e.g. racist perceptions, killing people, having servants) from what is moral and acceptable in real life while playing a game. At the same time players seem to become creative, imaginative, autonomous and able to deal with complex situations themselves.

The unreal representations of these games might confuse users with respect to environmental conditions and potential degradation. In two out of three games (CoD and Minecraft) the environmental dimension is quite clear. However, although the behavior of players in the game would cause serious damages on the natural or human environment, in the unreal setting of the game everything seems to be unharmed and unlimited. As with many games providing players with many "lives", here the environment seems to be regenerated. Fortunately in this study users realize that the real environment is more fragile.

Moreover, such games, and especially the Minecraft, help children to come in contact with economic sectors which are essential for sustainable development such as farming, agriculture and extraction of natural resources. Although the knowledge provided is shallow, some basic aspects are useful, especially for children living in urban areas. However, the dominant message emerging from LoL and Minecraft, that corresponds both to economic and environmental dimensions, relates to consumerism. Both of these games do not prevent players from acquiring a wealth of resources, materials and tools even if they are not needed. Without setting limits (e.g. economic, natural, moral), these games indirectly promote consumerism. In terms of appearance, children seem to adopt consumerist attitudes and accept that dressing is important in real life (LoL). Additionally, it is very interesting to note that children seem to be sensitive with regard to over consuming of some materials, a practice that degrades environmental aesthetics and exploits natural resources (Minecraft).

Conclusion

In conclusion, we consider that, in the light of a constructivist approach, online entertainment games constitute a significant link of an informal education chain which should be taken into consideration.

THE ONLINE LEARNERS IN MOOC SOCIAL ENVIRONMENTS

Udi Shimony, Anat Cohen, Rafi Nachmias, Tal Soffer, Tel Aviv University, Israel

Massive Open Online Courses (MOOCs) are the latest revolution in online teaching and learning. The world's leading universities, such as Stanford, Harvard, and MIT are offering MOOCs to the general public, worldwide, without any preconditions and free of charge. These MOOCs are offered by a variety of initiatives, such as Coursera, Udemy, MITx, edX, Udacity, and are taught by professors around the world, in various fields. They allow for flexible learning at any time and any place, integrating a variety of tasks into the course structure. A major emphasis is put on selecting suitable course subjects, instructors, high quality video production, and a friendly interface. These MOOCs may alter the conception of education and create a culture of collaborative social learning combined with peer assessment.

The literature emphasizes that MOOCs are based on active student engagement in accordance with learning aims and objectives as well as their early knowledge and skills. In online learning, Self-Regulated Learning (SRL) that is characterized by the ability to initiate learning and adapt to new learning methods is crucial. In addition, many researchers and educators (those who support the connectivism) claim that most of the significant learning in online courses takes place through the sharing of information, and interpersonal interaction. Thus, social learning is a central theme of online courses and especially of MOOCs. The main channel for this interpersonal interaction is the course website forums, in which the learning community can manage interactions on issues related to the course (but not necessarily). Hence, this study will examine the extent of forum usage in MOOCs and the patterns of students' activity using Educational Data Mining and learning analytics methods to analyze the data accumulated in Coursera log-files.

The presented study is part of a larger research that aims to characterize and promote effective online teaching and learning processes as well as assessment. In light of the claim that meaningful learning takes place through interpersonal interaction in discussion groups (forums) offered to learners, the fact that the percentage of participants in these discussion groups is lower than expected is not fully explained. This study focuses on large-scale discussion groups operated in connection with one MOOC offered by Tel Aviv University through Coursera. MOOC forums were chosen due to the wide range of activity of thousands of students who registered for this course, and the findings of this study will contribute to the developing body of knowledge on learner communities in other online learning environments as well as academic fully online courses. The aim of this study is to explore the students' participation patterns in forums and characterize them as well as to understand the correlated factors. Accordingly, the study questions were: i) What is the volume of students' activity? ii) What is the volume of students' weekly activity? iii) What are the student participation patterns reflected in the forums? iv) What are the factors which may correlate to the level of participation? and v) Is there a correlation between forum participation and passing the course?

The chosen MOOC was attractive to a large number of learners from different countries, especially from the United States, Europe and Asia. Of the 27,322 students registered for the course, approximately 4,500 registered to use the course's forums during the course, and only 1,257 of them were active in the forums throughout the entire course. Furthermore, when the data was reviewed at the student level, it was found that three quarters of students were hardly active. Most of the activity came from one quarter of the students. Taking a deeper look at student activity, we identified those who chose only to "view" and not to interact with their peers. Especially during the first couple of weeks, most students just "watched" and were "off stage". The volume of views throughout the course was much higher than the number of posts and comments (responses to posts). More students wrote posts than comments. Four clusters were identified while conducting Two-Step Cluster Analysis. Two clusters were characterized as more active (one with posts and the other with views). The other two had low activity, although one was more reactive to others by writing comments and giving points of evaluation and the second, which was the larger, did more posting, viewing and tagging. Active students performed similarly in each channel by writing posts, providing comments, and tagging. However, there are no correlations among the performance and the students' location or achievements. Observation of words used in discussion tags/posts/comments shows that intensive dialogue revolves around topics covered in the forums and related to the course subject. However, words related to learning management were triggered as well.

BUILDING BETTER MOOCS: USING DESIGN PATTERNS FOR MASSIVE OPEN ONLINE COURSE DEVELOPMENT

Steven Warburton, University of Surrey, United Kingdom; Yishay Mor, PAU Education, Spain

The range and number of MOOC offerings has continued to expand and MOOCs have now established themselves as an important part of the online educational landscape. This paper outlines how a design pattern approach was used to bring experts together through the participatory pattern workshop methodology and to explore the successful design approaches that have been deployed to design and deliver Massive Open Online Courses. The resulting set of 19 design patterns are offered as a way for those charged with creating and delivering MOOCs to build on expert success and help design better MOOCs.

The SNaP! (Scenarios, Narratives, and Patterns) methodology was implemented in the form of Participatory Patterns Workshops (PPW). The Participatory Methodology for Practical Design Patterns is a process by which communities of practitioners and experts collaboratively reflect on the challenges they face and the methods for addressing them. Participants share accounts of their experiences prior to the workshop series, which are formulated as design narratives, and collaboratively extract design patterns from these over the course of three workshop sessions.

The MOOC design patterns have been organised into six design decision domains which represent the key decision areas are integral to the majority of MOOC development projects:

Domain	**Patterns**
Structure	Adjacent Platforms; MOOC Legacy; Bring Them Along; Scaffolded MOOC; Checkpoints
Orientation	Induction; Bend Don't Break; Know Your Audiences
Participation	Fishbowl; Provocative Question; Chatflow; Sparking Forum Participation; Sharing Wall
Learning	Knowing The Story; Six Minute Video; See Do Share
Community	Crowd Bonding; Drumbeat;
Management	Engendering Teamwork

The work here creates a starting point for further design activity in the domain of MOOC design and development using patterns. We suggest the use of meta-design pattern or approach based on a simple design cycle to scaffold the MOOC design process to indicate where patterns and related design principles may be deployed.

THE BOOT CAMP MODULE IN MASSIVE OPEN ONLINE COURSES: EXPERIENCES IN TWO EUROPEAN INITIATIVES

Diana Morais, Maria João Leal, Maria João Spilker, Lina Morgado, Universidade Aberta, Portugal

Introduction

In recent years, the European Commission increased efforts in Open Education, Open Educational Resources (OERs) and Information, and Communication Technologies (ICT) in Education in Europe. The gateway of the European Innovative Learning offers access to institutions, resources, courses and MOOCs.

The Massive Open Online Courses (MOOCs) imply, for the educational institutions and the target public, i.e. the participants, the formulation of new goals and addressing unique challenges. In this sense, this paper intends to reach out for the meaning and importance, as a differentiator in the participants' perspective, of a familiarization module (Boot Camp Module) within a MOOC.

The European projects "EMMA" and "ECO"

The project "European Multiple MOOC Aggregator" (EMMA), is a 30 month pilot action that will offer open, massive, online courses in multiple languages from different European providers, promoting promote cross-cultural and multilingual learning. The main goal is to work as a central aggregator and host system of all the courses produced by the partners but also as a system that enables learners to construct their own learning paths using units from MOOCs as building blocks.

The European funded project "Elearning, Communication and Open-data: Massive Mobile, Ubiquitous and Open Learning" (ECO) aims to broaden the education and, on the other hand, to improve the cost-effectiveness of teaching and learning by designing and implementing MOOCs as a way to use OERs. Furthermore, it intends to expand successful experiences with MOOCs in Europe into a pan-European scale, contributing to the awareness of the advantages of open education in Europe.

The Study of the Boot Camp

In this paper we focus on the importance of a preliminary familiarization module ("Boot Camp") in context of a MOOC. This module was designed in conformity with a virtual pedagogical model and using a platform resulting from the integration of the Learning Management System (Moodle) and a social networking system (ELGG), giving the opportunity to acquire, develop and/or consolidate 21st-century skills such as collaboration, knowledge sharing and critical thinking.

The primary goal of the case study consists in the measurement of the importance of the familiarization module and the role of the facilitators' team, in the learning experience of MOOC participants, during this period of time. The messages posts in different spaces (The Wire, Blogs, and Forum) were collected and analysed, resulting in a clear indication as for the importance of this module for the early setting of sense of group and a learning community.

Conclusions and further research

The integration of a social media system (ELGG) with a learning management system (Moodle) seems to be a suitable environment to offer MOOCs. The use of these integrated systems enables the familiarization module used in this iMOOC, with a strong interaction element, which proved to be an essential component in participants learning success. In a future work it is worth investigating the impact of the Familiarization Module in the success of a MOOC by adding an initial questionnaire and interviewing a representative number of participants.

A PEER-MENTORING APPROACH FOR THE CONTINUOUS PROFESSIONAL DEVELOPMENT OF EDUCATORS IN A MOOC SETTING

Muriel Garreta, Universitat Oberta de Catalunya, Spain, Gemma Aguado, Consultant, Spain, Yishay Mor, Consultant, United Kingdom, Carles Fernandez, Consultant, Spain, Katerina Riviou, Ellinogermaniki Agogi, Greece

Introduction

The Massive Open Online Course (MOOC) called 'Learning Design Studio for ICT-based learning activities' was offered from May 19th to June 20th 2014 to teachers and teacher trainers as part of the second pilot of the European Lifelong Learning project HANDSON. The MOOC was aimed at promoting the inclusion of Information and Communication Technologies (ICT) in teaching and learning by empowering educators with digital competences. Following the Learning Design Studio approach (1), the MOOC was designed as a set of activities to walk educators in the design process of an ICT-based learning activity ready to be used in their classrooms.

The data presented in this paper explains how peer-mentoring was implemented for this second pilot of the HANDSON project and how it worked. Both the quantitative and qualitative data gathered show that feedback and comments from peers were positively valued. Also, the data show how peer mentoring generated a shift from the facilitators being at the center of the conversations to the participants being the leaders of conversations.

Peer mentoring in the LDS4ICT MOOC

Peer mentoring is a key element of the HANDSON project and was chosen as a way to create communities of practice among educators and offer ongoing support in the introduction of ICT in the teaching and learning processes. The targeted learners of this MOOC were educators from different sectors and countries.

Several concrete actions and tools were set during the course to involve peers in the learning and feedback process:

1. Explicit mention in the course description and methodology about the use of peer mentoring.
2. Include specific peer mentoring activities.
3. Look at the reviews others have done to your activity and reflect your peers' comments.
4. Comment participants contributions as part of the facilitators tasks.
5. Provide appropriate interactive tools.

The peer mentoring during the second pilot of the HANDSON project has been analyzed using the following indicators: i) number of messages among participants in the Moodle forums, ii) number of comments in the activities developed in ILDE (Integrated Learning Design Environment), iii) participants perception about peer mentoring and interaction during the MOOC. As a result, the data that follows has been gathered from the Moodle, the ILDE and the final survey that was sent to students. Besides, the qualitative comments from participants have also been taken into account.

Discussion and further work

The implementation of peer mentoring actions and strategies during the second pilot of the HANDSON project were successful in raising awareness of the value of feedback from peers and in the engagement of participants as active learners during the MOOC. However, more work needs to be done to make the contributions of peers enriching for the learning processes of participants and to maintain the community alive after the end of the MOOC.

Participants asked for clear indications and guidance regarding the activities of the MOOC. This was mostly provided for the individual activities but a framework also needs to be provided regarding the peer mentoring. Along with the need to be more clear with the process about peer mentoring, as MOOC designers, we faced other difficulties already existing in the MOOC literature: how to guarantee that students are skilled enough to validate the work of peers? Group assessment, creating eportfolios or using challenges are some of the possible answers we present to this question.

COURSES OF THE BAVARIAN VIRTUAL UNIVERSITY FACING MOOCS

Regine Prem, Christina Stötzel, Bavarian Virtual University, Germany

Introduction

The Bavarian Virtual University (BVU) was set up in May 2000. It supports its 30 state funded member universities in providing e-learning courses for high quality education for a growing number of students of higher education. More than 46,000 students were enroled in courses of the BVU in the academic year 2013/14.

The aim of the BVU is to share academic knowledge and therefore to increase cooperation between its member institutions on the issue of education. The courses of BVU can be completed entirely online, thus facilitating their exchange between the member universities. However the aim is not to replace but to complement the programmes of the traditional universities. Students can earn credit points in individual courses but they obtain their degrees at their home university as the BVU does not offer complete degree programmes.

International perception

The BVU was identified as one of seven particular innovative approaches in higher education worldwide in the "Study on innovation in higher education" of the European Commission (2014) "Lifelong Learning: Higher Education and International Affairs". The report aims to contribute to a better understanding of recent developments affecting higher education and provide evidence of how innovation can support higher education in times of change.

Innovative approach of the BVU

With the upcoming number of MOOCs the BVU also started to think about how to face this development. Access to MOOCs has allowed students to obtain a level of education that many only could dream of in the past. This has changed the way people gain knowledge. Just like MOOCs BVU courses offer their participants a very high degree of flexibility and students do not have to pay any extra fees.

The main difference throughout the running course between BVU courses and MOOCs can be found in tutoring. Students participating in MOOCs often complain about the impersonal learning situation, arising from extremely high numbers of students so a single instructor has to cope with a horrendous amount of requests. Interactive actions such as group discussions are almost impossible as well as getting in-depth feedback. In contrast students in BVU courses are intensively guided by online tutors.

Another important aspect for the students is the acceptance of the course at their home university and the degree they are awarded. In MOOCs students often have no opportunity to gain credits for completing the course. So although a student may have received an excellent education, there will not be a corresponding certificate. As a result only a small proportion of students who start a MOOC actually finish it. According to recent surveys MOOCs achieve completion rates of less than 10%, whereas nearly 60% of the BVU students finish their courses with an exam.

Also the teaching staff and the institutions benefit from BVU courses. By integrating them into their study programmes universities can enhance their teaching capacities. The cooperation of different universities allows teachers to team up with colleagues from other organisations, building networks and learning from each other. Also an elaborate quality management is applied to course development and course operation.

Conclusion

As a result of the increasing number of MOOCs the BVU faces the subject carefully and with great interest. Although there are substantial differences in the organisational construction – BVU courses are not always massive, only open and free of charge for Bavarian students and always closely connected to universities – the BVU can benefit from the trend. On the other hand advantages of the BVU concept and its impact for learners, teachers and the learning institution can be shown and transferred to other institutions of higher education.

WHAT TO DO ABOUT MOOCS? BEYOND THE FEAR OF MISSING OUT

Mark Brown, Eamon Costello, Mairéad Nic Giolla Mhichíl, Colette Kirwan, Dublin City University, Enda Donlon, Mater Dei Institute of Education, Ireland

The challenge of weighing up and prioritising institutional drivers for launching a MOOC should not be underestimated. There are significant financial and reputation risks. This paper provides an insider's perspective on the drivers, platform options and guiding questions around the development of Massive Open Online Courses (MOOCs) at Dublin City University (DCU).

MOOCs have the potential for promoting openness, life-long learning and increased participation in higher education. These goals align with DCU's institutional mission of *Transforming Lives and Societies*. Thus DCU's drivers for MOOC initiatives are firmly rooted within its institutional mission. In addition to these high level strategic drivers, DCU's interest in MOOCs is influenced by its commitment to fostering innovation, curriculum renewal and professional development in the areas of online and blended learning. DCU is keen to transfer pedagogical lessons from the use of MOOCs to enhancing the student experience. This university also sees MOOCs as a technological tool to support readiness for university study and successful transitions, particularly for at risk learners.

As with the challenge surrounding prioritising competing institutional drivers, there is a challenge surrounding the selection of the MOOC platform. To fully evaluate the strategic fit for purpose of the many MOOC platforms available, DCU recommends using a decision matrix. Questions that reflected the university's strategic drivers for MOOCs were developed and assigned different weights. This resulted in providing a thorough and trustworthy evaluation of the relative merits of the many MOOC platform options available.

DCU is determined to learn from, contribute to, and help evolve the MOOC movement. Simply put, it intends to continue to play a leading role in new models of online, blended and flexible learning. This paper offers insights into a number of strategic questions about MOOCs, which may help guide future decisions in other institutions.

GAMIFYING MASSIVE OPEN ONLINE COURSES WITH ELGG: AN EXPERIMENTAL STRATEGY DESIGNED FOR THE ECO PROJECT

Antonio Garcia-Cabot, Eva Garcia-Lopez, University of Alcala, Spain, António Moreira Teixeira, Universidade Aberta & University of Lisbon, Portugal, Luis de-Marcos, University of Alcala, Spain, José Mota, LEaD, Portugal

Massive Open Online Courses (MOOCs) are a disruptive new trend in education. They are so called because they brought together the scalability and the openness elements to non formal education. In fact, MOOCs are scalable as they are intended for several thousand participants; they are open, since enrolment is free of charge and there are no admission barriers, constraints or procedures; and they are online because participants use the Internet to access content, resources and assignments, and to interact with other participants.

Designing and running a MOOC involves also tackling several logistical, technological, pedagogical and financial issues, one of the most known and important being the dropout rate. Given the fact that participants do not invest money in enrolling in a course, it is even easier for them to drop it at any time without facing any of the consequences typically experienced in traditional courses. Participant expectations and goals regarding their learning output in MOOCs are substantially different from conventional formal education. This also implies that completion rate is extremely low (between 5% and 20%) when compared with traditional formats, which makes it challenging to determine whether MOOCs are successful.

On the other hand, over time education researchers have conducted many studies on the videogames subject, both theoretical and empirical. These studies have exposed many potential advantages of videogames in education like immediate feedback, information on demand, productive learning, motivating cycles of expertise, self-regulated learning or team collaboration; but also some issues related to educational content, learning transfer, learning assessment, teacher implication and technological infrastructure.

Due to the aforementioned issues, some researchers do not use only videogames to educate; they seek to export the positive aspects of videogames to non-gaming educational contexts. This concept is commonly called "gamification". Gamification has successfully been incorporated with commercial purposes into platforms (e.g. Badgeville, http://www.badgeville.com), in order to create relationships between platform and users, and to increase platform popularity. This success suggests that it could also be used in education as a tool to increase student engagement and motivation. Furthermore, because of its technological nature, one of the fields where gamification may have a greater impact is online learning, especially in its emerging open formats such as MOOCs. Its potential benefits may address some well-known key issues as, for example, the lack of student motivation due to the limited (sometimes even zero) capacity of interaction with teacher and classmates, in xMOOCs, or the need to create a strong and dynamic learning community, in cMOOCs. In addition, the monitoring and communication infrastructure of e-learning platforms (including some specific to MOOCs) provides the necessary tools to incorporate different gamification mechanisms and to measure their usage by students.

Gamification seems thus to be a natural next step towards the development of engaging and collaborative learning experiences, making it ideal for MOOCs, where learning experiences are of this type. Furthermore, since motivation is one of the advantages of gamification, it would be desirable to apply it to MOOCs in order to increase the motivation of students and to decrease the dropout rate.

This paper presents the gamification strategy developed by an international team for use in the sMOOCs developed by Universidade Aberta (Portugal) in the framework of the ECO project partnership which draw their pedagogical approach from the iMOOC pedagogical model created by Teixeira and Mota.

The gamification strategy proposed is divided into two approaches; the first one introduces basic game concepts that have been tested in different courses with positive results in the students. The second approach tries to introduce a more visible mechanism of appreciation of the achievements completed by the students (Open Badges). The aim of this strategy is to improve the motivation and engagement of the students in a massive open online course, increasing the level of sustained commitment by the participants.

OPENSNH – DEVELOPING AN OER OPEN REPOSITORY TOWARDS MOOC

Mats Brenner, University of Gävle, J. Ola Lindberg, Mid Sweden University, Sweden

This paper concerns how open repositories can offer complementary services in relation to institutional and discipline repositories. This paper describes how a service could be built to fill an identified niche and how it connects to related services. The approach taken for this specific open repository, OpenSNH (www.opensnh.se), will highlight the possibilities of offering open educational resources to the entire university sector in Sweden, thereby using the resources for education in a more sustainable way.

In the last 10 years, there has been an increased interest in sharing resources for education in a more sustainable way. One of the initiatives that have gained a worldwide response is the development and sharing of Open Educational Resources (OER), which are often provided through different forms of repositories belonging to the educational providers that have produced them. In the OpenSNH platform, materials are included from several other Swedish universities, based on an agreement with OpenSNH. In the development of OpenSNH, efforts were made to develop tools and didactical scaffolds in the repository, thus turning the collection of OERs and their uses towards the production of mOOCs (mini MOOCs).

The website OpenSNH has been created in collaboration with two commercial partners who both have experience in open source software and e-learning. The content for OpenSNH is related to a previous website for OER resources run by the network SNH, and today nine months after its launch, the site opensnh.se is in operation with 84 learning objects and four complete thematic topics. OpenSNH was created with the open source software OMEKA.org used by several universities for teaching purposes. The OMEKA open source system has also been translated into Swedish. For the process of selecting items and OER for the themes in OpenSNH, we used the following criteria: lifecycle, provenience, originality, broadness, depth, prominence, reliability, and solidity (Commonwealth of Learning, 2011). The OER had to have previously been used in an academic educational context before or as an educational resource or in academic courses at an academic library. OpenSNH uses the resource description and metadata model Dublin Core Extended (2014).

The aspect of accessibility is one criteria that we have prioritized so that both the website of the repository (OMEKA) and the content (OERs) will be accessible to all students (according to 508 compliance standards). We are now investigating and testing the site with the published OERs and theme pages via the web accessibility evaluation tool WAVE. This is ongoing work to ensure that "all" learners benefit from the contents delivered via OpenSNH. We have also produced images/symbols (icons) for OERs that communicate when an OER is a video or a film, has subtext or interpretations, sign language/dactylology, and when the sound in the video is read aloud. All these special accessibility symbols and other OER symbols are open to use, share, and remix for other purposes.

To allocate resources and support around accessibility is a long-term commitment to further quality assurance with the aim that nearly all learners will have their special needs fulfilled regarding searching, viewing, and learning from the OER, theme pages, and forthcoming mOOCs via OpenSNH.

To summarize, the main message in this paper is to demonstrate the possibility of using an open repository to gather OER from different educational providers and provide them in a thematic form for the entire higher educational system. This makes the materials more accessible and the resources for education are used in a more sustainable way. The steps towards the mOOC involve not only technical issues but also an understanding of the predicament about MOOCs' role in a broader educational context.

EXTENDING MOOC CAPABILITIES WITH DEDICATED NETWORKS: THE E-PORTFOLIO TRAINING CASE

Marcelo Maina, Loudes Guàrdia and Ivan Alsina, Univesitat Oberta de Catalunya, Spain

This paper presents new ways of expanding learning scenarios by means of an extended MOOC that differentiates from traditional ones in several ways. Firstly, it is the result of a coordinated effort of organizations, including three different universities. Secondly, it is inserted in a European project broader action of fostering e-portfolio adoption through the creation of a European network of experts, researchers and users. Thirdly, it makes use of innovative scaling up pedagogies for crowd learning, focusing on scaffold and self-regulated learning together with the implementation of the latest notions of social learning. Finally, it pretends to act as a synergy element of the network, both providing and nourishing from each other.

MOOCs variants, the search for novel forms of open education

Even if the MOOC movement recognizes a foundational moment in Siemens Connectivism and Connective Knowledge open course in 2008, it is widely known that AI-Stanford like courses (or xMOOC) has gained worldwide attention and impact. xMOOC are usually criticized as traditional ways of conceiving education packaged in new forms. But MOOC response seems to show capacity of adaptability. MOOCs' variants are starting to offer original solutions blurring boundaries between formal and new forms of education and blending open education with the traditional educational offer. Exploration of new formulas illustrate the case: embedding MOOC using a higher education blended approach or adopting a flipped classroom approach where MOOC video lectures, exercises and quizzes supplement secondary school courses. The Haggard, Brown, Mills, et al. (2013) report shows diversity in the intentions of enrolled people to MOOCs. The statistical analysis of the participants' behaviour let identified four distinctive profiles: auditing, sampling, disengaging and completing. Many participants in MOOC declare to enrol for specific (bits) units or parts of a MOOC. They do not all have the intention to complete the course or they do not sign for recognition, but instead they declare to be interested in concrete competence development or being curious about specific knowledge.

Exploring transformative ways of educational provision

The European EPNET (http://www.eportfolio.eu) project aims at fostering e-portfolio practices for different actors from an integrative approach. We focus on the intersection between learning and professional stages of an individual trajectory, and we situate the e-portfolio as an asset useful to different stakeholders as broad as teachers, employers, governmental administrators and professional bodies. The project plans the provision of a MOOC-inspired open set of modules for self-regulated learning. Our proposal stands on seven independent modules aiming at providing conceptual and instrumental knowledge for the creation of an e-portfolio strategy and prototype solution, regarding individual or institutional objectives. Modules are organized around activities linking theory and practice. Conceptual content is presented in rich media formats using a variety of sources including videos, online presentations, interactive content, and readings. Each activity is provided with illustrative examples showcasing diverse situations and cases of e-portfolio use. We follow principles of scaffold learning applied to online learning by means of supporting instruments. Most of the activities are accompanied with templates and guidelines. To support the sense of ownership the participant is encouraged to set its personal goals and decide on the number of modules to take and the pace for doing so.

The modules will be delivered in first place as a MOOC within the EMMA platform, a development of the homonym European project (http://www.europeanmoocs.eu). This MOOC is part of a greater effort within the EPNET project which has established a network of interested people and that interacts through the Europortofolio portal (europortfolio.eu) and a set of local chapters. We envision providing an environment that connects the learning space (MOOC) with the Europortfolio network. This environment will support lasting debate spaces, open folders for participant-productions' sharing, and functionalities for easing social interaction: RSS feeds notifying content addition, notifications of new messages to interest-focused groups, list of contacts with associated digital profiles. Once a person enrols and registers to this interrelated environment, it may benefit from previous participants contributions, and in turn contribute to the growing of the community and the publishing of its own productions and ideas.

THE POTENTIAL AND THE CHALLENGES OF THE OPEN WEB IN THE DOCTORAL JOURNEY: THE GOAL ORIENTATIONS OF ITALIAN AND UK PHD STUDENTS

Antonella Esposito, University of Milan, Italy, Albert Sangrà, Marcelo Maina, Open University of Catalonia, Spain

This paper is concerned with the exploration of the motivations of individual Italian and UK doctoral researchers dealing with the potential and challenges of the open Web in their doctoral journey. The paper takes cue from the peculiar situation experienced by current PhD candidates, who are challenged to act more as 'doctoral researchers' rather than as 'doctoral students' and are increasingly exposed to the unprecedented opportunities of the Web 2.0 tools and services for improving personal development and practicing innovative scholarly activities. The study assumes that the new learning scenarios for doctoral education should be more permeable to the emerging forms of knowledge production and distribution and should look at doctoral researchers' current self-organized practices in the digital as an informed basis to critically innovate research training. Building on selected, qualitative findings drawn from a wider research, this paper provides a snapshot of drivers, hindrances and concerns characterizing the digital engagement of two non representative samples of individual doctoral candidates. Focus of this paper is on the dispositions of the PhD students toward the open Web, as arising from the free comments received in the initial, exploratory online questionnaire delivered across three Italian and one UK universities. Data triangulation has been applied across diverse contexts, according to the grounded theory principle of the constant comparative method. This approach has allowed us to assess the empirical categories of Benefits, Criticalities, Inhibitors and Individual Perspectives, that respectively summarize the accounted advantages, the factors that are likely to prevent or slow down the uptake of new digital tools and the stated individual views about the role of the digital in the doctoral journey.

It has also scaffolded the identification of a set of PhD researchers' Goal Orientations toward the open Web. The Italian and UK survey respondents similarly see the open Web as an efficiency-enabler of the scholarly tasks and share the same critical issues (e.g. lack of legitimation, privacy, copyright, etc.). However, we have noticed the prevalence of a pragmatic approach among the UK PhD researchers, whilst the Italian ones in places push forward the benefits of the open Web as enhancing the quality of the research environment as a whole. Thus, the conceptual analysis of the open comments has allowed us to sketch four clusters of different individual dispositions (Goal Orientations) toward the potential of the open Web: Pioneering (aiming at exploring new digitally-mediated practice), Coping (dealing with the digital on the basis of occasional needs), Waiting for the mainstream (slowing down engagement because of reluctant academic context) and Rejecting (judging the open Web as irrelevant for research work). Among the differences, in the Italian sample the Pioneering approach seems to imply an ideology-driven attitude, in which the individual feels to be part of a collective movement towards not-yet-defined ways of doing and communicating research. Otherwise, the UK sample lets emerge a peculiar relevance of individual agency for future engagement in the 'digital' as the doctoral journey advances. Moreover, the 'Waiting for the mainstream' disposition is clearly shown only among the Italian participants, whilst among the UK participants the trustful attitude toward the institutional asset of the doctoral experience is linked to a strong sense of personal responsibility in the endorsement of the new clusters of digital tools and practices.

To sum up, the results suggest that the current learning scenarios provided by doctoral programs hardly consider the possible, fruitful relationship between the PhD students' self-organized forms of assistance and the institution-led research training's methodologies. In fact, the PhD researchers involved in the study actually struggle in reaping the benefits and face the challenges of the Web 2.0 and social media, only relying on individual enterprise and occasional experiences and aiming to be somewhat supported by the local formal context.

As conclusions, the suggested line of interpretation of the four Goal Orientations deserves additional investigation to gain insights on the contextual factors (e.g. presence of social media training, adoption of networked practices by the supervisors, etc.) affecting the motivations of individual PhD students researching in diverse subject areas and different national settings. The accurate mapping of the assembling activities carried out by newer researchers between institution-led and self-organized digital opportunities can help to prefigure new learning scenarios for the PhD students, where the use of Web 2.0 tools and social networks in particular can support existing practices as well as unprecedented pilots in knowledge production and distribution.

EVALUATING WEEKLY PREDICTIONS OF AT-RISK STUDENTS AT THE OPEN UNIVERSITY: RESULTS AND ISSUES

Drahomira Herrmannova, Martin Hlosta, The Open University, United Kingdom, Jakub Kuzilek, Zdenek Zdrahal, The Open University, United Kingdom, and CIIRC, Czech Technical University, Czech Republic

Identification of at-risk students

The work at the Open University (OU) focuses on improving student retention by predicting which students are at risk of failing. Our predictive models are trained on data from the previous presentation of the same course and predict whether the student will pass the next assessment. To build these models, 3 types of data are used – students' activity in the Virtual Learning Envirnoment (VLE); their demographics and results from the previous assessments. Four models are trained – CART, Naïve Bayes, kNN with demographic data and kNN with VLE data – and the final decision is acquired by majority voting. These models have been used as a basis for weekly at-risk student predictions for two courses in the summer term 2014 and ten courses in the winter term 2014. The predictions are sent every week to the course teams.

Evaluation of models and issues

In our paper we present an evaluation of the weekly predictions done in the winter term 2014 for one selected course. All 4 models and the voting classifier were compared using the F-measure. Two interesting facts can be noticed in the results – i) including the result from the previous assessment causes growth in the performance of the model that doesn't utilise VLE data and ii) the importance of the VLE features increases when approaching a cut-off date of an assessment and decreases in the first week after the assessment. We can conclude that for the next assessment prediction, it is more important what he/she does right before the assessment rather than at the beginning of the assessment period.

Although the performance of the models expressed by the F-measure looks promising, a decomposition of the F-measure into its components, Precision and Recall, reveals some issues. Although the F-measure increases before the cut-off date as expected, Precision and Recall do not comply with the expected trend. This effect is caused by a misalignment with the previous presentation of the course, which was used for training the model – the cut-off date for the second assessment was one week earlier than in the current presentation.

Towards new mapping strategies

We discuss the problem of mapping the previous presentation to the current one in more detail. We explain why the currently used strategy for synchronisation at the beginning of the assessment period can cause the performance issues. In the worst-case scenario both presentations have a different number of weeks between beginning and end of the given assessment period, and cut-off dates are not in the same days of the calendar week. To tackle this issue, we propose several mapping strategies, which of implementation and evaluation will be the subject of our further work.

STUDENT VULNERABILITY AND AGENCY IN NETWORKED, DIGITAL LEARNING

Paul Prinsloo, University of South Africa, South Africa, Sharon Slade, The Open University, United Kingdom

The increasing collection, analysis, use and possible sharing of student digital data not only promise to increase the effectiveness of student learning and the effective allocation of institutional resources, but also increase student vulnerability. In the context of the asymmetrical power relationship between higher education institutions and students, students are often seen as data objects with now insight or choice regarding the type of data collected, how the data are stored and used, and opportunities to verify collected data or provide context.

Against the backdrop of Privacy 2.0 and the ineffectiveness of regulatory frameworks to protect individual data privacy, as well as concerns that thinking in terms of the binary of either opting in or out, we need to critically investigate the collection, analysis and use of student digital data. This paper explores the promise and possible perils of learning analytics through the interpretive lens of student vulnerability. A framework is provided as basis for a student centred approach to learning analytics where students' agency is valued and optimised within the context of a fiduciary duty of reciprocal care.

STEMMING THE FLOW: IMPROVING RETENTION FOR DISTANCE LEARNING STUDENTS

Sharon Slade, The Open University, United Kingdom, Paul Prinsloo, University of South Africa, South Africa

Though concern about student attrition and failure is not a new phenomenon, higher education institutions (HEIs) have struggled to significantly reduce the revolving door syndrome. Open distance learning higher education is particularly susceptible to high student attrition. Despite a great deal of research into the student journey and factors impacting on likely success, we are not necessarily closer to understanding and being able to mitigate against student attrition. Learning analytics as emerging discipline and practice promises to help penetrate the fog…

This case study describes work undertaken at the Open University in the UK to investigate how a learning analytics approach allows the University to provide timely and appropriate student support in a cost-effective manner. It includes a summary of the establishment of curriculum-based student support teams and a framework which defines more standardised student support informed by both student data and an enhanced knowledge of the curriculum. The primary aim of student support teams is to proactively support students through their study journey and to optimise their chances of reaching their declared study goals.

Higher education institutions (HEIs) are making increasing use of learning analytics to support delivery of timely and relevant student support. The Open University in the UK, like other HEIs, knows a great deal about its students before they start to study and is able to track student behaviours once study has begun. Until recently, the university has not taken full advantage of the additional insight offered by such information. This paper describes the framework of support interventions established for all student support teams and describes the learning analytics approach used to support that framework.

CONTRIBUTION OF NORMATIVE STAKEHOLDER THEORY TO AN EDUCATIONAL DATA WAREHOUSING PROJECT

Gábor Kismihók, Dávid Szörényi, University of Amsterdam, Netherlands

With exponentially growing data quantity, the importance of succeeding in educational data warehousing implementation significantly increased. High level of system quality is more associated with succeeding in organizational- and project implementation than in technical implementation, therefore this paper aims to find a way to improve factors affecting organizational- and project implementation success. Majority of them is strongly people-related, but still there is a gap in literature on how these factors should be improved.

Many researchers in the discipline of stakeholder theory are engaged with stakeholder identification and classification. This research investigates how normative stakeholder theory can contribute to the improvement of these people-related factors by conducting an exploratory case study.

Stakeholders of a learning analytics project at the University of Amsterdam are identified and classified in accordance with a significant classification model, furthermore, presence of the previously defined factors is measured within the project.

As a result, this paper provides several recommendations on the improvement of these factors by linking them with the identified and classified stakeholder groups.

LEARNING ANALYTICS OF A MOOC WITH A TERMINAL EFFICIENCY OF 22.35%

Lorena Yadira Alemán de la Garza, Tecnológico de Monterrey, Mexico, Teresa Sancho Vinuesa, Universitat Oberta de Catalunya, Spain, Marcela Georgina Gómez Zermeño, Tecnológico de Monterrey, Mexico

Introduction

Massive Online Open Courses have revolutionized the offering of open and distance education to a large amount of people; however, this does not imply that classroom-based education is obsolete. Students who enroll in a MOOC are mostly self-motivated individuals who can regulate the pace of their own learning and interested in the topic of the course; nonetheless, desertion rates are usually high. One way to calculate the success of a MOOC is by measuring the terminal efficiency, which is the percentage of participants who received the declarative of achievement, divided by the total of registered participants. Another calculation is the dropout rate, which refers to the school's abandonment due to multiple factors. As consulted in literature, less than 10% of a MOOCs' participants finish the course, and due to the confidentiality and privacy regulations of this type of courses, it is difficult to have sufficient information regarding the causes of students' abandonment. This research aimed to evaluate the terminal efficiency of 12 MOOCs offered by a well renowned Latin American University through Coursera in different areas of study. The panel of statistical analysis shown on the Coursera Dashboard was consulted to observe the number of participants who accomplished the activities to obtain the declarative of achievement in relation to the total participants. For this research, terminal efficiency was calculated considering the participants who remained active the complete course.

Results

From January 2013 to the summer of 2014, the University received 208,871 participants in the 12 MOOCs on Coursera, compared to the 95,000 formal students during the term August-December 2014. Results were organized in the following way: analysis of the 12 courses' terminal efficiency, and the characteristics of the participants of the course with a terminal efficiency of 22.35%. Aside the atypical case, terminal efficiency for the rest of the MOOCs is between 1.2% and 10.5%; the courses with the lowest and highest terminal efficiency correspond to the courses with higher amount of participants. The atypical course had 10,161 participants, from which 506 received declarative of normal achievement with a final average equal or higher than 70 and the submission of all activities, and 1,765 received the declarative of achievement with distinction that required the compliance of all activities and a final average equal or higher than 90, which means that 17.37% of students presented a high level of commitment to the course. The characteristics of the participants in the MOOC with atypical terminal efficiency are calculated from the survey that was part of the registration process to the course. Some of the descriptive statistics obtained are: 39.82% male and 60.18% female; average age of 38; 65.58% reside in Mexico and 34.42% outside Mexico. 74.38% work in the area of Teaching / Pedagogical Technical Advisor and 56.13% work at a Public School. 69.99% of the participants expressed that the main reason for participating was the desire to upgrade knowledge about models of strategic educational management, 98.04% expressed intention of completing the course, and 36.81% expected to get a participation's certificate by the University.

Conclusion

The reasons leading universities to offer MOOCs are part of positioning strategies, of attracting national and international talent for projects of educational innovation and social commitment, to name a few. However, there must be parameters to evaluate success. The analysis for the terminal efficiency minimum and maximum rate in relation to the number of participants enrolled at the MOOCs showed that a low terminal efficiency expressed as a percentage is still attractive to the academic authorities in terms of total amount of participants. Among the most noteworthy findings of this research is the terminal efficiency rate of 22.53% in a MOOC, higher than reported by other courses of the same University, or even in the literature. Future research is proposed to expand the knowledge of how to increase terminal efficiency in MOOCs, one suggestion is the statistical validation of the correlation between the initial intention and the terminal efficiency rate. It is concluded that to evaluate the success of a MOOC, it is necessary to generate learning analytics metrics other than those employed in the evaluation of face-to-face or hybrid courses, to influence in on the quality and improvement of educational offering of MOOCs.

WEB-BASED ANALYSIS OF STUDENT ACTIVITY FOR PREDICTING DROPOUT

Anat Cohen, Tel Aviv University, Israel

Persistence in learning processes is perceived as a central value in education; therefore, dropout from studies is a prime concern for educators. Since the increase in student usage of online learning materials on course websites, as well as online courses, it is essential to address the dropout issue in a wide array of configurations from web-supported learning to fully online courses. Additional tools and strategies must be developed to allow instructors or other educational decision makers to quickly identify at-risk students and find ways to support their learning in the early stages, before they actually drop out. The ability to detect these students during the semester, and not at the end of the course, can also serve as a basis for the development of appropriate assistance mechanisms which will enable those students to complete the course and even to fulfill the curriculum for their degree.

In order to meet the challenge of identifying dropouts early, it is possible to use the large databases that are created automatically in the Learning Management Systems (LMSs) servers. These databases contain enormous amounts of data relating to learning processes and learner behaviors on course websites. This data can be analyzed in order to evaluate the learning processes; improve teaching and learning; optimize the construction of learning systems and their operation; and can even be used to predict potential dropouts and failures.

The presented study focuses on identifying at-risk learners who might drop out from specific courses or from degree studies in general, based on the analysis of student activity in the course website data which is accumulated in the log files of the LMS, Moodle. Student data from six courses in the disciplines of exact science were analyzed. In these courses, the dropout rate is usually very high. Furthermore, students who fail these courses occasionally drop out of their degree study as well. Variables and measurements regarding student activity on course websites that may alert to dropout based on student activity intensity were identified. Student activity intensity can be analyzed relating to different features available to students through the course website. Looking at one student's activity alone is not enough. A comparison between the activity of a specific student compared to the rest of a class is required, in order to understand whether the observed activity is expected or not, according to the course requirements.

While exploring the student activity on the websites, different kinds of patterns were found. The findings show that certain characteristics of student web activity can indicate potential risk of course dropout or even degree study termination. At-risk students might show changes in their behavior, unexpectedly, such as inactivity on the course website or a reduced amount of activity in relation to the rest of the class. Furthermore, a high percentage of predicted dropout was shown and there was a strong correlation between the dropout alerts, course completion status, and continued study status. Students who were flagged using the analysis did not complete their course and/or discontinued their studies the following year.

The results of this study show that our main hypothesis is supported. Students most likely to drop out of a course will first become absent from the course website. Essentially, a dropout's early traces will be manifested first on course websites; hence, they can be traced in the LMS log files. These findings are preliminary and may be used as a basis for developing a web- based analyzing tool for predicting potential dropouts.

The information obtained from the presented analysis may assist teaching staff and other institutional mechanisms in supporting and retaining their students. This analysis enables the instructors to monitor student activity on the website throughout the learning process during a course, not only at the end, in order to detect students who are not using the website, or students with unexpected behavior. The main purpose of getting this information is to allow the instructor to contact students who could potentially abandon their studies, and to understand the reasons why. Additionally, this analysis will allow instructors to understand the scope of course material usage and patterns so that they can make improvements. This analysis can be used by educational decision makers too, according to ethical guidelines, since it will allow them to see the information on a campus level; to identify students with potential for dropout in relation to different faculties, instructors, types of courses, or other chosen criteria. Thus, intervention programs for potential dropouts can be initiated.

WIN, WIN, WIN: AN ASSESSMENT SYSTEM THAT WORKS FOR STUDENTS, STAFF AND THE ACADEMY

Danny Carroll, UNSW Business School, Australia

This paper first briefly explores the current landscape of assessment and assurance management systems, before providing a case-study of Review, a direct-marking and assessment management system in use at the University of New South Wales (UNSW), Sydney, Australia. The current state of theory and practice in systems facilitating assessment for learning is discussed, before features of future oriented assessment management systems are proposed. The underpinnings and affordances in our experience of using Review for students, staff and administrators are then described. Review, designed by academics for academics, is used in several Australian universities and in over a hundred courses each semester at UNSW.

The system is used for both direct criteria based marking and as a marks repository for course and Program (Degree) assurance. Review connects course-based learning events, judgment against criteria and feedback with degree and PLGS across the length of student degree programs. Native affordances and limitations of the system are described. The focus of this paper is on how the system supports a holistic approach to assessment which is described as a 'virtuous cycle' of activity for markers, students and administrators.

This virtuous cycle supports and improves student learning, staff assessment and Program (Degree) assurance and reporting. This is exemplified with detail of the system's learning / assessment data structures, the intuitiveness of its interfaces and workflow designs, marking efficiencies and the personalised data recoverable by users according to their roles. Few university wide assessment systems carry granular marks data that tracks meaningful and mappable student achievement, an essential attribute of a future oriented assessment system.

This paper advances Review as a successful example of a 'future assessment' system, agile, user-centric and holistically designed to concord with institutional values (promotion of learning). In Review, activity (framing assessments), achievement (judgement outcomes of assessment) and feedback is explicitly, efficiently and ubiquitously mapped to learning progress against degree / program learning goals, benefitting all parties.

This national award winning software supports direct, criteria-based marking, self-assessment by students and improves clarity around assessment for staff and students. The software provides students with a more personalised learning experience via degree-long access to course feedback and the ability to run task or longitudinal self-reports at the criteria, task, course, year and Program (degree) level. Essentially, this establishes the basis of an 'inclusive' assessment feedback system, where learner needs are equal to institutional needs.

Staff report decreased marking times, easier administration and improved feedback quality. This is facilitated by a team-based Comment Library feature that accelerates the creation, collective improvement and re-use of feedback, one aspect of the 'virtuous cycle'. A range of visual 'home' screens that track marking activity, with high-level heat maps, visually signify the masses of data that lie beneath, easing administration, supporting in-built quality processes and enhancing staff experience of managing assessment.

'Review improves marking efficiency and helps me moderate and benchmark my tutors' marking more easily … criteria-based feedback has reduced my post-assessment correspondence with students.' Finally, the inbuilt querying interface enables course and program assurance reporting via bottom to top' data mapping. Marking criteria data is mapped to Program and graduate Attributes (such as Critical Thinking, Oral Communication, Digital Literacy etc), and this provides the basis for task data to be meaningfully represented at all levels, including course, School, Program or university graduate attribute reports. The reporting on student's actual achievement from the very granular base of marking criteria systematises a description of assessment in a way that better represents their actual learning and charts the progress of their graduate attribute development.

All in all, let's not forget what this is all about – better learning experiences for our students. As assessment directs and drives learning, we have to design holistic assessment systems that support improvement in the experience of assessment, the associated learning and the development of self-regulating, professionally oriented graduates.

10 KEY CRITERIA TO MANAGE AND SUSTAIN E-FEEDBACK IN WRITTEN ASSIGNMENTS

Teresa Guasch, Anna Espasa, M. Rosa Mayordomo, Open University of Catalonia, Spain

Introduction

This paper contributes the body of research evidence in order to clarify how to sustain and maintain online formative feedback in online learning environments from a dialogical perspective. Feedback is not a static action of providing support to the learner in one direction; on the contrary, it is a complex process which includes how the feedback is received and used by the learner. Following Dysthe, Lillejord, Vines and Wason (2010), feedback is defined as a loop which includes the process of giving or delivering feedback (by teachers and/or peers), processing it and implementing it in the final output. This paper will present different strategies focused on feedback when developing written assignments. It will suggest how to design, deliver and provide feedback to learners in online learning environments in order for feedback to become an effective support which contributes to implementing changes into the final texts and consequently to students' learning.

Methodology

This proposal presents preliminary results of the analysis of a university teacher-training seminar about feedback processes in online learning environments which were held four times between 2012-2014. This training seminar consisted of a virtual hands-on workshop addressed to lecturers from all Faculties of the Open University of Catalonia (UOC), a fully-online university since its foundation. The participants were 113 university teachers, each an expert in their subject area, and with experience in online university teaching.

To collect information, different techniques were combined so that the data could be contrasted from different sources. First, an online survey was administered to the students in order to find out about their previous experiences of designing their method of feedback in online environments, particularly in relation to writing tasks. Secondly, participants' interaction in the groups was recorded to understand their difficulties in order to design and give feedback; this task was developed in each group. We also collected the learning outputs submitted by participants in the first assignment. Finally, participants had to answer a satisfaction survey. This study is focused specifically on the analysis of the learning outputs of the first assignment of the course. A content analysis of the documents was carried out from an inductive perspective identifying the topics related with how feedback should be carried out in order to contribute to learning. The data analysis is based on a previous study taking into account different dimensions, such as the planning process of designing the feedback method, the nature of the feedback, its function, the medium to provide the feedback, and students' use and implementation of the feedback.

Results and conclusions

From a triangulation of the different data sources, ten key criteria were identified covering the whole feedback loop (giving-processing-implementing). Examples of the strategies will be presented in order to provide scaffolding in their implementation into the teaching practice in online learning environments. Among the criteria are:

- Planning feedback; timing feedback (it should be given when the students are working on their assignments and also once they have submitted it); matching feedback to learning aims; personalising feedback; and designing feedback for self-regulation.
- Giving feedback by the teacher, a team, a peer, a technological system or an external expert. Depending on who gives the feedback, some strategies are identified: a) Co-assessment or peer assessment, b) Self-assessment and, c) rubrics for giving feedback.
- Choosing the appropriate medium when delivering feedback: audio, video, written.

360° E-ASSESSMENT: AN ONLINE COLLABORATIVE PROCESS IN THE SCENARIO OF THE OPEN UNIVERSITY OF CATALONIA (UOC)

Montse Guitert, Teresa Romeu, Marc Romero, Universitat Oberta de Catalunya, Spain

Based on the theoretical principles of assessment in virtual environments, this paper approaches e-assessment defined as any assessment process in which ICT is used in order to introduce and carry out assessment activities and tasks, register the answers and evaluate them from different perspectives: learners, teachers, institutions. The variety of applications of e-assessment and its innovation and efficiency reaffirm its potential as a booster of the learning process and learner outcomes.

The experience presented in this paper focuses on the subject "ICT competencies" (ICTC) which is part of all the UOC university programs. This subject helps students to develop key methodologies and skills to work in digital environments from a rational and critical perspective, and its objective is that students begin in a gradual and integrated way with the acquisition of transversal competencies at the UOC; «Use and application of ICT in an academic and professional environment» and «Online team work». The methodological approach is project-based learning, concretely; the developing of a collaborative digital project is contemplated. To undertake it, students form groups of four, and have their own group space which integrates a variety of tools.

During the development of the subject, student learning is assessed from two dimensions provided by the continuous assessment paradigm: on the one hand, based on the analysis of the process followed during the development of the activities and, on the other hand, based on the final outcome

Considering this perspective, the concept of 360° e-assessment can be formulated from the bases of the 360° Communication, and be defined as following

- Strategic: considering the totality of the learning experience and competency acquisition,
- Comprehensive: seeing the learning space as a live, changing and dynamic system that affects all of the agents of the teaching and learning process,
- Holistic: takes into account all the internal agents –understood as work groups- and external –the whole classroom- in order to understand collaborative learning as more than an addition of several parts,
- Transversal: it affects all of the learning actions and activities and the interactions that take place during the learning process,
- Coherent: it coordinates and gives sense to the whole teaching-learning process,
- And dynamic: it conceives assessment as a constant interaction process among students and between students and teachers that can be redefined depending on the inputs received.

Following this definition, the aim of 360° e-assessment is to reinforce and motivate the students' learning process in order to help them to acquire the competencies of the ICT competency course.

This paper highlights different typologies of e-assessment in the 360° paradigm, considering process and final outcome assessment from both teacher (Assessment of the process of the groups followed during the learning activities, and result of the assessment based on the analysis of the outcome of each phase of the subject) and student's perspective (carrying out self and peer assessment processes; reflection and dialectic assessment of the final products of other teamwork).

In conclusion, what provides the 360° vision to e-assessment is the fact that it is carried out collaboratively and each student has an important role in both self and peer-assessment processes. In order that this collaboration becomes authentic, it is necessary that all of the participants show some attitudes like those of constant participation, periodicity in communication, commitment and transparency. In addition, it is a great resource to improve online teaching and learning processes.

OPEN BADGES, A NEW STANDARD IN THE EXPANDING LEARNING LANDSCAPE

Eric Rousselle, Discendum Oy, Finland

From a lifelong learning perspective, our learning landscape can't be reduced to educational institution's formal learning environment because most of our learning is informal and actually happens in "real life"; at work, at home, in different kind of activities and in interaction with different kind of people. The expansion of the educational landscape is much more than the adoption of new technologies and new methodologies in the field of formal learning. The replacement of massive Learning Management Systems by lighter solutions such as MOOCs, PLEs, social media services and mobile apps shows that the traditional formal learning environments are beginning to become less formal, less institution centric and more decentralized and learner centric. The borders between formal and informal learning are slowly but surely vanishing, and the fragmentation of traditional learning environments requires a new approach to the recognition of learning. With the Open Badge standard our educational landscape can be expanded but still remain consistent and meaningful.

The Open Badges concept is a new way to recognize, acknowledge and make visible the skills and achievements acquired by formal and non-formal learning. It is an open standard developed by the Mozilla foundation. An Open Badge is a digital image that includes metadata about the skills of the receiver of the badge. The digital form of the badge enables the use of the badge in online services such as social media applications or one's own ePortfolio. Badges offer a way of increasing engagement and efficiency of working with ePortfolios.

Several national and international projects (such as Badge Europe, Badge Alliance, DigitalME) have been set up to promote Open Badge awareness and develop badge ecosystems recently. In this presentation, we will introduce a Finnish project called Open Badge Factory, and its efforts to develop an active badge community and a badge management platform. The project's core team consists of five Finnish organizations from non-governmental, corporate and educational sectors. The work on the Open Badge Factory project was started in 2013 and is now in a piloting phase, with 101 organizations from around the world taking part. The piloting organizations are committed to reporting their user experiences and feedback to the project team.

One of the key drivers in the project is to develop methods to prevent badge fragmentation and inflation in organizations. In our presentation, we will discuss how a centralized Open Badge library and a clearly defined badge strategy aligned with an organization's competencies can lead to improved credibility and adoption of the badge concept.

We can state that the interest in the Open Badges concept is global. However, many organizations are still at early stages with their badge system and they are just testing the concept. We have trained several Finnish organizations and we have learned that badge creation is a demanding process, which requires teamwork, assessment of organizational operations, changes and strategic decisions. One of the challenges is that pioneers taking part in the piloting phase cannot raise the organization's management's interest in the matter.

The pilot shows remarkably how the Open Badges can function as an agent of change in an organization. When an organization embarks on the journey of badge design, they will have to actively reflect on their current ways of working, spell out what kinds of competencies are required. In the process, they may start to question things that have been previously taken for granted, which opens doors for developing and validating new ways of working. Employees could be an integral part of the badge implementation process: they could bring their views of future knowledge and competence needs to the table and also build up communities of practice in an organic way.

We will conclude our presentation by sharing the usage statistics and feedback from the piloting community, and based on those will also present the challenges which have become apparent when implementing the Open Badge concept. We will also present our views and possible solutions to these challenges.

MEASURING A CRITICAL IMPACT ON TECHNOLOGY IN EDUCATION: A TOOL FOR OERS EVALUATION

Antonella Poce, Francesco Agrusti, Università Roma TRE, Italy

This paper is part of a wider research project and focuses on the model adopted for evaluating the impact and effectiveness of online teaching and learning, enabling students to adopt a critical approach which could be extended to any online resource which they may use for their lifelong learning. Otten and Ohana, in their *The Eight Key Skills Competences for Lifelong Learning (2009)*, a document issued under the support of the EC DG Education and Culture, focus on the identification of a set of skills needed to overcome present youth unemployment and social exclusion in developed countries. The central concepts referred to are: "critical thinking, creativity, initiative taking, problem solving, risk management, decision taking and managing feelings in a constructive manner" (p.10). There should be a closer connection between the above skills, education and digital education in particular. Technology plays a fundamental role in everyone's life and must be approached critically, especially by young people entering the labor market for the first time. In the information society, the amount of online content is constantly increasing, and more content is becoming readily available online. Open Educational Resources (OER) are assuming an ever increasing importance in national educational policies. Between 2005 and 2007 UNESCO identified priorities for the spread of OER (OECD, 2007).

The Laboratory for experimental pedagogy (LPS) based at the Department of Education – Roma Tre University has been working, since 2010, on research focusing on the enhancement of students' critical thinking skills to foster the development and promotion of the critical use of technology in education. A series of departmental projects, coordinated by LPS researchers, have been funded from 2011 to achieve these aims (Poce et al. 2011, 2012, 2014). The projects use specific models and coordinated approaches to teaching and learning across a range of disciplines. Students are invited to engage in learning activities, which involve analysis and reflection, individually and in groups, taking into considerations the differences in learning, according to the specific situation. Students work on the different tasks focusing on the identification of cultural and disciplinary contexts, within the *lectio magistralis framework*: i) *Distinctio* – presentation of the context; ii) *Divisio textus* – analysis of the text; iii) *Collatio* – discussion; iv) *Quaestio* – critical interpretation.

The same analytical method is used on a variety of texts, including Descartes and Rousseau, working online on a dedicated platform. The main aim of the study has been to provide students with the opportunity to approach online learning in a structured way, which can be applied in a variety of contexts.

This paper describes how giving students the tools to carry out an evaluative analysis of the resource they are accessing can enable them develop their analytical and critical thinking skills. It can also help them to gain insight into the importance of 'learning to learn'. These students also gain the ability to identify the impact of OERs on Higher education teaching and learning. The main scope of the present research project is that students could independently evaluate the quality of online digital resources both as learners and future educators. Doing so it is possible to overcome "brief term instrumental characteristics" of tools and promote long term evaluation processes (Vertecchi, 2012). This proposal concerns an area of research into distance learning which has not been explored in this way previously. The study does not explore the quality of learning in online environments. Rather, it investigates how students should approach the online resources at their disposal, facilitating their critical and reflective skills and adopting a model for analysis.

REALIZING THE POTENTIAL OF COMPETENCY-BASED LEARNING AND BADGES

Deborah Everhart, Georgetown University and Blackboard, United States of America

Though not new, competency-based learning (CBL) has recently captured the attention of the education community – and for good reason. When millions of people have been unable to attain credentials while juggling work, families, and other responsibilities, learners need flexibility in their educational opportunities. The large segment of first-generation, low income students also benefit from innovative pedagogical approaches and lower cost options, and in this arena CBL provides many advantages. However, CBL is not one specific thing, and when combined with the potential of badges and micro-credentials, it is part of a growing range of opportunities for learner-centric innovations in education policy and practice.

As part of a joint research initiative, the American Council on Education and Blackboard have generated a series of resources to foster broader understanding of CBL and how various types of CBL practices can contribute to degree completion and workforce readiness. The research deliverables include

- Clarifying Competency-based Education Terms: A Lexicon, contributing a shared vocabulary that facilitates discussions among stakeholders
- a framework of CBL models
- a series of case studies
- guides explaining CBL practices
- a white paper, The Currency of Higher Education: Credits and Competencies, analysing how learning outcomes attain value in educational ecosystems
- a public forum
- a series of roundtables among CBL thought leaders.

The research is not simply describing the current state of CBL, but more importantly raising challenging questions about scalable, learner-centric approaches that include assessing learning in non-academic settings and the use of open badges to record, certify, and accumulate evidence of learners' competency achievements. The research prompts us to consider critically the role of courses, credits, and other traditional educational structures as CBL provides a different lens for understanding learning achievements, authentic assessment, evidence of learning, and lifelong learning practices. This presentation addresses how evolutions in policies and practices are changing the landscape of educational delivery and attainment.

This presentation will provide a review of the research results, interwoven with a series of challenging unanswered questions. The presenter will prompt the audience with potential scenarios depicting different approaches to CBL that lead to innovative changes in policies and practices. Participants will be challenged to consider how CBL scenarios could challenge existing structures and/or lead to innovative, learner-centric evolutions at their own institutions.

Participants will benefit from this presentation by:

- articulating scenarios that cause reconsideration of traditional educational units and structures
- formulating challenging questions about the opportunities of CBL and badges
- being challenged to consider the potential impacts of CBL at their own institutions.

PDPIE FRAMEWORK: ONLINE COURSE DEVELOPMENT QUALITY CYCLE

Afsaneh Sharif, University of British Columbia, Canada, Merce Gisbert, Universitat Rovira I Virgil, Spain

Introduction

The growth of online education, new approaches for its delivery, its convergence with on-campus learning, and its global impacts have created considerable discussions in quality of online learning all around the world. This has also brought educators' attention into the practice of those professionals involved in online course development including instructional designers who are the key professionals involved in online course development. Planning, Design, Production, Implementation, Evaluation (PDPIE) Framework is an online course development quality framework which is the result/outcome of a PhD study conducted in Spain and Canada. The study and observation of the evolution of technology, instructors and learners' roles, and instructional designers' cultural and educational differences led to development of a flexible online course development guideline within this field. The guideline can be found at http://wiki.ubc.ca/Design_Quality_OnlineCourse.

PDPIE Quality Framework

The framework consists of five sections; each section covers one of the five phases of the course development cycle: planning, design, production, implementation and evaluation. PDPIE shares many qualities with ADDIE model. The first phase of the PDPIE calls for conducting a needs analysis, which covers learners' characteristics, context, and instructional goals. In the second phase, the main content and instructional strategies are determined and developed. In the production phase, the content is developed fully online. The implementation covers instructors' training, teaching/delivery, learners' support and resources. Finally, the last phase covers evaluation in both formative and summative formats. In each phase, the roles and required tasks are discussed and different guidelines, and checklists are developed and shared. The terms and steps are explained in detail to avoid misinterpretations. Supporting documents developed for each phase include templates, samples and guided questions that help designers and instructors to do their jobs more efficiently with the timeline given. The resource has been accessed by 2107 individuals so far and has been used in different universities in Spain, Canada and Australia.

In the online resource in which the framework is presented, each phase starts with an overview, a descriptive image, and a list of tasks suggested to be performed by an instructional designer within that phase. The resource is based on team approach course development; however, there are instructions for lone ranger approach as well (for those instructors who do not have any resources or support to develop their online course). The resource is flexible in the sense that it is accessible online and is licensed under creative commons. Those who decide to adapt it should be able to customize and update it regularly. The resource was developed in Wiki so that the content can easily be transferred to a website, a Learning Management System, or a course. It is also user friendly and easy to update.

A QUALITY SCORECARD FOR THE ADMINISTRATION OF ONLINE LEARNING PROGRAMS IN HIGHER EDUCATION

Kaye Shelton, Lamar University and Online Learning Consortium, United States of America

The delivery of education online has forever changed higher education and distance learning programs throughout the world. Many institutions experienced quick success in this new method for teaching and learning; however, there was much concern expressed regarding quality and how it compares to the traditional method for teaching and learning. In fact, both administrators and faculty have questioned how to measure quality in online education and what evaluation methods should be used for continuous improvement strategies and accreditation requirements. This six-month long Delphi study produced an answer to this important question: a fully developed instrument for online administrators to use for program evaluation that may be used at the program, college, or system level — *The Quality Scorecard for the Administration of Online Programs* (QSC). *The Quality Scorecard* may be used to demonstrate elements of quality within the program as well as an overall level of quality. In addition, weaknesses are identified that can be used to support program improvement and strategic planning initiatives. *The Quality Scorecard* was developed to be utilized by an administrator as the researcher believed that the only the administrator would have a large enough perspective and knowledge of all elements of the online program.

The QSC is organized into nine categories: Institutional Support, Technology Support, Course Development and Instruction Design; Course Structure; Teaching and Learning, Social and Student Engagement, Faculty Support, Student Support, and Evaluation and Assessment with a total of 75 quality indicators. Each of the 75 indicators is worth one, two, or three points and corresponds to a provided rubric. The administrator will determine at what level their program meets the intent of the quality indicator after examining all procedures and processes. The following guidelines are provided as part of the coversheet for the scorecard:

- 0 points = Deficient. The administrator does not observe any indications of the quality standard in place.
- 1 point = Developing. The administrator has found a slight existence of the quality standard but difficult to substantiate. Much improvement is still needed in this area.
- 2 points = Accomplished. The administrator has found there to be moderate use and can substantiate the use of the quality standard. Some improvement is still needed in this area.
- 3 points = Exemplary. The administrator has found that the quality standard is being fully implemented, can be fully substantiated, and there is little to no need for improvement in this area.

The following scoring guidelines are also provided as a general recommendation for the online education administrator:

- 189-210 points – Exemplary (little improvement is needed)
- 168-188 points – Acceptable (some improvement is recommended)
- 147-167 points – Marginal (significant improvement is needed in multiple areas)
- 126-146 points – Inadequate (many areas of improvement are needed throughout the program)
- 125 points and below – Unacceptable.

Quality is a perception that varies within industries, including that of higher education whose traditional indicators for quality are changing. The results of this study provide an industry agreed upon tool by creating a scorecard for determining levels of quality in online programs, which satisfies a great need in the field. This study provides just such a process, which is now being used throughout the United States, in Latin America after a norming process, and Mexico. The assessment of quality online education has never been more important as fierce competition from for-profit programs as well as many non-profits programs continues to increase and students all over the world are clicking to find a quality online degree program.

HOW ASSESSMENT TECHNOLOGY CAN DEVELOP TO ADDRESS THE CURRENT CHALLENGES OF ACADEMIC INTEGRITY

William Dorman, Kryterion Inc., Rick Shearer, Penn State University, United States of America

Academic integrity is essential to the reputations of our institutions as well as the credibility and perceived value of our degree programs. Of particular interest in recent years has been the increasing use of online assessments for both distance education and resident instruction students and the associated challenges and opportunities this relatively new methodology might present. How can software systems streamline the assessment process, ease the burden on faculty and students while maintaining the high standards of academic integrity we require? Further, how can new test development and delivery tools, coupled with online proctoring services, present secure exams that surpass the assessment and measurement abilities of traditional multiple choice and short answer type strategies?

In general, criterion-referenced tests and assessments measure student performance against predetermined criteria or learning standards (i.e. specific written descriptions of what students are expected to know at a specific stage of their education). Typically these are used to evaluate whether the student can perform at or above the established expectations. For example, by answering a certain percentage of questions correctly, they will pass the test, meet the expected standards, or be deemed "proficient". Further, our norm-referenced tests are designed to rank test takers on a "bell curve." Thus what we end up with is a small percentage of students who perform poorly, most trend towards average performance, and a small percentage perform above the average (one standard deviation). This result would imply that test questions are designed to accentuate performance differences among test takers, rather than identifying whether students have achieved specified learning standards, learned required material, or acquired specific skills.

So how can today's technologies help shift the assessment strategies from ranking test takers against each other to more meaningful assessments of knowledge gained? How can our systems employed in online proctoring expand to include essays, open-ended questions, and case-based learning that work to uncover levels of deep learning?

This session will explore assessment strategies and try to answer some of the key questions:

- How can technology address "open-ended" questions or a combination of question, or item, types?
- How can learning gaps or academic deficiencies be captured and analysed?

How can technology assist with the evaluation of a course by using "pre-tests" and "post-tests" to measure learning progress?

USING MOOCS TO TRAIN THE NEXT GENERATION OF WEB ENTREPRENEURS: CHALLENGES AND OPPORTUNITIES

Eulalia Canals, Universitat Oberta de Catalunya, Spain, Yishay Mor, P.A.U. Education, United Kingdom

There is an increasingly growing gap between the skills required in most web related jobs and the skills recent graduates possess, especially in the technology sector. MOOCs and other open online courses are beginning to be considered as suitable training options, although employers have yet to acknowledge their value as a proof of the knowledge and/or the skills acquired.

This paper presents the main activities conducted within the framework of a European project which aims at providing training opportunities for aspiring web entrepreneurs in Europe by encouraging the use of Massive Open Online Courses (MOOCs) focused on web skills. Within the scope of the project, we carried out several activities to explore and promote the use of MOOCs to develop web skills. The project started with a scoping study that examined the total amount of existing webMOOCs and provided a precise mapping of the platforms and the countries that were offering them, whilst comparing the provision in European and in North America. Next, a survey was carried out amongst students, entrepreneurs, leaders of innovation support programs, developers, and MOOC providers with the aim of offering insights and data to help strengthen and enhance the use of MOOCs for web talent across Europe. In addition to these two research activities, the project created a network of MOOC providing institutions and MOOC experts that met in several networking events, including a webinar around the topic of certification and recognition of MOOCs, a workshop session at EC-TEL 2014, and a final conference in Helsinki during the 2014 edition of Slush.

According to the project's findings, MOOC participants are mostly interested in acquiring or improving web design skills and claim that taking a MOOC helped them develop the skills they needed, although this did not necessarily result in them finding a job. MOOC providers expressed their interest in the extra dissemination opportunities that MOOCs bring, as well as the fact that MOOCs can help improve blended learning pedagogy. They also stated however that cost remains the biggest barrier for the provision of MOOCs. Developers, entrepreneurs and innovation leaders stressed the fact that in the current market it is especially difficult to find employees with web and mobile application design skills, audio/video authoring, game design, web animation skills, and web programming languages. They think that MOOCs and 'on-the-job' training could be the most effective training methods in providing those skills and closing any skills gap.

Amongst the project outcomes, there are several that have some implication for policy-makers. MOOC providers need to address the concerns of students regarding recognition of MOOCs as valuable learning practices. Potential participants are struggling to find the MOOCs they need. Policy makers should consider offering MOOC providers specific mechanisms that can help them reduce the cost and raise the quality of the MOOCs they produce, in order to better meet the demand for courses based around specific areas of content.

COMPETENCES AND SKILLS FOR 21ST CENTURY DIGITAL MEDIA PROFESSIONALS

Mathy Vanbuel, ATiT, Frauke Hein, ATiT, K.U.Leuven, Belgium

The 2014 iProfessional survey with over 1100 participants from eight EU countries collected data about the skills and competences of professionals working in digital media and arts, including industries such as eLearning design. This highly diverse group of professionals consists of designers, creators, writers that are working across all media: radio, TV, press, web, multimedia, film, theatre, print, games etc. and not only in the artistic realm but in all segments of the society: information, news and press, advertisement and public relations, industry, commerce and education.

The rich and complex data that are the result of the survey are sufficient to come to meaningful conclusions, especially with regard to the impact of education and training on this worker in his professional environment. The survey has allowed us to make a quantitative and limited qualitative analysis of the profiles of media workers with regard to the competences, skills and attitudes they possess, such as artistic skills, technical skills, business processes knowledge, communication skills, project management, structuring of content, teamwork, problem solving, time management, etc.

The survey resulted in a comprehensive list of transversal skills and competences that are required by the professional digital media and arts worker set off against those acquired in formal education as well as on the job, identifying in that way the existing gap between what education offers and what the industry expects in this particular domain.

- The very high degree of variance of results demonstrates one of the assumptions that were at the origin of the survey: the fact that a significant number of employees are streaming in to the job without sufficient qualification in the specific professional field and/or with no relevant education or professional experience.
- A higher educational degree seems to have a positive influence on the "skills and competences gap": a higher education results in a smaller gap.
- Male respondents show a lower average gap than female respondents.
- Company size does not show any correlation with the average skill gap.
- The average skill gap is lower with those respondents that are not in their first job, and even lower again where their previous job was also in the digital arts and media domain.
- Internships have a very positive effect on the skills gap if they last at least one year. This effect is amplified when the internship is supervised.
- There is also a relationship between the skill gap and the secondary school degree: those secondary education degrees that contain certain digital arts and media competences and skills have a positive effect on the skills gap later on in the professional career.
- To reduce successfully the skills gap the educational system should already focus on secondary level and on early specialisation in digital media in higher education. General higher degrees do not reduce the skills gap in the section of digital arts and media.

Besides the very specific, directly job-related and highly specialised subjects, the professional worker in this domain is expected to build his/her competences in a number of well defined following areas that can be found in the full presentation.

THE 'BOOMERANG EFFECT': HOW OUTSOURCING IMPACTS ON THE WORKLOAD OF ACADEMICS

Thomas Hülsmann, Britta Zawada, UNISA, South Africa

Various institutional reports at the University of South Africa (UNISA) indicate, not only an increasing workload for academics, but particularly a shift in the composition of the workload towards more administrative tasks, i.e. to tasks not belonging to the core academic tasks of teaching and research. The proposed paper looks at the reasons for this.

The conceptual framework of the analysis takes as point of departure the cost-structure of distance education. Cost structure here refers to the composition of fixed and variable costs in the total costs equation (TC=F+v*N). Distance education (DE) is traditionally commended for its ability to capture scale economies. This means that variable costs per student (V) are assumed to be lower than those of alternative modes of teaching and learning. This leads to a certain elasticity in DE provision to expand and cater for more students without the total cost rising in a lockstep manner with the number of students, and at the same speed as in delivery models characterized by higher variable costs per student. While total costs (TC) increase more slowly under expansion in DE than in other systems, average costs per student (AC=TC/N) may even fall. This led to the famous Daniel 'iron triangle' and the Daniel's argument in favour of mega-universities as the best format to capture economies of scale (e.g. Daniel et al., 1999).

UNISA is such a mega-institution with close to 400 000 enrolments and individual courses sometimes exceeding the enrolment numbers of a middle-sized university. In the post-Apartheid years UNISA grew considerably and had to absorb many more students. While it is true that course development costs are invariant with respect to increasing enrolment other teaching costs do impact on costs per student. Such costs are related to assessment, such as marking assignments and examination papers, as well as student support through various kinds of interaction.

The safety valve which kept the UNISA model going was, and is (i) the reduction of various kinds of interaction, and the (ii) outsourcing of marking. Since the affordances of digital technologies increase pressure on the institution to accommodate more features of student interaction (widely seen as a quality indicator and expected also to bring down drop-out rates), there is a move to employ online tutors (e-tutors, teaching assistants), which is also done through outsourcing on a part-time contractual basis.

This paper takes a recent UNISA report as point of departure. The report says that UNISA academic staff perceives a massive shift of their workload away from core academic tasks to tasks related to academic administration. According to the report the core academic tasks decreased between 2009 and 2013 by 6.7% (from 67.5% to 60%) while the non-academic tasks increased by 8.3% (from 32.5% to 40.8%). The boomerang hypothesis explains this as being due to increased outsourcing. It is found to be consistent with other institutional data (HEDA). While these data do not confirm that student enrolment at UNISA grew much quicker than the academic workforce the data confirm a massive shift in the composition of academic staff away from staff on long term contracts and staff on short term contracts. While in 2009 only a small percentage of the staff was on short term contract (about 6%) this figure did rise dramatically until 2013 and 2014 (to close to 50%). This shows a marked increase in outsourcing since the category of staff with short term contract comprises the markers, e-tutors and teaching assistants.

While there are other factors contributing to the perceived increase of academic administration (such as ethical clearance or an overall increase in institutional performance measurement activities) the major shift in the composition of the workforce clearly comes with additional management tasks for faculty on long term contract to manage the staff on short term contract.

TEACHING 21ST CENTURY ENTREPRENEURIAL COMPETENCES USING A PROBLEM BASED APPROACH

Ingrid le Roux, University of Pretoria, South Africa

Background to study

Throughout the world, shifts in populations, demographics, technology changes, fluctuating economies and other dynamic forces have transformed societies as never before, bringing new challenges and opportunities to the forefront, causing interest in entrepreneurship by governments and the public. These changes have a far-reaching implication for the workforce and population at large, with many activities taken over by computers with subsequent job losses and increasing unemployment statistics. Youth unemployment and under-employment have become key concepts for both the developed and developing world. Youth unemployment is enormous with a quarter of the world's young people (290 million) neither working nor studying. Due to the harsh picture painted above, it has become important to re-visit the entrepreneurship education (EE) and skills debate. The inclusion of entrepreneurial competencies as a generic skill in the 21st century skills debate has never been more critical. The field of entrepreneurship and EE are gaining prominence in a changing economy. Entrepreneurship in general proves to be popular in business schools, engineering schools, universities and educational institutions.

This study focuses on the *how* or method to transfer entrepreneurial learnings and competencies. Using PBL (project based learning) in an entrepreneurship or business classroom is one option to reach the desired outcome. Therefore, the purpose of the study is to investigate if entrepreneurship concepts and skills can be transferred using a PBl approach linked to a real life event. PBL provides the students with an opportunity to experience, to apply theory in practice and receive feedback as they develop new abilities.

Methodology

The study is qualitative in nature, using a single case study to capture the reflection of student experiences after the completion of a PBL intervention. The results indicate that PBL enables students to become active participants in their learning and provide an opportunity to practically experience the entrepreneurial process. Mastery of more than entrepreneurial competencies and theory were reported as benefits gained, including the 21st century skills. A focus group discussion was held three years later to determine the long-term effect of the intervention. The outcomes of the focus group confirmed that the intervention had long-term benefits. Two of the respondents were self-employed and mentioned that the project developed their ability to scan the environment for opportunities. They also referred to their ability to take calculated risks because they understood and experienced the entrepreneurial process. One of them mentioned that he still uses the window of opportunity as a guiding principle. The other six respondents were working in the formal employment sector. They mentioned the benefits they gained from working in a group, understanding others, adapting to new situations and their ability to critically look at their environment and work content.

Conclusion and recommendation

The value of the PBL intervention reaches far beyond the classroom and gives the students valuable insight into the action, processes and activities of an entrepreneur. The study concludes that a PBL approach linked to a real life problem gives the students an opportunity to hone their entrepreneurial competencies, master entrepreneurial concepts in a practical way while they also nurture generic and survival skills across disciplines. The study has implications for both educators and practitioners. A PBL approach linked to an authentic task benefit students by exposing them to the world of work and practice. It can be applied across disciplines and is therefore ideally suited in many higher education subject areas. It also helps students to understand and develop not only content but also 21st century skills needed in todays' competitive working environment.

DESIGNING APPLICATIONS TO SUPPORT MOBILE WORK BASED LEARNING IN THE CONSTRUCTION INDUSTRY

Graham Attwell, Pontydysgu, United Kingdom, Joanna Burchert, Bremen University, Germany, Raymond Elferink, Raycom, Netherlands, Gilbert Peffer, CINME, Spain

This paper focuses on the use of technology for (mainly informal) learning in Small and Medium Enterprises (SMEs) in the construction sector. It is based on work being undertaken by the EU funded Learning Layers project. The project is aiming to develop large scale take up of technology for informal learning in two sectors, health and construction. The project includes both research and development strands, aiming to facilitate and support the development, testing and deployment of systems and tools for learning. The wider goals of the project are to develop sustainable models and tools for supporting learning in other countries and sectors. The paper describes the outcomes of empirical research undertaken in the construction sector as well as the co-design process contributing to the development of the Learning Toolbox, a mobile application for apprentices.

Any use of mobile technology in and for work depends on the very specific situation and general conditions within a business sector. Hence research and development for mobile digital media includes both peoples' needs and practices as workers and learners as well as specific business challenges, directions of development and needs concerning knowledge, skills and competencies. Testing and guiding the introduction of such solutions in enterprises and organisations could be understood as one kind of action research. Thus in researching and developing mobile learning applications and digital media for use in SMEs it is important to examine the possible impacts on employees and work processes as well as just the impact or potential for learning. The research in enterprises differentiated four lines of argumentation around the use of digital media: a) anxious-avoiding, b) critical, c) optimistic and d) pragmatically oriented.

Our interviews confirmed that technology is fast changing the world of construction, with increased work pressure and the demand to document work. Mobile devices are increasingly being used to produce a photographic record of construction work, as part of quality assurance processes. However, there was pronounced scepticism towards what was termed as "VET researcher fantasies" for instance in developing knowledge exchange networks. Companies were not prepared to share knowledge which was seen as giving them a competitive advantage over others.

The initial interviews were followed up with a survey of over 700 first, second and third year apprentices. The survey confirmed the desire for more use of mobile learning and a frustration with the limitations of existing commercial applications. Whilst only a limited number of companies permitted the use of mobile devices in the workplace, 53% of apprentices said they used them for learning or for obtaining work related information, explaining this was in their own time in breaks or after work.

The project is developing a 'Learning Toolbox', designed as a comprehensive framework for apprentice training and continuing training. Rather than training the main interest craft trade companies in web tools and mobile technologies is related to real-time, knowledge sharing, communication and problem-solving. Experience with earlier web tools has shown that they do not necessarily contribute to optimisation of work and business processes. However, flexible framework solutions like Learning Toolbox can be customised to their needs. Supplier companies (vendors of machinery, equipment and materials) want to customise user guidelines, maintenance manuals and instructional media for different users. They also need to develop real-time feedback to improve error control mechanisms.

The implementation of Technology Enhanced Learning in SMEs will require capacity building in organisations, networks and sectors. This includes the capacity of trainers to support pedagogically the implementation of technology for learning, the development of technical infrastructure and the capacity of organisations and managements to support the use of technologies.

Finally is the importance of context in work based learning. Mobile learning applications need to be able to adapt to different contexts. These include, but are not limited to, the context of what kind of work is being undertaken, different forms of work organisation and different locations and forms of learning. The Learning Toolbox application is particularly designed to bridge formal and informal learning and to take account of the different contexts of learning in the vocational schools, learning in the industry training centre and learning on the construction site.

BUILDING AND MAINTAINING OPERATIONAL SKILLS DURING COMPLEX CHANGE – A WORLD BANK GROUP STAFF LEARNING CASE STUDY

Darlene Christopher, East Asia Region, Jennifer Ross Gildee, Europe & Central Asia Region, Jeanette Murry, South Asia Region, World Bank

Rapid and ongoing organizational change

Beginning in 2012 and continuing until the present, the World Bank Group has been going through a complex process of rapid change. This includes a new president, senior management, organizational structure, operational reforms, IT systems and changing policies. Furthermore, greater pressure was directed at making sure that World Bank Group operations were achieving intended development results effectively and efficiently, which is often referred to as project quality. This effort requires staff to keep ahead of a plethora of revisions to operational policies and practices while at the same time maintaining the specialized, technical excellence required by clients.

Breaking down silos and a new approach to learning

In response to the rapidly changing organizational environment, the Regional Learning Coordinators (RLCs) of the World Bank launched a highly successful Global Operational Clinic program to keep staff up to date on operational changes through a centralized learning approach. Three key components made this program possible: a new outreach strategy, a plan to rapidly produce materials using cutting edge content, and a new content repository strategy.

Historically, learning was "siloed" by region. RLCs determined that through collaboration they could reach staff from more than 100 countries on a regular basis with synchronous training. The collaboration began with building one "global" schedule of clinics. This means clinics are held in Washington, D.C. at 7:00, 9:00, 14:00 and 21:00. Additionally, each clinic is delivered to both face-to-face and webinar participants. By utilizing a common web-based webinar platform, staff can choose to participate from the office or from home during one of the clinic times that is most convenient to them and they can also connect using a mobile device even when travelling.

Another benefit of the Global Operational Clinics is the development of standardized content. The RLCs work with one or two subject matter experts to develop the clinic materials and ensure institutional vetting of the content for alignment with policies and procedures. Maintaining the quality of clinic materials is simplified since there is only one set of standardized materials. From a pedagogical standpoint, a learning professional can review the materials to ensure key learning objectives are covered, the scope is appropriate for a short, web-based clinic, and participant engagement activities are embedded in the delivery.

The process of sharing content across regions has led to the development of a content repository where regional learning teams store and access clinic materials. This required reaching agreement on a taxonomy that matched the content topics in the corporate learning management system and content types such as slides, hand-outs and recordings. Finally, naming conventions were designed to keep content organized so users could locate the latest version of materials.

Outcomes

The results of this collaborative effort to offer Global Operational Clinics include major improvements in participation and in overall quality of learning content. Within 6 months of commencing the series, staff from 101 countries and from across all regions had attended at least one clinic. Overall, 34 percent of these participants were based in World Bank country offices. Shifting learning delivery from a regional to a global focus also required developing new ways of communicating with staff about upcoming offerings. Rather than each region announcing regional clinics to their specific audience, a global announcement is sent to all operational staff, regardless of location.

The three part focus of developing new and more coordinated ways to reach out to staff in country offices, standardizing and developing training materials, and building an effective and shared repository, have all contributed to early success of the program.

TEACHERS' CPD PROGRAMME IN FOSTERING COMPETENCES – COMMUNITIES OF PRACTICE SUPPORT MECHANISMS

Katerina Riviou, Sofoklis Sotiriou, Ellinogermaniki Agogi, Lamprini Kolovou, Antonis Ramfos, Intrasoft International, Greece

Key competence acquisition is one of the long term objectives of the updated strategic framework for European cooperation (Official Journal of the European Union, 2009). The concept of key competence originated with the adoption of the Lisbon Strategy in 2000 and it resulted in the European Reference Framework (European Commission, 2006). Key competences in the EU framework are those that 'all individuals need for personal fulfilment and development, active citizenship, social inclusion and employment'. The Framework identifies and defines eight key competences, among which the five are considered transversal. Most of the EU Member States are beginning to implement policies that move their school systems from being predominantly subject-oriented towards curricula which include competences, active and individual learning, as well as a focus on learning outcomes. One such example is Greece, where in the school year 2011-2012, pilot curricula for competence driven education have been introduced. In Austria however, the promotion of holistic teaching methods has been supported at policy level for several years. In other countries (e.g. France, Netherlands) innovative policies are already embedded in national strategy documents and in some cases these have already led to major structural changes, such as the introduction of new qualifications frameworks or the reform of the curriculum around the Key Competences (European Commission, 2009). In general, there are a variety of different models of competences in European countries (European Commission/EACEA/Eurydice, 2012). Yet, these developments do not necessarily result in significant, widespread changes in practice – that is, in how schools actually organise and provide learning experiences for pupils. The difficulty is in all cases translating these policies into practice. To this end, two initiatives active in the field of teachers' professional development under which the specific research has been undertaken; thus Open Discovery Space and TRANSIt have been initiated.

In this study we present the current state of Competence-Based Learning policy and practice in Greece, the results from the needs analysis study, the design and localisation of the Training Framework and Environment based on the collected responses and the specifications set from the Greek Curriculum, the user/community support services that have been developed, as well as indicators from the user exploitation of these services and feedback collected by users with the use of online questionnaires and interviews. Our needs analysis confirms that, given the limitations imposed by the official curriculum in Greece, teachers are generally motivated to make a paradigm shift. The profile of the participants demonstrates that there is a strong interest especially by secondary education teachers to get trained and exchange practices within peer networks and communities of practice. This is aligned with the literature findings that the situation is even worse for teachers of secondary education since their training has not prepared them for the most part for holistic methods and cross-curricular teaching (European Commission, 2009). The preference of teachers and head teachers to learn primarily from demonstration of tools and instruments, practical assignments and examples of good practices, demonstrates the need of stakeholders to undertake hands-on training, and that teachers need support in their everyday practice. The training content developed includes specific examples/good practices and tries to address training needs with an emphasis on assessment methods and tools, as well as the national context requirements. Collaboration and exchange of practices needs to be encouraged through training, let alone since participants refer to the benefits of collaboration with colleagues. Events such as contests and webinars and wide dissemination of such activities have proven to be a valuable tool for the support and population of these communities. Time is needed so that a new user proceeds from the basis of consuming content to the process of contributing. The feedback we got though from the interviews conducted so far is that teachers would be eager to contribute their resources on the portal. As shown by contributions per user, participants are quite hesitant in sharing their resources; therefore such a culture needs to be fostered. Further work remains the creation of a long-lasting Virtual School on the theme of competence development exploiting the under study Communities of Practice. The possible ineffectiveness of top-down approaches in providing support and training for teachers makes the support and role of online communities such the ones presented in the current study even more crucial.

Acknowledgements

This research has been undertaken under the Open Discovery Space project funded with support from the EC.

INCLUSION'S FINAL FRONTIER: UNIVERSAL DESIGN FOR LEARNING – ICT AND INNOVATION IN TRANSFORMATIVE EDUCATION

Alan Bruce, Universal Learning Systems, Ireland

Differential access and learning

The last two decades have produced ample evidence of the extent to which ICT permeates social structures, economy and generation of knowledge itself. Social change is shaping our understanding of the role and potential of ICT – which can affect an emerging emancipatory dialectic. Historically, the teacher played a major part in this framework, given that these were the people who taught those that did not know. This 'banking conception' of education was one in which the student was an empty container that had to be filled with content, opposed to a candle to be lit (Freire, 1970). Traditional economic systems and market driven learning policies have undergone a fundamental challenge in terms of relevance and ability to meet the needs of individuals and communities. The 2008 crisis puts a new focus on innovation – this has a direct impact on learning for those working in inclusive education, in particular disability. One of the central questions in international contexts is how to work with the needs of specific communities to create a new matrix of opportunities for inclusion. This affects learning specialists and educators in terms of professional training, best practice and standards in community diversity. Social inclusion and educational provision can provide a dynamic synergy of perspectives and possibilities.

Universal Design for Learning

The roots of UDL (*Universal Design for Learning*) are in the early civil rights legislation that emphasized rights of all students to a free, appropriate public education in the least restrictive environment. The UDL framework was conceived in the United States by those who later established the *Center for Applied Special Technologies* (CAST) in the late 1980s using three conceptual shifts: Advancements in architectural design; Developments in education technology; Discoveries from brain research and neuropsychology. CAST defines *UDL* as "a set of principles for curriculum development that gives all individuals equal opportunities to learn". The existence of advanced technologies created a powerful synergy of creativity and innovation that began to question traditional curriculum design itself as being potentially discriminatory.

UDL provides a blueprint for creating instructional goals, methods, materials, and assessments that work for everyone - not a single, one-size-fits-all solution but flexible approaches that can be customized for individual needs. One key idea of UDL is that new materials and technologies should be designed *from the beginning* to be flexible enough to accommodate the unique learning styles of a wide range of individuals. Examples of UDL include: accessible web pages; captioned and/or narrated videos; word prediction; speaking spell checkers; talking dialogue boxes; voice recognition; picture menus. In UDL diversity originates in disabilities – sensory (visual and auditory), physical, neurological, developmental/intellectual and psychiatric. But diversity also includes those other dimensions: gender, ethnic origin, religious belief, migrant status, sexual orientation. UDL aims to create barrier-free environments that enable today's teachers to apply universal design concepts in ways that support the needs of the widest range of learners. UDL considers ways of developing course content in a manner that is proactively accessible to as wide of an audience as possible.

In Europe the UDL Network (*UDLnet*) project commenced in 2014. *UDLnet* aims to the collect and create best practices under the framework of UDL from a wide range (generic guidelines down to more specific ones) of four envisaged themes: inclusive learning environments, accessible resources, teachers' and school leaders' competences, examination of barriers and identification of opportunities.

The implementation of a UDL framework has the potential to open doors in education to all students, especially those not effectively served by current systems and structures. This embeds inclusion as both a method and valued outcome, a critical resource in times of significant structural transformation.

DISTANCE EDUCATION IN EUROPEAN HIGHER EDUCATION INSTITUTIONS: ANALYSING MECHANISMS FOR INCREASING PARTICIPATION OF ADULT LEARNERS

Angela Owusu-Boampong, UNESCO Institute for Lifelong Learning, Germany, Carl Holmberg, ICDE, Sweden, Monique Udnæs, ICDE, Norway

The Impact of Distance Education on Adult Learning (IDEAL) project is a joint project of the International Council for Open and Distance Education (ICDE), the UNESCO Institute for Lifelong Learning (UIL) and StudyPortals (SP). It examines the interrelations of adult learning, higher education and distance education, exploring if and how higher education institutions can contribute to adult learning by means of distance education. The project seeks to offer policymakers and distance education providers insights into the needs of adult learners and to increase the participation of adult learners in higher education through distance education. The adult learners targeted by the IDEAL project are adults who have completed their initial education and training and are returning to further education.

The IDEAL project views 'distance learning' as a generic term for different organizational forms of education in which students and teachers are separated by time and space. This definition encompasses distance education of any length and includes 'dual-mode' institutions that offer both campus-based and distance education. It also includes online education (where more than 80% of the content is delivered online) and blended education (where 30-79% of the content is delivered online) as well as modes of education that use printed material delivered by post and/or other tools for bridging distances and facilitating learning.

Three separate research studies were conducted as part of this project:

- Study 1 examined the distance education *offer* of European higher education institutions.
- Study 2 consisted of a survey of *enrolled* distance education students in Europe and outside Europe.
- Study 3 focused on *potential* distance education students, examining who they are, what they look for and what barriers they face.

At this stage, the meta-analysis of the three studies has produced the following results:

- Increasing attainment levels, improving career prospects and self-fulfilment are the major motivations of adult learners who engage in distance education.
- Provision of online education as the main mode of distance education responds to most adult learners' demands for more flexible learning opportunities.
- Transparent information on recognition of prior learning and possible alternative access modes need to be provided.
- Students need more guidance on selecting courses as well as support throughout their studies.
- Funding opportunities need to be diversified, eligibility criteria need to be more visible and more information on credit sand the transferability of qualifications should be available.

One challenge that has been encountered is that the results of this study are biased by the offer on the study portals.

The meta-analysis of Studies 1 to 3 will be available in the final report, which is to be published in June 2015. The online reports presenting the first results are available on the project's website: http://idealproject.eu

VIDEO-BASED LEARNING IN HIGHER EDUCATION: THE FLIPPED OR THE HANDS-ON CLASSROOM?

Laia Albó, Davinia Hernández-Leo, Jaume Barcelo, Luis Sanabria-Russo, Universitat Pompeu Fabra, Spain

Nowadays Higher Education is adopting new ways of teaching such as ways of Video-Based Learning (VBL) with the aim of moving away from the traditional classrooms. The interest in VBL has increased as a result of new forms of online education, most prominently in the case of Massive Open Online Courses. VBL has unique features that make it an effective Technology-Enhanced Learning approach. Furthermore it seems to support a rich and powerful model to improve learning outcomes as well as learner satisfaction, but it is necessary to choose an appropriate instructional approach when designing VBL environments. One of the latest methods that use video as a tool for learning is Flipped Classrooms – or inverted classrooms- and, in many cases, it is showed that the result of introducing videos in a learning design eventually converges in this type of methodology.

To explore this context, this research presents a case study that uses a combination of the VBL and Project-Based Learning methodologies. The classes are face-to-face but there are no lessons: the students develop small projects in labs. A set of teaching explanations are recorded in videos provided together with the descriptions of the projects. The objective of this research is to study the behaviour and satisfaction of the students using the videos, their utility as well as the position of the professors. Participants were the students of the course "Wireless sensor networks" that took place in April to June of 2014. This was designed as an optional subject in the 3rd and 4th year of the Bachelor Degrees in Computer Engineering, Electronic Engineering and Audio-visual Systems Engineering. Two professors were in charge of the course, one of them acting as a coordinator and other as a teaching assistant.

The study was conducted using a mixed methodology and used five instruments to gather data: two surveys (students, teachers), an interview (teachers), an observation protocol and two types of system log files (course delivery platform and video server). The gathered qualitative and quantitative data were analyzed and triangulated. One of the main results is that students interacted with the course content mainly during class hours, despite the fact that they had the opportunity to watch the videos before the sessions. Hence the flipped classroom was not present though it was the expected situation. Students used videos as support material within class while they were working on the projects at their pace. On the one hand, the incorporation of videos in class allowed students to enjoy a great flexibility to access the professors' explanation. The advantage of this flexibility questions the use of oral teacher presentations in class because of the latter are governed by schedule, meaning that the students cannot access to this explanation beyond the class in the moments when their application is more significant. These conclusions are somehow in line with claims by other researchers saying that the role of presence-based learning may be re-thought, standard lectures do not take advantage of having the students personally present in the class. However, the use of video allows access to content "on demand". Moreover, the use of videos has helped students to become more autonomous. In a learning design based on the student as in our case, the flexibility and autonomy that provide videos -used as support material during classes- help students to have more control over their own learning process and, therefore, the role of the teacher as facilitator is reaffirmed.

Contrary to common belief, the use of video-based learning may not only converge in the use of flipped classroom methodology. It is also possible to use the videos in a hands-on class as a support tool that encourages a more autonomous, flexible and significant learning. The application of a flipped or a hands-on classroom approach depends on diverse aspects, including the nature of the course (with practical or theoretical orientations), the behaviour emerging from the students (depending on their needs and preferences, time constraints, etc.) and the design of the activities proposed by the teachers (strongly requiring students to watch videos in a certain timeframe, e.g. previously to the class, or offering flexibility). Future research considering variations of these parameters will help to understand the benefits and limitations of both approaches and to what extent they may coexists in VBL.

MASTERING THE BLEND: STUDENTS' VALUE OF CLASSROOM AND ONLINE COMPONENTS IN A BLENDED ACCOUNTING COURSE

Lynette Nagel, Louwtjie Venter, University of Pretoria, South Africa

Introduction

In order to improve student success in pivotal courses, the promise of technology needs to be harvested. Blended learning should incorporate course redesign in a way that integrates online and classroom activities in the most beneficial way to provide every student the best chance of success. Coordinated design research can indicate how particular sections of the "blend" can add particular value to learning. We examined the strengths of activities in the two main delivery modes and how they complemented each other, drawing on the Garrison and Kanuka approach to blended learning being "the thoughtful integration of classroom face-to-face experiences with online learning experiences". Benjamin Bloom laid the foundation to improving student outcomes. Inspired by tutoring, he showed significant improvement on average in student outcomes after providing personalised corrective feedback in the areas where students had not mastered the requisite concepts or skills. The Mastery Learning process that builds on his principles, is widely accepted and has been consistently successful in tutoring students in subjects such as mathematics. This approach translated well to computers as tutors, becoming an effective instructional aid. There is little research on how the blend of delivery modes actually tap into the way students construct knowledge. In order to compile the most successful blend of delivery modes for each learning component, designers should also take into account students' preferences.

Context

First-year chartered accounting students often underestimate the importance of theory, resulting in poor marks and pass rates. Therefore we adopted a mastery learning process using blended learning. Ten minute formative online quizzes were deployed in the LMS and addressed the content of the past week or two's theory and focused on known misconceptions and troublesome concepts. Each question had feedback in non-technical terms to benefit the students who were unfamiliar with the terminology. Supportive documents including administrative resources and sample questions and answers from multiple sources were provided in the LMS to coincide with current lecture topics. Some resources supported homework and preparation for classroom discussions, and formed an integral part of the expected learning process. Others provided enrichment and extra practice. We examined which lecturer characteristics were most valued in the blended environment and how the online tests and supplemental material were used by the students.

Findings and Discussion

The formative online quizzes were beneficial to 98% of the students, specifically for confirming how well they understood the work, learning the subject, and learning from the feedback. They had relatively less value in preparing for formal tests. Online resources were grouped into those that helped with understanding and those that helped with preparation for summative assessment; the latter were deemed significantly more useful. Lecturer teaching characteristics were grouped according to helping students understand the work and preparing for assessment. Students rated teaching for understanding as significantly more important, particularly high-achievement students.

We propose that mastery learning in a blended learning environment take students' learning preferences into account. For understanding new work students prefer the classroom and a teacher who explains theory and concepts well. The higher the student's own standards, the more they value this expertise. The next step is to monitor understanding, for which students prefer online formative assessment that explains misconceptions and shows gaps in knowledge, for which online resources are used. Thirdly, students value lecturers that help them prepare for tests, but they also prefer to use high quality online resources to practice and exercise their skills before tests and exams. Our findings illustrate the integrated way that students prefer to learn, moving between contact and online environments for preferred activities in mastering the outcomes.

EVALUATING THE QUALITY OF STUDENTS ACTIONS IN A DISTANCE LEARNING PROGRAMMING LANGUAGE ACADEMIC DISCIPLINE

Elizabeth S. Carvalho, Adérito F. Marcos, Universidade Aberta, Portugal

Online learning (OL) has grown in importance as a direct consequence of the rapid development taking place in information and communication technology (ICT). This development has pushed OL agents into finding new methods of teaching and learning that could explore the technological media to the limits that ICT could actually offer. Due to the evolution of OL, it is difficult to find a precise and current definition. Nichols describes OL as “education that occurs only through the Web, that is, it does not consist of any physical learning materials issued to students or actual face to face contact. Purely online learning is essentially the use of eLearning tools in a distance education mode using the Web as the sole medium for all student learning and contact.” Though this statement is still valid, the notion of OL has evolved to include aspects such as collaborative learning, connectivist learning and online participation.

This form of teaching and learning is very often based on the principles of student-centered learning; learning flexibility (spatial, temporal); and online interaction, in particular, asynchronous interaction, which blurs the temporal barriers imposed by communicational synchronism, and is consistent with the flexibility principle. Interaction is absolutely fundamental for the teaching-learning process so that students can effectively acquire the corresponding knowledge and skills. It occurs when students are actively participating in learning activities involving peer-to-peer and teacher communication, be it contributing in a discussion, solving an exercise, analyzing a result, simply exchanging views with their colleagues, or clarifying questions with the teacher.

When teaching computer science in an online learning environment, we usually face increasing problems promoting student participation, when compared with other teaching fields (e.g. humanities). Students face natural inhibition in presenting publicly questions or issues that they consider to be of lower value or that expose their ignorance on more technical subject matters. Student’s participation is often more than communicating a verbal opinion but to demonstrate a very specific technical issue. In fact, experience has shown that discussions are usually dominated by a small core of students with a greater mastery of the subject areas or who are less inhibited, which results in a reduced level of student participation.

To teach how to program with an object-oriented language (like C++) is normally not a simple task. It is especially true when the students do not have any programming background or previous experience with any other programming language. Even those students that are used to program in a procedural approach find some difficulty to change the way they reason to solve a problem under the object-oriented paradigm. This reality is quite recurrent in any programming language teaching class anywhere around the world where the students are on-campus studying. Things can become a little bit more complicated when you have to teach object-oriented programming in a totally e-learning environment.

Despite recent advances of electronic technologies in e-learning, a consolidated evaluation methodology for e-learning applications is not available. Maybe the main cause for this is the complexity that the evaluation of an e-learning environment demands. Many different perspectives and thus dimensions, in the analysis process can be considered, such as the quality of: learning, teaching, learning environment and interaction. Each of these dimensions can be evaluated according a group of pre-defined and chosen indicators. In the case of interaction, we may consider that the quality of students’ interaction is one of the most relevant indicators.

This article presents the main results obtained through the analysis of the students’ actions while interacting and using the object oriented programming discipline available on the Moodle platform of Open University (UAb) of Portugal to the students of the 1st cycle in Computer Science degree. All teaching and learning activities were developed online (emphasis on asynchronous communication) and this discipline is taught in the first year of the graduation (second semester).

THE URBAN GAME MOBIGEO: STUDENTS PERCEPTIONS ON POTENTIAL AND CONSTRAINTS OF AN MOBILE OUTDOOR EDUCATION

Liliana Vieira, Clara Coutinho, Minho University, Portugal

Mobile technologies are increasingly rooted in society and, therefore, intuitively, teachers begin to take advantage of devices that students carry with them daily in a logic of 1:1 bring your own device (BYOD). In fact, it becomes crucial to use this media to promote/increase new pedagogical activities to motivate and challenge students to acquire and discover knowledge. Our research is based in the emergence of a new paradigm for learning, the Mobile Learning that bring to education the advantages of "just in time" and "anywhere", breaking the classroom barriers and extending the process of teaching and learning to a custom context where the virtual and real worlds merge.

This was the inspiration to create the MobiGeo, an Urban Game, for Geography teaching, that arose from a partnership between the Basic School ("Agrupamento de Escolas de Vila Verde") and the Knowledge House of Vila Verde (Casa do Conhecimento de Vila Verde). In this Urban Game participated all classes of the 7th grade of the Public Basic School, a total of 173 students (82 boys and 91 girls), with ages between 12 and 15 years. Each school class was divided in four teams – GeoFronteirs, PDA, Support and Wallpaper – and the geographical area was bounded between the school and the Central Square of Vila Verde a space with wireless system (Digital Plaza). Mobile phones were also available for each of the teams to communicate and receive instructions of the path to go (GPS) and the tasks were associated with QR codes. In the end of the route, the team that concluded all the points and performed all the tasks had to raise the European Union flag as a symbol of victory.

The theoretical background of the Urban Game designed in our research is based in four pillars: Constructivism (the student takes an active role in the production/construction of knowledge), the Situated Learning (authentic context is a sponsor of knowledge); Connectivism (which puts mobile devices as a source of connections available for the acquisition of knowledge) and Conversation Theory.

The research question that guided the project was to understand whether the implementation of an urban game – Mobigeo – that enhanced collaboration and interaction among peers could influence the process of learning geography in an outdoor education context. After reviewing emerging research on mobile learning, this article presents the results of two open questions of the survey to the participants in the activity. To assess students' perceptions on the MobiGeo the researchers developed and validated a questionnaire based on the motivational model of Kirkpatrick (level1) and embraces three major dimensions: Motivation/Interest, Interaction and Perceived Learning.

Data obtained allow us to conclude that Urban Games, like MobiGeo are potential agents of motivation and interaction that predispose students to learn geography in informal learning environments. Mobile technologies offer a range of learning experiences that may involve and effectively involve students in learner-centred activities. We can also say that the success of Urban Game MobiGeo was due to the challenge of finding out what is hidden in the georeferenced location using mobile phones to uncover the information needed to conclude the game. In fact, students said that "the use of mobile phone motivated the commitment of the group" also assumed the strengths of MobiGeo, "the points are located at the GPS", "the use of QR codes" and "have used wireless internet ". So, we suggest that the roles of teacher and student should not be abandoned but recycled and adapted to this new reality that requires more personalized and diverse activities of learning.

TYPES OF PARTICIPANTS' BEHAVIORS IN A MASSIVE OPEN ONLINE COURSE

Tali Kahan, Tal Soffer, Rafi Nachmias, Tel Aviv University, Israel

In recent years, there has been a proliferation of Massive Open Online Courses (MOOCs). Initiatives like Coursera, edX and Udacity provide platforms for higher education institutions to develop and deliver online courses to the general public. These courses are usually offered free of charge, with no preconditions or commitment, and attract massive numbers of registrants from around the world. Yet, a central criticism about MOOCs refers to the relatively low completion rates of participants, with 10% or less of the course registrants earning a statement of accomplishment. Ho et al. (2014) argued that certification rates are a misleading representation of the diverse ways in which registrants are engaging with MOOCs. Kizilcec et al. (2013) argued that the categorization of MOOCs learners into those who pass the class, and everyone else, makes no allowances for learners who choose to stay engaged with the course and participate in some aspects of it, without earning a certificate.

Subsequently, the purpose of this study was to gain more insights into different types of participants' behaviors in MOOCs, by analyzing non-certificate earners' and certificate earners' behaviors. The study examined the different types of participants' behaviors in one MOOC, based on the participants' activity in the main learning resources of the course. The research questions were:

- What are the types of engagement in the course?
- What are the types of behaviors in regard to the course video lectures, discussion forums, and assessments?

The study examined a MOOC on plant biology, which was offered by Tel Aviv University in Coursera. The course began on October 2013 and lasted 7 weeks. Each week, a different topic was covered via the course learning resources, which consisted of: professor announcements, reading recommendations, 50 short video lectures, around 40 interactive in-video questions, 7 discussion forums, 6 quizzes, and a final exam. 32,007 people registered for the course, and 68.4% of the registrants (21,889) started it. 10.6% of the participants who started the course (2,319) completed it and received a certificate.

The study was conducted using a data mining methodology. The data mining was applied on a data set that documented the participants' actions during the course. The data was received from Coursera in database tables. Using MySQL queries, a set of variables were computed for each participant, displaying their use of the course components. Using a Two-Step cluster analysis, the course participants were then classified into clusters, based on their activity in the main learning resources of the course. The following 8 variables were chosen for the analysis: *unique video lectures viewed online, unique video lectures downloaded, unique in-video questions answered; total threads views, total threads opened, total comments; unique quizzes submitted, and final exam submitted.* The cluster analysis was applied separately for the non-certificate earners and for the certificate earners groups. This separation was essential in order to gain better insights into the different behaviors between the groups and within each group.

The analyses revealed 8 clusters in total; 4 clusters per group. The clusters are presented and discussed in detail in the paper. The different types of engagement and behaviors that emerged in the clusters were analyzed. Five major types of engagement in the course were identified: Tasters, Keepers, Partially Persisting, Committed participants and Completers. With reference to criticism regarding relatively low completion rates in MOOCs, significant numbers of non certificate earners who demonstrated some level of engagement, ranging from the Moderately Persisting participants to the highly committed participants, were identified. Regarding video usage, three types of behaviors were identified: online, offline, and combined. These types may indicate different participant preferences for watching the videos and may have significant implications on the learning process, as they facilitate different pedagogies. Regarding the discussion forums, two prominent types of behaviors were identified: passive and active participation. Consistent with the literature, the vast majority of discussion participants were found to be passive, whereas only a small group, consisting mostly of certificate earners, held the on-going discussions. These findings raise questions regarding the extent to which the social learning potential of MOOCs is realized. Finally, three levels of participation in the assessments were identified: negligible, moderate, and extensive.

This study was conducted on one MOOC. More research is required on other MOOCs, in varied disciplines, target audiences, and structures.

AN APPROACH TO DIGITAL LEARNERS IN A CATALONIAN PUBLIC FACE-TO-FACE UNIVERSITY

Eliana E. Gallardo-Echenique, Luis Marqués-Molías, Universitat Rovira i Virgili, Spain, Mark Bullen, University of British Columbia, Canada

Introduction

Until recently, the argument that the generation born between 1980 and 1994 has different ways of using and making sense of information, approaches to learning, and expectations about life and learning had been accepted uncritically by many educators. This changed in 2007 as researchers began to take a critical look at this claims and found there was little empirical support for the idea that exposure to digital technology had fundamentally changed this generation.

Aim and research questions

Despite the lack of empirical support for the digital generational claims, it is clear that the ubiquity of digital technology is having an impact on society and, more particularly, education. The central aim of the study is to investigate this impact at the post secondary level and understand how university learners use digital technologies and what the implications of their use for Higher Education are. The study was guided by the following research questions: (a) Do postsecondary students distinguish between their social and educational use of digital technologies? (b) What impact does students' social use of digital technologies have on postsecondary learning environments? and (c) What is the relationship between social and educational uses of digital technologies in postsecondary education?

Methodology

An interpretivist methodology was used to guide our research to emphasize interpretation and to focus on the meanings of the researcher and the participants. This study used a sequential transformative mixed methods design - a mixture of both quantitative and qualitative research, consisting of two distinct phases.

Finding and Discussion

RQ 1: Do postsecondary students distinguish between their social and educational use of digital technologies?

All the students distinguish between their social and educational use of digital technologies (devices and softwares). This suggests that within an identified set of digital technologies, students were able to identify which was better suited to a given task. All students can distinguish social practices (e.g. Facebook) for academic purposes, choose technologies according to their need (social and/or academic purposes), and can see the affordances of technologies for various purposes (e.g. for entertainment, communication, interaction, etc.). Learners are able to recognize what technology they can and cannot use given a specific context.

RQ 2: What impact does students' social use of digital technologies have on postsecondary learning environments?

There is insufficient evidence to identify the actual impact of such technologies upon learning either in terms achievement or final academic results. Results from this study do demonstrate some impacts in their learning by improving the communication between them and peers. We could declare that some digital technologies impacted on the way they collaborate with their peers. The findings show that while learners are using some digital technologies for socializing, they are clearly being used in multiple spaces, including the formal contexts of the school setting.

RQ 3: What is the relationship between social and educational uses of digital technologies in postsecondary education?

At a general level there is a close relationship between social and educational use of some ICT. In theory, the social and academic lives remain as separate activity systems; however, our findings suggest that there is also a significant overlap in their use of some digital technologies (e.g. mobile phone, WhatsApp, Facebook) for academic and social purposes.

LEARNERS' BEHAVIOURS AND AUTONOMY IN LIVEMOCHA AND BUSUU ONLINE COMMUNITIES

Maria Luisa Malerba, Open University of Catalonia, Spain

Language learning in online communities

This paper reports on a broader study about learners' construction of opportunities for second language (L2) use in online communities designed for L2 learning. These environments, designed for a potential language improvement and based on the social web, raise some questions about the use that online users make of their tools and the behaviours enacted when inhabiting the communities. In particular, this paper focuses on learner autonomy and learners' main goals and behaviours when inhabiting online communities for L2 learning.

The main objectives of this paper are to explain the dynamics generated within online communities designed for L2 learning, to describe what types of experience learners make of these communities and, accordingly, what kinds of behaviour they enact. In addition, the paper examines the degree of autonomy that learners exhibit when they operate and construct their actions in this environment.

A socio-cultural framework and an online ethnographic approach

The theoretical underpinning of the study reported in this paper is Socio-Cultural Theory, which focuses on the social aspect of learning and which sees the language as a very important mediational tool between human mind and the environment.

Another valuable conceptual tool adopted for this study is Activity Theory, which is included in Socio-Cultural Theory and which permitted to describe learners' actions, oriented goals and social roles within the activity system of the two online communities selected for the investigation, *Livemocha* and *Busuu*.

The methodology adopted to pursue the aforementioned objectives is mainly qualitative and relies on an interpretative paradigm and on online ethnography. The methods of the investigation ranged from fieldwork, to online survey and online interviews, which allowed the cross-checking of the data obtained.

Learners' behaviour and learner autonomy in online communities

The results reported in this paper describe the presence of different profiles of learners, oriented towards different goals, different beliefs about learning and, as a consequence, different modalities of participation in the online communities. These differences generated "tensions" when they were interpreted under the lens of AT.

The findings, obtained through the analysis of learners' perceptions, also revealed that learners are aware of the limitations of the online platforms and that one of the main limitations is represented by the didactic affordances of these online communities. In addition, results revealed that learner autonomy is a pre-requirement for an effective and more complete L2 learning experience in online communities.

The study reported in this paper is expected to shed more light on lifelong and informal learning practices and to provide more information about affordances and constraints of online communities for L2 learning.

MOBILE TECHNOLOGIES AND CHANGING LEARNER CHARACTERISTICS AND PREFERENCES: TEACHERS' PERCEPTIONS

Kwok-Wing Lai, Lee Smith, University of Otago, New Zealand

In 2014 the authors conducted a study in one New Zealand University, investigating teaching staffs' use of mobile and digital technology in their teaching practice. A survey form was sent to all teaching staff at the University whose contact email addresses were listed on departmental websites. A total of 308 respondents filled in the survey forms, and 30 undertook a follow up interview. One of the research questions guiding the study was:

What are the perceptions of university teachers on the learning characteristics and preferences of their students, as compared to ten years ago due to their use of mobile technologies and applications?

It is on this question that this paper focuses. Survey and interview participants reported that due the ubiquity of mobile technologies nowadays, students have developed a preference for online resources and more 'traditional' ways of accessing information such as libraries and printed texts had become secondary to online information. Many participants stated that students demanded immediate access to online lecture materials, which meant that they often skipped lectures. Numerous interview and survey participants described how students were now surface learners who simply took online information as factual without discerning the creditability of the resource. Participants also reported that students are now adept at multitasking and developed a preference for information being divided into smaller pieces to accommodate a shorter attention span. However, participants also stated the use of mobile and digital technologies had resulted in students becoming more independent learners who could solves problems for themselves, while at the same time setting up online study groups through social networking sites such as Facebook. The paper concludes with a discussion of how some of the University teachers are adapting their classroom pedagogy to meet the change in students learning habits, which have resulted from their reliance on, and preference for online learning.

FLIPPED LEARNING: THE GATEWAY TO LEARNER AUTONOMY

Amany Atef, Hamdan Bin Mohammed Smart University, United Arab Emirates

Over the last two decades, the concepts of learner autonomy and independence have gained momentum; this shift of responsibility from teachers to learners is the result of a concatenation of changes to the curriculum itself towards a more learner-centered kind of learning. What is more, this reshaping, of teacher and learner roles has been conducive to a radical change in the age-old distribution of power and authority that used to plague the traditional classroom. *(Little, 1991: 4)*, learners, autonomous learners, that is, are expected to assume greater responsibility for, and take charge of, their own learning.

Recent advances in pedagogy and educational technology have pointed to the need to rethink the traditional in-class, lecture-based course model, and unlocked entirely new directions for more models that boost autonomous learner.

The flipped learning is one of those models, a new pedagogical method, which utilizes asynchronous video lectures and practice problems as homework, and push all online for learners to learn on their own. While class time is dedicated to engaging learners in learner-centered learning activities, like problem-based learning, exercises, and inquiry-oriented strategies.

In Hamdan Bin Mohammed Smart University (HBMSU), we applied the flipped learning by integrated it with our blended learning model, therefore; we pushed online all lectures to self-paced online videos and used class time to engage students in active learning exercises.

This paper addresses Hamdan Bin Mohammed Smart University' Flipped Learning model, by illustrating the model anatomy and how it boosts the learner autonomy and encourage the learner-centric environment; intending to serve as a guide to instructors to develop, implement, coach/monitor, and evaluate innovative and practical strategies to transform learners' learning experience.

It also provides a comprehensive survey of prior and ongoing research of the flipped learning; these include; the type of in-class and out-of-class activities, the measures used to evaluate the model, including; but not limited to: increase learner participation, learner autonomy, engagement and motivation; improve students' critical thinking/creative problem solving, improve learners' team-based skills and peer-to-peer interaction; make learners the center of learning/encourage learner ownership of learning; better faculty to learner interaction; encourage faculty collaboration and improve learning outcomes.

EMPOWERING STUDENTS BY CO-DESIGNING EXPANDED LEARNING SCENARIOS

Iolanda Garcia, Elena Barberà and Ingrid Noguera, Universitat Oberta de Catalunya, Spain

For many years researchers have been calling for a transition from teacher to student-centred environments and instruction. However, many features of teacher-centred models still remain in higher education practices. In this paper we sustain the transactional view, according to which teachers and students are jointly responsible for the success of the learning process. This means that teachers and students negotiate and decide together the tasks and roles that each one will assume in the process and, thereby, each other's level of control over the learning process.

A critical factor for the adoption of this kind of student-centred transactional model is the students' capacity and readiness to self-regulate their learning process. On the other hand, many studies prove that student engagement constitutes an essential means for generating positive learning experiences in higher education.

Our research is based on the assumption that empowering students to feel more autonomous, competent and connected with their teachers and peers may result in greater involvement in their learning processes, and in turn this may have a positive impact on the adoption of a student-centred transactional model. We sustain that student empowerment may require intervening in different directions, some of the more fundamental ones could be stated as follows: a) improving students' knowledge and expertise with the learning methodology; b) proposing a rich, compelling and authentic learning scenario and tasks, providing opportunities for active learning; c) promoting interchange and negotiation between students and teachers regarding their respective tasks and responsibilities throughout the learning process.

The Design2Learn project intends to involve students in the co-design of learning scenarios that are inquiry-based and expanded by technology. In this paper we focus on the potential of empowering the student voice through student involvement in the joint process of designing learning scenarios with teachers and researchers. We believe that these participatory design practices may also increase students' engagement and facilitate the adoption of student-centred and expanded learning scenarios.

The study applies the methodology of design-based research. The object of study is therefore the very process of co-designing involving teachers, students and researchers, taking as key agents both the teachers and the students to whom those practices are addressed. A mainly qualitative approach is used for data collection, analysis and interpretation although quantitative measures have been used for specific results.

The specific research questions raised by this study have been formulated as follows:

- Is co-design an effective approach for empowering students' voice and promoting student engagement?
- Can the student voice approach bring relevant contributions to the design of expanded learning environments?

In this paper we refer to the foundations of co-design as a means of empowering students by integrating their voice into the design of expanded learning environments. Next, we present the D2L research framework and purpose. Finally, we discuss the opportunities and pitfalls observed so far in the experiences of students co-designing expanded learning scenarios.

MAKING IT MOBILE: CHANGING APPROACHES TO CLINICAL LEARNING ENVIRONMENTS

Daniel Puntis, Laura Delgaty, Jennifer Hoban, Newcastle University, United Kingdom

Background and Aim

Mobile technologies are increasingly being adopted: institutionally by medical schools and independently by students in order to support learning in the clinical environment. Whilst the ubiquitous nature of mobile technologies brings us one step closer to Sharples vision of "learning anytime, anywhere", the theoretical basis of mobile learning (m-learning) is poorly understood, inadequately researched and as a result, often poorly supported. This research was a direct result of these concerns.

Aim

To explore how students are using mobile technologies in a clinical context to develop a theoretical understanding of m-learning and pragmatically inform academic practice.

Methodology

A broadly qualitative methodology was adopted. Data collection consisted of six semi structured interviews of medical students and was analysed via thematic analysis.

Results

Four broad themes were identified including: the nature of m-learning, multiplicity of functions, the effect of technological factors and sociocultural acceptability. Facilitators to m-learning in a clinical environment were highlighted (portability, speed, collaboration, control) as were barriers (rules, acceptability, trustworthiness, limitations).

Discussion and Conclusions

These results provide a detailed exploration of students' experiences of m-learning in a clinical environment. Medical student's value m-learning and use mobile technologies as a supplementary clinical learning resource, gathering small chunks of information in a timely manner. Use is influenced by convenience, ease and functionality of the device. Immediacy of information, integration of learning activities and intuitive designs promote m-learning although sociocultural factors impact upon their use and there remains a pervasive negative perception of mobile devices within the clinical environment. Students are using and institutions are ostensibly supporting m-learning. However students in this study describe a lack of support and understanding from staff. For m-learning to become mainstream within medical education, a shift of attitudes is required. Negative perceptions must be addressed whilst barriers to access, adapting resources for mobile technologies and disseminating rules of 'mobiquette' are essential. This research provides both practical guidelines to clinical academics and a novel conceptual model of the m-learning process in a clinical setting.

MEDICAL STUDENTS' PERCEPTIONS OF SOCIAL MEDIA (SAMPLE OF HACETTEPE UNIVERSITY)

Baris Sezer, Sukriye Ece Abay, Hacettepe University, Nezaket Bilge Basusta, Mersin University, Turkey

Face to face communication has been replaced by technology-oriented ways of communication with Internet's becoming an indispensable component of life. This situation has introduced new relationships established via Internet. Social networking sites present themselves in the center of this kind of communication established on a virtual platform. Social media, which has entered out lives as an expansion of "Web 2.0", can be described as platforms expanding with social interaction by using Internet and web-based technologies, with high accessibility and including contents and sharing.

In Turkey, there are not many studies on the use of social media sites in the educational context. Some of the present ones focus on social media users' habits, the impact of the use of social media on individuals' motivations and purposes of the use of social media. In this context, the point of departure of this study is the need arising from the former completed studies on social media because there is not a single research that metaphorically focuses on the ideas of students. Metaphors are a means of perception. Metaphors are described as a strong mental scheme and modeling mechanism that enables individuals to understand and shape their worlds. Metaphores involve the transfer of information to a relatively unknown domain. Existing in every part of life including languages, ideas and activities, metaphors consist of explaining a subject via another or experiencing it. Metaphors provide a mental framework for thinking about a concept. In this context, the main purpose of this research is to analyze systematically the metaphors related to the social media concept, used by 1st term students of Hacettepe University, Faculty of Medicine. It is considered that these research results would open up an opportunity in the body of literature to look at the social media concept from another perspective.

The mixed method has been used in this research. Study group includes the students (N=336) of the Faculty of Medicine of Hacettepe University in the 2013-2014 academic year. Research data was collected both via questionnaires and the analysis of the data collected from recorded focused group discussions. All data gathered during the research process were analyzed with frequency (f) and percentage (%) values related to metaphors and acquired conceptual categories.

According to the findings gathered in the research, 202 metaphors related to "social media" were read and analyzed using the content analysis technique. Content analysis is described as determining, counting and commenting on recurring subjects, problems and concepts in qualitative data. In the process of creating conceptual categories, related literature was examined by 3 researchers; and taking into consideration the studies containing social media descriptions and structured focused group discussions, the metaphors created by first term medical students were separated into 4 categories. Of these categories (i) communication tool; the use of social media by individuals as a tool to interact with people they want, (ii) source of information; the use of social media by individuals as a tool to get information about any people or event, (iii) a threat; misuse of the social media and its possible harms and (iv) stirrer; the fact that social media has both beneficial and harmful features.

PEDAGOGICAL MODELS STUDENT VOICES: INNOVATIVE FOR COURSE DESIGN

June Breivik, The Norwegian Business School BI, Norway

How do students in higher education respond to the use of video as a substitute for the lecture?

Many argue today that students – called the net generation, digital natives and homo zap pines – are learning differently compared to previous generations of learners, and thus require different approaches to learning and methodology. Others claim that this is a misconception. By asking students themselves about their expectations and experiences regarding learning and use of technology for learning we can get a better understanding of how they learn, the basis for their expectations, and their feed-back on various methods. This is especially relevant when it comes to the flipped model vs. traditional lecture.

Advocates of the lecture emphasize the personal connection and communication that happens in the lecture hall, even though studies question the effectiveness of the lecture when it comes to learning. It can be claimed that videos are non-personal, and over-rated as learning tools because of the non-personal format as compared to the interaction that happens in the lecture.

The present study aimed to get a better understanding of how students experience change from traditional lecture to the flipped model.

This paper reports in depth interviews and research with students, addressing their experiences, competence and expectations regarding use of digital technology in higher education. The paper includes students from three different higher education institutions and from different study programs.

Some of the students were part of a larger project aimed at flipping the lecture, meaning all lectures were replaced with video instructions, and the “lecture time” used alternatively. The findings show that students' expectations on pedagogy and use of technology in higher education are strongly affected by current practice as well as students' prior experiences in K1-13 education. Students, however, quickly embrace new ways of learning when introduced to them. The paper reviews differences in the student use of digital technology for learning.

LECTURE VS WEBINAR: ENGAGEMENT AND DISTRACTION IN DISTANCE LEARNING ADULT TEACHERS

M. E. Cigognini, INDIRE, G. Paoletti, R. Fattorini, M. Boscarol, University of Trieste, Italy

Enabling conditions and key elements to sustain technology enhanced learning for teachers training: Engagement, Motivation, Distraction

The movement for openness of learning content and courseware is pushing a change of paradigm and a need for new approaches in using ICT for smart environment. A new thread of investigations recently emerged regarding quality and efficiency of MOOCs: they were born with a promise of democratization and of teaching quality improvement and now provide us with information on huge numbers of subjects and on courses repeated several times, thus granting strong external validity to the performed studies. Moreover, the line of research dealing with study motivation is also reviving, in considering motivation and volition in distance learners and also in exploring causes and consequences of nowadays study environments, in which students make use, with multiple goals, of their own electronic device (BYOD – Bring Your Own Device). Here we propose an investigation on data collected in the past academic year within a blended course for adult students aimed at a post-graduate training, who were prevalently, and simultaneously, full-time engaged as high school teachers. The reflections we suggest are based on the analysis of the answers provided by the students to a questionnaire for the final evaluation of the course. We shall devote attention to the problem of the complex interplay among engagement, motivation and study context. Research on BYOD, on multitasking and on volition displays a framework of problems of attention which may affect blended students. One in particular is concerned with the problem of interference due to the multi-purpose use of the available devices and the consequence of being always connected and available. Our investigation is aimed at describing the context of elaboration and study of students dealing with various kinds of learning materials, which enabled, or not, interaction (webinars, classroom lectures) and control on the pace of the presentations (the recorded resources). Our expectation was that interactive tools should alleviate the isolation and distance feelings reported by studies on MOOCs. Interactivity may increase engagement and retention of attention on the material and on the lesson. The material under the students' control might have diminished the elaboration difficulties linked the difficulties of concentrating on a single task in a multitasking environment. The data collected concern the effectiveness of the resources as perceived by the students. We investigated their initial motivation, their study habits and preferences, how these fitted with different study resources and difficulties experienced because of internal and external sources of distraction during attendance and study.

Method: subjects, material, questionnaire and procedure

The questionnaire was completed by 83 students on 97 enrolled. They (26 male students and 57 females) were specialized in several disciplinary fields (36 in the area of Science, 32 in the area of Human Studies, 15 in the area of Music). The full-time employed subjects were 63. The transfer burden was reduced by allowing (not forcing) in-presence attendance, which is the format preferred by the majority. The availability of recorded material (either used in synchronous modality or retrievable later on) seems to meet the needs and preferences of students. The difference between ideal duration of resources (as indicated by our subjects) and the one resulting from research on online courses, MOOCs especially may appear surprising. While in the latter attention drops resulted after 6', our students indicated as ideal duration 1-2 hours. Explanations may be various and multi-faced. In-presence lecture, as stated by participants, is more involving, it forces and fosters attention and (at least) external disturbances are avoided. A recorded lecture, and asynchronous, allows repeated review of the material. Differences among resources are clearly acknowledged. When asked about ideal duration, the one for in-presence lectures is more extended than the one for lectures at a distance or for video-lectures.

Regarding concentration, students believe to get distracted rather frequently, with all kind of resources and especially by internal factors. Personal worries, tiredness, low attention/distraction, fatigue are the main perceived obstacles. Less disrupting are considered job and family related calls and texting, being sudden and short. Some limitations of the present investigation are acknowledged and may be ascribed to diverse factors. Some of them are expected to be overcome in subsequent stages of this study.

TEACHER'S TECHNOLOGY USE AND ATTITUDE TOWARDS E-LEARNING IN HIGHER EDUCATION

Sandra Kučina Softić, University of Zagreb, Croatia

Introduction

Today, teachers are confronted with two big challenges: with the need to learn about new technologies and how to integrate them into the teaching and learning process, and with the need to change course design from content-oriented to active and engaging learning settings. This is not an easy process as teachers are faced with technologies with which the most of them are not familiar. Numerous studies have been dealing with teachers' problems in accepting new technologies, focusing mainly on the how to use technology and only lately on its integration into the teaching and learning process. Studies show that successful implementation of educational technologies depends largely on the attitudes of educators and that their attitude is a major enabling/disabling factor in the adoption of technology (Albirini 2006; Mahdizadeh et al. 2008; Al-Zaidiyeen et al. 2010; Krishnakumar and Rajesh Kumar 2011; Babić 2012).

Teacher's Attitude towards e-learning

There have already been some studies on teachers' attitudes towards the ICT and e-learning implementation process in education. Studies show that successful implementation of educational technologies depends largely on the attitudes of educators and that their attitude is a major enabling/disabling factor in the adoption of technology (Albirini 2006; Mahdizadeh et al. 2008; Al-Zaidiyeen et al. 2010; Krishnakumar and Rajesh Kumar 2011; Babić 2012).

In his paper, Buabeng-Andoh (2012) identified personal, institutional and technological factors that influence teachers' adoption and integration of ICT into teaching. Apart from age, gender, educational level and educational experience, personal factors also include ICT competence, experience with ICT for educational purposes and teachers' attitude towards ICT and e-learning.

Teachers' attitude towards ICT and computers can greatly influence their adoption and integration of these technologies into their teaching (Albirini 2006; Al-Zaidiyeen 2010; Buabeng-Andoh 2012). It cannot be expected that teachers will automatically accept that they need to change their teaching methodology and embrace technology as they have to first understand why technology should be used in teaching and how it can be used to make teaching better.

Among the most important factors in the implementation of e-learning are training and support for the teachers. The institution needs to support teachers, ensure that there is a positive environment and encouragement, organize various types of training, provide the infrastructure and transparently value teachers' efforts and work invested in teaching. In such an environment, teachers will have a more positive attitude towards new teaching methods.

Conclusion

The conducted research examined, from the perspective of teachers at the University of Zagreb, their attitude towards ICT and e-learning in higher education. The research found that teachers have a positive attitude towards e-learning. Permanent and reliable organized support and promotion of e-learning has contributed to this attitude. Teachers find that ICT and e-learning enable education adjusted to meet the needs of today's students, collaborative learning, better achievement of learning outcomes and knowledge management. A small number of them think that ICT and e-learning merely represent more work for teachers, that they underestimate teachers' role in the education process and that they have no impact on teaching and learning. This confirms that teachers' attitude towards technology influences their perception of the usefulness of technology and how it can be integrated into teaching.

EXPANDING BLENDED LEARNING SCENARIOS: HOW TO EMPOWER ADULT LEARNERS TO PERSIST?

Ellen Van Twembeke, Katie Goeman, Luc De Grez, Jan Elen, KU Leuven, Belgium

Introduction

Blended learning refers to the integrated online and face-to-face organization of educational content, activities, assignments and meetings. The flexibility peculiar to this instructional format especially appeals to adult learners. However, learners' persistence or completion of a learning program when facing obstacles, tends to be low in blended environments. It was repeatedly shown that insufficient self-regulation skills considerably account for non-completion. This issue gives impetus to the exploration of retention efforts in adult education. Drawing on the theoretical framework of self-regulated learning (SRL) by Barry J. Zimmerman, this study is concerned with the interaction between formal training and learners (meta)cognitive, motivational, behavioural and environmental processes related to persistence in blended learning settings. More specifically, this research initiates the quest for effective interventions on adults' SRL aimed at improving their persistence in blended learning.

Methodology

This paper presents the results of a systematic literature review. The objective was to identify effective interventions that focus on self-regulation which improve adult learners' persistence in a blended learning context. Articles were included when (a) written in English, (b) peer reviewed, (c) experimentally designed, measuring the effect of self-regulated learning interventions on persistence or retention of learners, (d) targeted at adult learners and (e) situated in the context of blended learning. Information retrieval (without date restrictions) was conducted between November 2014 and January 2015 using the databases of ERIC, PSYCArticles, Web of Science and EBSCO. These databases were searched using a combination of key terms. The concepts of adult learners and blended learning, as well as related keywords, were simultaneously used in the search. These were alternately combined with terms referring to SRL and persistence and verbs describing the act of improving SRL.

Conclusions

Firstly, our literature search revealed that current studies seldom address simultaneously the SRL-persistence relationship in the instructional context of blended learning targeting adults. The review results demonstrate that most studies fail to match this original problem setting. Either the research context is different from adult or lifelong learning settings, the applied methodology is non-experimental in nature, or the central concepts do not deal directly with the SRL-persistence question. Secondly, our literature search indicated a lack of research in which SRL interventions are tailored to address the obstacles faced by learners in relation to persistence. While two studies did focus on the problem, these could have been methodologically improved. Particularly, these studies fail to capture and act upon the dynamics of the learning process. Stemming from the use of aptitude-centred, self-report measurement instruments and pre-fixed intervention designs, these gaps highlight the need for further research that i) will help identify those moments when students' persistence is challenged in a blended learning programme, and ii) will define which online or face-to-face SRL interventions could be implemented at these different points in the learning process to support retention. Therefore, before we can build on current SRL intervention guidelines aimed at improving adult learners' persistence in blended environments, these are fundamental issues that require further reflection.

USER PERCEPTIONS ON RELEVANCE OF A LEARNING MANAGEMENT SYSTEM: AN EVALUATION OF BEHAVIORAL INTENTION AND USAGE OF SCIPRO SYSTEM AT UNIVERSITY OF RWANDA

Jean Claude Byungura, Henrik Hansson, Thashmee Kharunaratne, Stockholm University, Sweden.

Since the introduction of computer in everyday human life, there has been a dramatic change in the way activities are performed and the education sector has not escaped this phenomenon. With the emerging use of technological interventions in education systems, e-learning systems contribute immensely in education delivery. However, with substantial efforts from the Rwandan Government, there are still claims about the lack of online support systems especially for thesis process in Rwandan higher education. Furthermore, the experience has proved that some systems implemented at University of Rwanda have failed because the adoption is loath. Therefore, one of the reasons is that some innovative systems are fully diffused and deployed in the university without prior test to its future users to predict the user behavioral intention and usage of a particular system.

This study follows the introduction of one learning management system called Scientific Process abbreviated as "SciPro" which mainly supports thesis process by enabling communication and resources sharing among students (authors) and thesis supervisors. The system was developed at Stockholm University, Department of Computer and Systems Sciences, DSV (Hansson & Momberg, 2011). After getting information on the features and capabilities of SciPro system in supporting thesis process, the University of Rwanda has been interested in implementing it in its six colleges in order to improve research activities in Rwandan public higher learning system. It is in this framework, that a number of pilot tests and studies are planned and the first test was conducted in June to October 2014 to get perceptions and views from participants (teachers, system e-learning coordinators) and the senior management of the university on how they perceive the relevance of this system. Therefore, the aim of this study was to evaluate supervisors' perceptions about the relevance of SciPro System in improving thesis process at University of Rwanda by determining the user's behaviour intention and usage of SciPro.

As a theoretical framework, a research has applied the Unified Theory of Acceptance and Technology (UTAUT). Hence, four independent variables of UTAUT model are used to accommodate all thirteen SciPro resources mentioned above in order to determine the degree of behavioural intention and usage. These variables are Performance Expectancy (PE), Effort Expectancy (EE), Social Influence (SI) and Facilitating Conditions (FC). Thereafter, this predicts the behaviour intention and use when the system will be full implemented. Embedded Case study (Yin, 2003 & Denscombe, 2010) was used as a research strategy to collect data from 31 out of 42 participants using a questionnaire with a mix of close and open-ended questions. Afterwards, convenient interviews were conducted at 5 colleges during and after testing some features and functionalities of SciPro System. The study population was composed of teachers (64.5%) and e-learning coordinators (35.5%) with the experience in academic institution ranging from 2 to 22 years. Both categories are involved in the supervision of both bachelor and master's research projects and they represent 5 of the 6 colleges of the recently created University of Rwanda.

Results show that future users express a reasonable level of behavioural intention (90.78%) and use (87.34%) of the system and this can predict a high degree of successful implementation. This was determined from their perceptions in regard to the importance of SciPro resources, which is also at a higher level. But on the other side, this will depend on if other conditions outside the system are fulfilled. That is the reason why the information from this figure is not enough to confirm this affirmation from quantitative data about the future use of this SciPro system at University of Rwanda. The reason is that some respondents posit that other external factors out of SciPro should be taken into consideration. Interviewed participants expressed some of the key factors such as basic ICT infrastructure in place, a clear E-learning Policy and motivation of early adopters and the degree of involvement from the top management that should be considered to ensure success integration of SciPro System. Thus, on the other hand, one concludes that proposed customization of SciPro in accordance to Rwandan education system should be considered for some features such as peer review process and anti-plagiarism control functionalities.

EXPLORING CAUSAL RELATIONSHIPS AMONG TEACHING, COGNITIVE AND SOCIAL PRESENCE IN INTERNATIONAL COLLABORATIVE SEMINARS: INITIAL FINDINGS USING THE COMMUNITY OF INQUIRY SURVEY

Helga Dorner, Central European University, Hungary

This paper discusses the causal relationships among the three presences in the Community of Inquiry (CoI) framework that has been used extensively in the research and practice of online and blended learning. Both the framework and the CoI survey have been validated in multiple studies, and yet, the causal relationships among the presences require empirical demonstration. In particular, the overarching effect of teaching presence on the contextual dynamics of the presences needs further investigation. Similarly, the question whether social presence makes significant contributions to the prediction of cognitive presence has been addressed but is still in need of exploration. Hence, this paper aims to advance research on the CoI through the investigation of the contextual relational dynamics of the three presences in the redesign model 'international collaborative seminar'.

Telecollaborations served as a methodological precedent to our redesign model of 'international collaborative seminar', which refers to a university course involving two in-person learning communities located at two simultaneous teaching sites collaborating through web-conferencing and asynchronous online work. In such courses students experience the complex dynamics of international, interdisciplinary, online and face-to-face, synchronous and asynchronous learning. Hence, this unique instructional set-up with the synergy of experiences necessitates our focus on the nature of causal relationships among the presences that are at play.

Relations among social, cognitive and teaching presence were explored in the context of a series of course redesign experiments (2012-2014) in higher education. With the CoI survey we tested the hypothesized causal relationships among the three presences. Results of the regression model on the predictive relationship of social and teaching presence with cognitive presence (F (2, 50) = 86,968, p = .000) confirmed the relationship that teaching and social presence have a significant perceived influence on cognitive presence, but interestingly, as further analyses demonstrated (F (2, 50) = 64.584, p = .000), teaching presence is perceived to influence social presence less than cognitive presence. These results underline the overarching importance of teaching presence in facilitating cognition in a formal online learning community however they also direct our attention to further exploring its role in the social dimensions of the instructional processes. Details of hierarchical regression, conducted to identify the statistically significant predictors among the items of the CoI will be also presented with the aim to further refine our understanding of the contextual dynamics among the presences and to also arrive at the pragmatic and functional implications for the purposeful instructional design of similar models in the higher education context. We also intend to discuss the limitations of the applied research tools.

TOWARDS A COLLABORATIVE SPACE FOR LEARNING DIGITAL SYSTEMS

David Baneres, Open University of Catalonia, Spain

Practical skills such as Programming Languages or Digital Systems Design are learned by experience. Such skills are not mechanical processes, but rather creative ones. For this reason, students should practice repeatedly and receive constant feedback in order to further progress in their learning process. Nevertheless, it is difficult for instructors to give constant and individual feedback in this type of exercise, as there are many different correct strategies to construct a valid solution. Intelligent tutoring systems can be used in order to automate individual feedback, however the lack of intervention of the instructor or other students in the process of solving the design hinders the learning process.

Most of the degrees in Computer Science or Engineering have subjects related to the specialty of Digital Systems. Several skills are acquired in the area, such as the design of digital systems. In our university, the first course of the specialty is Computer Fundamentals. The student has to acquire the skills of analysis and synthesis of small digital circuits and to understand the basic computer architecture. The course combines three types of learning resources: i) The material of the course is organized as a textbook; ii) there is an online discussion forum moderated by an instructor, where the students can interact; and ii) an intelligent tutoring system, called VerilUOC to practice the design of digital circuits. All the three learning resources are combined in order to provide a successfully learning experience. The potential benefit of collaboration during problem-solving is that a deeper elaboration can be reached. Although students may produce non-canonical solutions or even incomplete solutions, detecting differences between solutions or comparing erroneous and correct examples can guide the students to a higher level of knowledge construction.

Students started tending to study individually and few students used the forum to post messages. The instructors also complained that there was an increment of individual messages via the instructors' email address that students posted in the forum on the previous semesters. This is a serious concern since the knowledge acquisition is no more shared among students. Additionally, we observed also a decrement of the number of exercises performed using the tutoring system. The students have difficulties on solving exercises and they asked directly of the instructor instead of asking on the forum.

On 2014 spring semester, we decided to try to amend this tendency to the total individual study by reorganizing the structure of the course. We propose to connect the students who seek collaborative learning by adding a new space. This space that we called laboratory class is basically a plenary new discussion forum where all the student of the course (of every classroom) can post messages and it is moderated by another instructor. We are interested in forums where students can freely communicate without any restriction. The previous forums were not removed, we only change their orientation. The theoretical aspects and questions related to the organization of the course are discussed on the small group forums, whereas the new forum is only intended for the practical activities and the exercises proposed using the intelligent tutoring system.

Although, this system can be used individually to learn the design of circuits, the analysis performed in this paper shows evidences that the skill of circuit design was not properly learned with this standalone tool and, therefore, the cohabitation with this new organization of the communication channels impacts in the learning engagement of the students. Many advantages have been showed: increment of the engagement of the student in the classroom activity, (slightly) increment on the students' performance and increment on the collaborative knowledge construction in the course.

CREATING THE DIGITAL UNIVERSITY: OPEN, COLLABORATIVE MODELS FOR STRATEGIC PEDAGOGIC AND TECHNICAL

Sheila MacNeill, Glasgow Caledonian University, Keith Smyth, University of the Highlands and Island, Bill Johnston, University of Strathclyde, United Kingdom

The notion of the Digital University has gained traction in the last few years as a key topic in the discourse of organisational and educational development in Higher Education around the world, and as a focus for academic research in areas including learning literacies, teaching practice, and technological developments.

We felt that exploration of this overarching term offered the potential to act as a catalyst for fundamental change throughout an institution from administration to teaching and learning.

Our starting point in 2011 was trying to provide answer to 'what do we mean by the Digital University?' We challenged the assumption that this was a largely trouble free concept driven by technological innovation and infrastructure developments, which could be managed through existing institutional structures. Emerging narratives included an overly techno-centric view that technology alone constituted an environment that could be nominated as "digital". We felt a need to acknowledge the human and social processes involved and proposed that a truly digital university can only be fully realised where there is a fusion between technology and staff/student developments driving innovation and creativity.

Our approach involved: discussion; generation of models that we shared openly via a blog; presentations, workshops, publications; and a major collaborative effort with a Scottish university. This open process characterised by its collaborative, generative, pro-active nature.

Our paper describes the development a strategic model that provides a multidimensional, holistic view of the concept of the Digital University and offers a flexible tool for engaging staff in identifying and formulating systematic programmes for change through harnessing, or developing, digital spaces, practices, and provision.

The resulting conceptual matrix can be used by institutions to:

- Analyse policy documents.
- Channel strategic discussion.
- Focus on specifics whilst retaining a broader perspective.
- Shape the division of labour to best effect.
- Co-ordinate projects, debate, decision making and action.

We will describe how this approach has been used to develop digital strategy in a number of UK universities.

TELEPRESENCE WITH IPADS: LEARNING AND COLLABORATION IN LOWER SECONDARY SCHOOLS

Bente Meyer, Aalborg University, Denmark

Introduction

In the spring of 2013 I was asked to research an ongoing school development project in a rural part of the west of Denmark, where three schools had for a year been using videoconferencing for teaching basic subjects such as maths, German, science, history and literature. The purpose of the project, which was initiated by the local municipality, was to explore how the use of videoconferences in schools could support community and curriculum developments through increased collaboration between schools, access to experts and the establishment of links between schools, industry and community. Within these broad aims the municipality sought to respond to a variety of community challenges, for instance the depopulation of specific rural areas and the consequent limited access to resources such as specialized teachers and experts. Following a municipal reform in 2007, the municipality had increased in size and incorporated several rural school districts which necessitated a local strategy for linking schools and reorganizing available resources. As a result, the municipality initiated the project and at the same time schools invested in iPads for all students in lower secondary school (age 13-16).

The research project specifically explored the potential of videoconferences as a supplement to classroom teaching for qualifying lower secondary students' learning, with the three local schools as an empirical case. Research was done as an ethnographic, multi-sited study that included observations in all three schools as well as interviews with students. Research is ongoing and the following reports from the initial phase of the project from the autumn 2013 to 2014. The project ends in the summer of 2015.

Some conclusions

The paper identifies some of the challenges, issues and potentials involved in connecting schools through telepresence understood as different kinds of mediated practices in everyday schooling. Whereas videoconferencing – according to the literature – has extensive potential for redistributing learning resources in rural communities and enriching learning - actually making the connection(s) is, as the examples show, still affected by both logistics and issues of proximity and distance. In terms of logistics, the schools in question must aim to adapt their organizational and cultural specificities to the community of schools with regard to for instance timetables and teaching styles. When this adaptation is successful, three school organizations may to some extent become one and can act as one in the synchronous learning environment. What works against this, however, are not only organizational structures in the individual schools, but also the lack of familiarity and feeling of community between students and teachers who are in many senses effectively strangers inhabiting the same local municipality. Therefore, connections between students and teachers in the schools must in future be supported and enhanced in order to establish engaging learning forms in the mediated environment that can create this feeling of community.

Another issue that acts in the telepresence with iPads activities is the co-presence of several teachers and learners in restricted synchronous learning environments. As argued by the literature, synchronous interaction can be an extremely challenging framework for learning in terms of both logistics and effectively making the connections that support interactive learning practices (see for instance Anderson & Rourke 2005). This is an aspect of videoconferencing that schools should address and take seriously in their development of telepresence activities. In the schools in question, one of the challenges identified by the research is exactly these brief and fragile synchronous learning spaces that to a large extent fail to connect distributed students and teachers. Therefore, the synchronous activities in these schools might be enhanced by extending and supporting them through asynchronous and face-to-face activities that could establish a more solid and meaningful basis for collaboration by bringing real connectivity back into the picture. This will entail looking at collaboration – and telepresence - as a broad framework for learning between the schools, in which different kinds of connections – both synchronous and asynchronous, mediated and face-to-face, large screen and desktop interaction, can support the placement of schools within the community and in the global context of learning. One of the exciting aspects of telepresence is thus the ways in which the potential of mediation changes the directions of learning – i.e. brings them out of the brick and mortar environment and into communities that are both global and local and in which collaboration is directed at real world communities. One of the interesting issues to be taken up by the research described in this paper will therefore be a further study of the consequences of these new directions and connections of learning, i.e. how a deeper study of these connections between schools and communities can bring more learning potentials into the picture.

CREATIVE COLLABORATION IN ONLINE COMPUTER-SUPPORTED COLLABORATIVE LEARNING

Margarida Romero, Université Laval, Canada, Elena Barberà, Universitat Oberta de Catalunya, Spain

Creativity is a key competence for facing the society challenges of the post-industrial knowledge society (Garrison, 2011). Despite the importance of collaborative learning in the 21st society (Bates & Sangrà, 2011; Hesse, Care, Buder, Sassenberg, & Griffin, 2015), creativity in educational settings has been mainly analysed individually. Moreover, the collaborative aspects of creativity have been not developed in the context of online collaborative learning (Romero, Hyvönen, & Barberà, 2012), despite being a part of the 21st century skills. There is also a lack of assessment methodologies for the collaborative creative assessment (Wishart & Eagle, 2014). This study aims to contribute to the analysis of creative collaborative learning in online distance context through the conception and analysis of the Assessment Scale for Creative Collaboration (ASCC). The scale is evaluated in the context of an online learning course on Creativity in Advertisement in the virtual campus of the Universitat Oberta de Catalunya (UOC) in Spain.

MOOCS UNDERUTILISE VIDEO, SELF-ASSESSMENT, TEACHER GUIDANCE

Jack Koumi, Educational Media Production Training, United Kingdom

Description – and relevance to the conference theme, *Social Media, Digital Collaborative Learning*

The paper questions the efficacy of MOOCs for learning, arguing that peer/peer discussion forums are inadequate to counteract the following pedagogic paucity of the other MOOC features.

Firstly, the paper considers 34 techniques and teaching functions for which video is outstandingly capable – in four domains: Cognitive, Experiential, Affective, Skills. A selection of these 34 will be illustrated with video clips. These potent roles are in contrast to the paucity of video roles in the typical MOOC – often just a talking head.

Secondly, the paper describes a style of UK OU video-print hybrid that is divided into short segments, interspersed with self-assessment questions (with suggested answers). The depth of these questions and answers are contrasted with the typically superficial, multiple-choice quizzes after each MOOC video segment.

Thirdly the paper decries the poor teacher presence in a MOOC due to the massive student/teacher ratio.

Finally, the paper questions the efficacy of the MOOC peer discussion forum, in which the rich get richer and the poor (may) get poorer.

Summary of novel characteristics

The transmissive elements of a MOOC (Massive Open Online Course), are typically short narrated videos interspersed with on-screen printed quizzes (Glance, 2013; Conole, 2013); that is, video-led self-assessed video-print hybrids. However, the vast majority of MOOCs' videos are 'head and shoulders' lecture-capture. Hence they use few of video's rich presentational attributes and potent pedagogic roles (described in Koumi, 2015).

Self-assessment in MOOCs is usually through multiple-choice quizzes, which cannot hope to enable the intensity of reflection and retrieval practice enabled by the SAQs and suggested answers in the above UK OU illustration.

A paucity of pedagogically potent video, reflective nudges and retrieval practice would severely undermine learning outcomes. As would the minimal interaction of the teacher with the students.

The digital collaboration between students benefits those who are already good learners and may cause poor learners to lose hope – due to the so-called Matthew Effect: *For unto every one that hath shall be given, and he shall have abundance: but from him that hath not shall be taken away even that which he hath. (Gospel according to Matthew, XXV, 29)*

ADDED VALUES AND CHALLENGES SOCIAL MEDIA REPRESENT IN THE HYBRIDISATION OF TEACHER TRAINING

Anders Grov Nilsen, Aslaug Grov Almås, Stord/Haugesund University College, Norway

Today digital technology plays a central role within important areas of society such as business, entertainment, transportation, art, education, and of course the media industry. The interesting question now becomes: How do student teachers of our time acquire information? How do they find their way to knowledge?

Students and newly qualified teachers establish, maintain and develop digital networks as an important source of development in the school subject and subject didactics. In a teacher education context, it is important to know this new interaction patterns that occur between children, adolescents and adults. Teachers must also consider how the information gathering and learning that occurs in the informal learning context can be used in a school context.

Unifying factors associated with the recent Web 2.0-technology are related to sharing, collaboration, networking and community. The characteristics of the content have changed to a more dynamic state, with a higher degree of participation and influence. Key pedagogical questions related to these changes in content and pattern of use is what learning competencies, knowledge and practices that develops. This means that the educational foundation is challenged and a revitalization of pedagogy is in progress. With this background this article discusses how teacher trainers can orchestrate and facilitate learning with new technologies.

Norway is ranking third highest among European nations for posting to social media platforms. Our student teachers arrive equipped not only with individual technologies that they maintain and improve, but also with their own personal learning environments and social networks. The Web 2.0-technology has provided affordances which cause a rethinking of the tasks and learning goals we set for our students. But it is not about finding one tool that increases learning outcomes in one learning objective. This involves a constructive process consisting of communication, learning and reflection.

Students' use of digital technologies can be seen as a media ecology. Usage is woven into the social contexts in which technology is integrated. Activities are created between technology and its users' subjective intentions. This means that the technology will be a part of, and should be understood in the social context. A broader interpretation of knowledge and teaching requires a perspective where teaching and learning takes place in very complex educational ecosystem. A sociocultural learning perspective emphasizes that interaction and cooperation are fundamental for learning. It further highlights the context, environment and culture around the pupil. In this perspective we discuss how teachers can design their teaching and learning activities in higher education in the ecology of Web 2.0 and social media. We are using the three key points; participation, personalization and productivity to focus our discussion to contribute to developing new practices.

The methodological approach is based on a theoretical review, previous empirical data and our own experiences as teachers in teacher training courses. The previous empirical data includes respondents (n=56) from teacher education enrolled in net based courses at Stord/Haugesund University College.

Our findings related to the tree Ps indicate potential and challenges for teachers and institutions to cope with. The triangle of Ps is framing the complexity in a constructive way. Findings and discussions related to the characteristics of each of the angles indicate we have to change practice and task descriptions. This mean we have to implement our web 2.0-pedagogy and design learning (environment and activities) which supports purposeful activities, possibilities for reflection – spaces and tools which facilitate communication and sharing of ideas and understandings.

THE CORRECT USE AND THE DANGERS OF MISUSE OF SOCIAL NETWORKS AND DIFFERENT WEBSITES WITHIN/OUTSIDE THE CLASSROOM

Gyula Hegyi, Hungary

To commemorate the 70th year of the liberation of Auschwitz, the BBC showed just how haunting Auschwitz-Birkenau remains, by flying a camera-equipped drone over the empty buildings and grounds. This short video is a reminder of the horrors humanity is capable of inflicting on itself. It uses the visual language of our days, can be watched on laptops, mobile phones or other devices, and the other hand this video gives a deeper and more emotional picture on Auschwitz as long quotations from history books.

Speaking about WWII, Wikipedia provides us interesting details and serves as the main source of information, favoured by many students and hopefully not so many teachers. The Hungarian version claims that Edvard Benes, the former president of Czechoslovakia was rescued from the German-occupied Prague to London by a KGB commando. It is totally nonsense, he left his country before the Nazi occupation, and why would the Soviet KGB flee him to London?

These two examples show us the correct and incorrect use of the social media in the teaching and studying of the history. The drone over Auschwitz uses the modern technology to provide a deeper picture on the well-known and well-documented historical facts. The second one is a simple lie, written most probably by somebody who hates Edvard Benes because of his anti-German and anti-Hungarian decrees after WWII.

Somebody collected the fifty craziest lies in Wikipedia, but of course we can find similar lies on other social media as well.

There are two types of information on the net. Digitalized versions of already existing texts, documents, films, etc. and original contents made for the net. Social media prefers the latter one, but of course new contents are also based on former information. Digitalization is always a selection, motivated by political, cultural, practical or other consideration. Concerning history, the first selection is usually made by the state (archives), the science (universities, institutes), or lobby groups and private activists. Selecting certain documents to digitalize and ignore others leads already a biased explanation of the history. The second selection is a practical decision. Technical, financial poblems of digitalization and the royalty issues (legitimacy) matter a lot. The third selection is made by the consumers, directly or indirectly. In principle the students can find everything on the net, but usually they choose what their teachers, fellow students, media or in the worst case different hate groups suggest to choose.

But there is a fourth and crucial selection, the linguistic one. Wikipedia has roughly 4,900,000 articles in English. German is the second with 1,800,000 articles, while Spanish is the third with 1,170,000 articles, which is less than one fourth of the English articles. Catalan students have to use frequently either the English or Spanish version, as there are only 460,000 articles in their mother tongue. Most probably there are different accents on the Catalan history in the Catalan and Spanish (Castilian) texts. Latvia is an independent Member State of the European Union, but there are only 60,000 articles in Latvian. They can choose between almost 5 million English or 1,200,000 Russian articles, as one third of the population speak Russian as first language. No need to say that this choice is not only a practical one; it leads to different interpretation of the history. And Wikipedia still tries to work on so many languages as possible. YouTube and other social media can be reached only or mostly in English. Facebook has 1.35 billion active users per month, and even if they use their native language, many terms and phrases exist mostly in English on Facebook. If you target a global audience, you use English, using your own language means you can reach only your compatriots.

I don't want to speak about the political control of the social media, which country and intelligence service has the real power to control the internet. The almost total control of the net by a certain country and the censorship of the internet by some other countries are two sides of the coin. The pure fact is that without proper English everybody is handicapped person on the net and in the social media. It impoverishes our knowledge on history, culture, national identity. On the content side, more and more information should be put on the net in different languages. On the user side teachers, professors should encourage and even oblige their students to mix the net information with other sources like libraries and oral history. It is not a polite but very useful way of the information diversification if the educators check the sources of the thesis written by their students, and refuse it if totally based on the net. It is not against the net society. However as the mankind had a history before the digital age, studies in history should exclude pre-digital sources as well.

OPEN SOURCE LEARNING STREAMS IN SOCIAL MEDIA IN YEAR 11 MATH TEACHING

Thomas Kjærgaard, Elsebeth Korsgaard Sorensen, Aalborg University, Denmark

The students' use of social media during lessons and in group work is a general concern amongst teachers especially from secondary school and onwards. The blurred ecotones between private, social and academic life brought on by the always present online mobile technology makes utilization of social media in teaching a balancing act. On the one hand the teachers in this study welcome the possibilities for communicating, sharing and producing academically relevant products, and on the other hand they fear that the rhizomatic connection between what is academic and what is regarded as non-academic is disrupting the learning process. Hence, teachers take different measures in order for the ecotones to either separate or engage in fruitful synergy. In this study two very different approaches are taken within similar pedagogical designs in a highly comparable context. In theory the outcome of the pedagogic design should be the same but in practice the two teachers achieve very different results. The study utilizes the deleuzean notion of 'interest' and 'desire' and problematizes the common use of 'motivation' in pedagogy. The study analyzes what appears to be a conflict between the institutionalized 'interests' of the educational system and personal 'desires' of the student. In one case the institutionalized interest and the personal desire of the student share a significant intersection; whereas the other case shows a clash of 'interest' and 'desire'. The study also shows a clash between content driven teaching and learning driven teaching. Finally the study shows that if a pedagogic design is imposed upon a teacher without his acceptance or full understanding of the design then the outcome is questionable. The study suggests a different approach to motivation that acknowledges that the process of learning is a desire of 'becoming' not the 'pleasure' of satisfaction through entertaining activities.

At the school, where this study was carried out almost every student brings their own devices to class. For the most part the students live in a state of omnipotent onlineness where postponed replies in social media is considered impolite therefore controlled and restricted use of social media in particular and smartphone in general result in conflicts. The teachers at this school take different measures in the fight for getting the students attention; some teachers are very proactive, they collect smartphones in the beginning of classes and so forth, while other teachers resignate in inaction. But for the most part the teachers try to incorporate social media in the pedagogical design (blogs, google drive, socrative etc.). The incorporation of social media is done in many ways; one is to create intrinsic motivation through accommodating to the means of communication that the students use in their private lives, another is to try to move the academic tasks into social media. In both cases the use of technology is blurring the ecotones between academic and non-academic life. The blurring of ecotones brought on by online, personal devices is a general concern in this study. Case 1 shows a teacher (referred to as teacher 1) who tries to utilize the academic affordances of social media, while case 2 (referred to as teacher 2) tries to maintain a well-defined ecotone between private and academic. In this study social media has the role of; hand-in folder, feedback channel and assignment distribution. It is merely a tool that is in everybody's shared repertoire and not so much an attempt to create extrinsic motivation through accommodation to youth culture.

The theory of science behind this study is Critical Realism. The methodology is design based research.

WHAT DO STUDENTS SAY ABOUT EPORTFOLIOS: UTILIZING SOCIAL MEDIA TO EXPAND LEARNING SCENARIOS

Lori L. Hager, University of Oregon, United States of America

Purpose

The purpose of this research is to understand how students value implementing open source ePortfolios as a 21st century learning strategy. This paper presents findings about how students and alumni value ePortfolios for connecting formal and experiential learning, and professional preparation in academic programs. The project reached hundreds of students, suggesting possibilities for an integrated technology approach to education and expanded learning scenarios in a global learning environment.

The graduate student learning ePortfolios connect curricular and co-curricular learning and achievement, provide evidence of the development of professional skills, and a means to critically reflect about and analyze the learning process while embedding technology-rich strategies in research and professional practice. Results of the project suggest that "eportfolio learning" fosters habits of mind conducive to 21st century skills and are fundamental to addressing challenges in education as alternative, technology-rich educational structures replace traditional classroom learning environments.

Project Description

The *ePortfolio Project* began with the idea of creating and fostering a digital neighbourhood, or "commons," as the point of daily departure and return, where learning is fostered through sharing thoughts, ideas, events, and professional development. The project sought a way in which what was happening in classes could be made visible, and to

- generate a forum for students and faculty to share how they were extending their thinking and applied practices to outside the classroom
- create a virtual community where students articulate value, and where students, faculty, and professional partners foster connections between curricular and co-curricular work
- make evident how students transfer skills and knowledge across a range of experiences

Students post their academic plan, and are encouraged to utilize the system in order to provide evidence of achievements, and to document their growth over time. In this way habits of reflection, evaluation, and documentation are embedded in the learning process. Students are also encouraged to document and provide evidence of their professional growth through their internships, practicums and other professional activities, and are encouraged to engage as thoughtful digital citizens. At the end of the term, students then reflect on their course learning objectives, and analyse how they participated in working towards their objectives, identifying transformative moments, and discussing and providing evidence of how their thinking has changed relevant to their future growth.

Findings

The inclusion of open source social media ePortfolio approaches to learning are valued by students for their support of making learning visible across the curriculum and in connecting co-curricular learning and professional development. ePortfolios support a more student centered pedagogy that thrives in experiential, and experimental, education. The proliferation of education technologies liberates education from traditional pedagogical and classroom structures, and the use of ePortfolios across the curriculum supports the development of skill sets necessary for the next generation of meaning makers, such as critical thinking and collaboration. ePortfolios can provide a means to both practice and to demonstrate transformations in thinking and learning, and to make the applications of learning (and knowledge generation) visible to students, to peers, to faculty, and to professionals. The ability of students to document and demonstrate what they learned, and their problem-solving process, can lead to transformations in learning and outcomes. As educators, fostering learning in this way not only has the potential of preparing students for the new 21st century workplace, but of opening up the learning landscape to fuel global education rich in international connectivity

DIGITAL IDENTITY AND PERSONAL LEARNING NETWORKS (PLN) IN A PHD RESEARCHERS COMMUNITY

Nuno Ricardo Oliveira, Lina Morgado, Universidade Aberta, Portugal

Abstract

The Web 2.0 has been increasingly used by the academic community - teachers, students and researchers - to create, stimulate and expand learning in an informal way, even when knowledge is acquired in a formal context. The appearance of emerging environments and pedagogies has enabled the introduction and adoption of new practices and behaviours of individuals in the university academic context. In the context of lifelong learning and as a complement to formal learning, there is a new reality for the 21st century researchers - the personal learning network. This research project addresses issues related to the researchers' digital identity in the field of Online Distance Education and e-Learning and their personal learning environment, researching the genesis, management and dynamics of the personal learning network of each member in a community of researchers. Within this background, this research aims to analyse how a community of researchers uses social networks to deepen their knowledge, as well as to understand how they create, manage and stimulate their social networks to acquire knowledge based on their contacts.

Digital Identity

In a society that lives increasingly networked and in constant online interaction, it becomes necessary to have an awareness of digital presence. In the context of this study, the researchers mark their digital presence through their sharing, collaboration and dissemination of their work through the social network(s). Through the network and what is shared, each person will disclose their digital identity. Oliveira & Morgado (2014, p. 469) assert that "the digital dimension of identity is understood as the total information about the individual, from credentials that allow access to the closed system, to the representation of the complex "I" in an open digital space[16]". The concept of Digital Identity is recent and derives from the practices that individuals have been developing on the network. It's an important element because it is the reflection of the personal, academic and professional life of the researchers.

Personal Learning Network

The evolution of technology creates new challenges to education and researchers, as we nowadays live increasingly networked. The network is composed of individuals who are part of our everyday life, who we share interests, resources, thoughts, links, insights and jokes with, among many other things, but the most important thing is that they enrich our professional, academic and personal life. This sharing is taking place, most of the times, through social networking and web 2.0 tools, which motivate and facilitate the edition, simulation, reviews, sharing of text, sound, image and video, by promoting and valuing the Personal Learning Environment (PLE) and a networked learning (Mota, 2009b), enabling a social learning which is collaborative and open, through their Personal Learning Network (PLN) (Brown, 2002). The Personal Learning Network (PLN) is the social dimension of a Personal Learning Environment. For Castaneda & Adell (2013a) the PLN emerges as a relationship tool and strategy, which consists of environments where the researcher relates to others and that by means of this relationship, feedback and interaction that may exist, there is a production of knowledge, and therefore there is a network of learning. The PLN is defined by the connections that the researcher establishes through the means available and at their disposal, with the purpose of improving mutual learning, through feedback, ideas, documentation, new contacts, thus building a network of learning and acquisition of new knowledge. In short, the main elements that characterise the relationships developed between members of the network are reciprocity and trust, which encourage the exchange of information with the aim of learning. The PLN describes habits of informal learning and creates opportunities for learning through relationships and interactions. They are not social networks, since the incentive to participate in them is in learning. They are referred to as the sum of social knowledge and connections that help people create their own environment for autonomous learning. Throughout their network, each individual serves the needs of personal learning, which is not limited by collective objectives.

ICT INTEGRATION IN EDUCATION: THE GREEK AND SPAIN PERSPECTIVES AMIDST AN ECONOMIC CRISIS

Munir Abbasi, Georgios Xydopoulos, Masoud Fakhimi, Lampros Stergioulas, Maria Fragkaki, University of Surrey, United Kingdom, Luis Anido, Manuel Fernandez, University of Vigo, Spain, Panayiota Vassilopoulou, University of Liverpool, United Kingdom

Information and Communication Technology (ICT) and its applications are becoming increasingly prevalent in European education systems thus attracting the interest of the European Union and individual governments. However, due to various recent developments, including rapid and intensive changes in digital learning technologies, innovation, disruption, cloud computing, and mobile learning but also unclear policies, and economic constraints, some European countries lack effective pedagogical integration of ICT in education.

This paper focuses on the use of ICT in the educational systems and practices in Greece and Spain, aiming to highlight not only the barriers imposed under the pressures of the current economic crisis in both countries, but also the main drivers for funding mechanisms and actors that can influence the future development of ICT in Education. During the past decade, these two South-European countries have been seriously affected by the economic crisis. In both cases, education is primarily supported by public funds and, therefore, cuts imposed by the crisis have impacted directly on the development, infrastructure, training, delivery and quality of education. Hence, although ICT- based education is a priority for both countries, it is questionable whether the investment required for ICT in education to develop in this direction may be realistically secured.

What follows is a summary of the main outcomes of research in the integration of ICT in European educational systems carried out under the EU-funded Open Space Discovery project (2012-15), of which the authors of the present paper are members. ODS is an open innovation and collaboration environment for K-12 teachers that facilitates educational content and tools for the creation, co-creation, use, re-use, sharing and retrieval based on OER as well as for networking and further collaborating among K-12 stakeholders (teachers, learners, parents, content and technology providers, and policy makers etc.).

In both Greece and Spain, there have been several initiatives with different types of action programmes for the integration of ICT in Education. Educational Institutes in both countries are responsible for the integration in ICT in Education (e.g. CTI & Press- Diophantus in Greece and Educational Technology Institute in Spain). One main difference between the two countries, is that while in Greece the same centralized policy applies to all regions, in Spain, different policies are followed in each of the regions thus responding to their specific educational needs and provision; in this way, Spain, unlike Greece, facilitates continuity and development to be built on previous achievements (as illustrated by Galicia's case, which is discussed in detail in this paper). In principle, all schools in both Greece and Spain have Internet access, but while in Spain about 70% of schools have technical personnel responsible for coordinating ICT technical functions and dealing with related problems, this is not the case in Greece, where for the most part such issues fall under the responsibility of the teacher. We argue that, educational reform is needed in both countries with regard to the content and the methods of the integration of ICT in Education able to meet the relevant challenges, including, for example, sustainability, the need for the adoption of critical/reflective perspectives, ICT and OER integration, and financial allowances. Such reform, however, is seriously undermined by the significant reduction of public funds observed in recent years.

With regard to training, both in Spain and Greece teachers are trained at higher education level, during their undergraduate studies and further through in-school programs that are organized as part of CPD. Most teachers receive face-to-face training, while others are trained through e-learning, and thus through a less blended training process. However, both Spain and Greece need to address problems of inclusivity and to overcome the divide, much accentuated by the dire economic conditions evidenced in both countries, between privileged and challenged members of their respective population, in respect to access to ICT and education more generally. It is thus of paramount importance and urgency, as we hope this paper shows, that significant changes be made to policy mechanisms, distribution of budget and investment that would need to focus on teachers training and how they could use ICT in order to promote innovative, creative and constructive education, affording them with the necessary skills to secure a stable position in the 21st century landscape across Europe and globally

BOLDIC – OPEN LEARNING RESOURCES ONLINE

Ulf Sandström, Swedish Association Distance Education, Ebba Ossiannilsson , Lund University, Sweden, Torhild Slåtto, Flexible Education Norway, Norway

Background

The general purpose of the "Boldic – open learning resources online" network is to deepen and bring further the co-operation between Nordic and Baltic organizations dealing with distance education, flexible learning and e-learning by opening the community for new partners from both the Baltic and the Nordic countries. The network has been supported by Nordplus (Founded by The Nordic Council of Ministers) for ten years and we want to disseminate results, discussions and future issues during the EDEN Conference in Barcelona 2015.There is a continuous increase in the demand for technology supported learning material, and especially so for material developed for on-line learning. Most of this material is developed in such a way that it normally is quite easy to change language and in other ways fit the material for use in different countries. I.e. the field is very well set up for exchange of material and for continuous cooperation in development, marketing, etc. In short, we have a demand, what we need is better marketing and simpler exposure of the material between the potential exchangers of the materials. The intention of the network is to establish a major Nordic and Baltic integration project supporting open learning resources online. Apart from better quality in learning, the project proves the benefits possible by simple cooperation between the learning organizations of the different countries. The Boldic network also works for supporting cultural exchanges as the materials often contain cultural parts.

Description of the Boldic work

The Boldic Award work seeks to recognize outstanding organisations and people in the open and distance learning field. The Boldic Award winners should support any ODL-activity connected to adult learning meeting one or more of the following criteria: teaching/learning arrangements, support systems (for delivery of learning content or/and learning support), development of activities, content or understanding within the ODL area and the activities should be transferable to other countries and be learner focused, facilitate blended or flexible learning, be innovative, be scalable, have a sustainable strategy, have a sensible and appropriate approach to technology and involve continuing evaluation. Both persons, projects and organisations can been nominated for the Boldic Award. The following topics are discussed and tested in the Boldic network. Webinars, preparation, advertising, implementation, common start-up problems and list of meeting and conference platforms.

Future work

Practically the network now stands on the good results from the previous completed Boldic network projects, Nord Plus Voxen, Flexible Learning Network (2005-2007) and – Nordic- Perspectives online (2008 -2011) and the ongoing project Boldic Open learning resources online. We work for bringing in new players from the Baltics and Nordic countries and from other sectors of educational and working life. It will also improve on the contact system as well as the Boldic-award system. The Boldic-award system – i.e. to hand out a special award to the project found most interesting in the partner countries – has been a success.

Partners

Swedish Association Distance Education (SVERD) http://www.sverd.se (project coordinator)
Flexible Education Norway (FuN) http://fleksibelutdanning.no/
Aarhus University (Denmark) http://www.au.dk/
Vilniaus Kolegija/University of Applied Sciences (Lithuania) http://www.ekf.viko.lt/
BA School of Business and Finance (Latvia) http://www.ba.lv/lv/
University of Jyväskylä (Finland) https://www.jyu.fi/
Tallinn University (Estonia) http://www.tlu.ee

OER, OPEN ACCESS AND SCHOLARSHIP IN PORTUGUESE HIGHER EDUCATION

Paula Cardoso, Lina Morgado, António Teixeira, Universidade Aberta, Portugal

The present paper is part of a PhD research, which is being developed in the scope of the Doctoral Programme in Education, specialisation in Distance Education and eLearning at Universidade Aberta, the Portuguese Open University. The theoretical framework for the research is Open Education, particularly the specific fields of Open Educational Resources (OER) and Open Access (OA). The main objective of the research is to identify and understand the awareness, knowledge and attitudes of scholars in Portuguese public Higher Education Institutions (HEI), regarding OER and OA and, in particular, to compare scholars' awareness, attitudes and perceptions towards OER and OA in the context of their teaching and research practices.

Similarly to many other society spheres, Higher Education Institutions have been facing several challenges, which have led to various changes, not only in terms of scholarly practice, but also in the role of higher education in the current 21st century. There is currently the need of identity management and more collaborative behaviours, which, consequently, pressure institutions to increasingly innovate, cross-collaborate and design new business models, focusing on students and innovative practices. Within this context of change in higher education institutions, the role of scholars and how they perform their scholarly practice is also facing opportunities and challenges, particularly when we consider the relationship between information technology and scholarship. Based on the multidimensional nature of scholarship proposed by Boyer (1990), we analyse how the current use of Web 2.0 digital tools has been shaping the research work of scholars in different ways, and, similarly, this influence has been characterised in different terms in the literature, depending on the behaviours or practices each perspective intends to highlight. In this context, scholarship in the digital age has been termed as social scholarship (Cohen, 2007), digital scholarship (Pearce et al., 2010) open scholarship (Burton, 2009), digital scholarship (Weller, 2011) and networked participatory scholarship (Veletsianos & Kimmons, 2012). Even though scholarship has been termed differently in the literature, the apparently diverse definitions place the focus beyond the use of technologies, highlighting the values that are embraced and promoted by that same use. What is common to all definitions are the principles of openness, collaboration, networking and sharing, and thus, scholarship in a digital age is influenced by different factors, such as networking, sharing of digital data, increased collaborative work and increased emphasis on openness and benefits from the Web 2.0 affordances, by connecting traditional formal scholarly practices with more informal, open and collaborative practices. Within this background, it is, thus, fundamental to understand the specific role of scholars and to analyse their educational and research practices within the framework of these global movements and within the current situation of Higher Education Institutions. Even though there are multiple and diverse perspectives on how to characterise scholars, scholarship and the scholarly cycle, what is common to all perspectives are the concepts of sharing, networking and openness.

In a first empirical stage, data will be collected through a questionnaire survey, targeting teachers/researchers of public Higher Education Institutions in Portugal. The main dimensions are based on previous national and international surveys, concerning OER and OA in Higher education institutions and the indicators will be adapted, based on an analysis of common grounds for comparability in the measured dimensions. A second stage will be carried out, with the objective of achieving a deeper understanding of the data collected in the previous stage, by means of focus groups. The purpose of the focus groups is to corroborate possible findings and explore in greater depth the relationships suggested by the previous analysis.

The revision of literature carried out so far has allowed us to preliminarily acknowledge two aspects: first, that there aren't many studies focusing on addressing the awareness, knowledge and attitudes towards OER and OA practices, even though they represent two functions of scholarly practice; second, that some Portuguese institutions have participated in several initiatives regarding the two movements, but it is necessary to understand the current situation of the Portuguese scholars in the movement of openness to knowledge.

THE IMPLEMENTATION OF ICT IN SECONDARY SCHOOLS IN CATALONIA

Jordi Serarols, Albert Sangrà, Nati Cabrera, Universitat Oberta de Catalunya, Spain

Theoretical framework

Students need new skills and competences to be fully integrated in the 21st century society; this is why ICT must be integrated in curricula and why the implementation of ICT in schools has been enhanced by European, national and regional programmes. Despite the use of ICT in schools, there has been little improvement or innovation in the teaching and learning processes. To take advantage of the educational opportunities of ICT, schools need both a global educational model at professional development, organization and curricular levels and a strategic and effective use of ICT to improve outcomes. When organisations make strategic and effective use of ICT to improve educational outcomes, they can be considered e-mature. To become e-mature, schools pass through different stages of ICT implementation: initial, e-enabled, e-confident and e-mature. It has been shown that the role of the principal and the quality of teaching have arisen as key elements in the setting of e-maturity in schools.

Methodology

This research is based on three study cases, three secondary schools from Catalonia, whose head teachers have already been interviewed using a semi-structured interviewed to know the school vision and organization of ICT, the role of the school leader, how the school evaluates the use and impact of ICT and how national educational policies can guide the use of ICT in schools.

Analysis of the first results

The first results of this research are organized into four categories: school organization, school leadership and management, impact and evaluation of ICT, and educational policies. Regarding school organization, these schools consider themselves as innovative, with ICT embedded in their daily activities, which makes them invisible. Concerning school leadership and management, in all schools there is an ICT committee where strategic decisions are made. All schools have organised ICT professional development courses, being in-house training and individual support the most valued. With respect to the impact and evaluation of ICT all schools pass questionnaires to measure progress. The head teachers agree that students' outcomes cannot be related to the use of ICT in their schools. Finally, with reference to educational policies, the three school leaders agree that at present there are few educational policies that foster the use of ICT in schools in Catalonia and they would like more advice and support.

Discussion and first conclusions

The first analysis of these three interviews to school head teachers seems to confirm some points of the studies on e-maturity and the role of principals in the implementation and use of ICT in schools. In these schools there is a shared clear vision of ICT by all stakeholders. ICT is embedded in their daily activities using a wide variety of digital tools and resources to support, facilitate and personalise learning. The head teacher in these schools has a key role in the implementation of ICT; they were the person who decided to start using ICT in the teaching and learning processes, but they have developed a distributed leadership, with an ICT committee in charge of making decisions. Finally, the head teachers point out the importance of teacher professional development and teacher support.

UNLOCKING THE POTENTIAL OF PUBLIC LIBRARIES IN SUPPORTING TEACHING AND LEARNING IN OPEN AND DISTANCE LEARNING IN MAKERERE UNIVERSITY

Harriet Nabushawo Mutambo, Makerere University, Uganda, Jessica Norah Aguti, Commonwealth of Learning, Canada, Mark Winterbottom, University of Cambridge, United Kingdom

This study examined the nature of services and facilities available and accessible in public libraries to ODL students in sub-Saharan Africa and the challenges these services face.

Library services are central in teaching and learning processes because they expose the students to a variety of resources which facilitate in-depth study and lead to development of intended competencies. However, according to Pernell (2002), traditional library services often fail to adapt to the needs of Open and Distance Learning students especially in dual mode universities. This in the end affects students' final grades as well as the quality of education they receive.

Using a cross sectional survey, from 422 respondents who include students, staff (both on campus and off campus) and librarians, data were collected though questionnaires, interviews, focus group discussions and documentary analysis. The findings reveal that due to inadequate library resources in study centres where ODL students are meant to receive remote support, the students have been utilizing library resources from the public libraries.

This support from public libraries however needs to be acknowledged and fully integrated in the University policy provision for effective collaboration and knowledge sharing to ensure smooth coordination of library activities.

This paper seeks to examine the potential of public libraries in supporting distance learners in Makerere University and the need for policy to guide the collaborations and while sharing library resources.

HIGHER EDUCATION IN BRASIL: ACADEMY AND OPERATION, A CHALLENGE OR A PARADOX?

Susane Garrido, Universidade Tuiuti do Paraná, Brasil

Information (and consumption) Society: Is that a good thing, by the way?

The perspective thought for this paper is to show a part of Brazilian reality at universities trying to survive in a world where the academy and the market are different worlds and the survival depend on this understanding. We are changing so fast in higher education but not at the same time like community, including students, teachers and managers.

In a world where the "means" becomes the "end", when I refer to the "massive use of technologies", determining the speed of changes, behavior, mood, or even economic level, being such phenomena originated from needs or fads, certain things are enhanced, while others, such as a country's Education take a crucial time to endure any kind of change (exceeding patience or survival).

There is no need to bring up the famous jargons applied to Education, especially here in Brazil, where it has been facing a stationary state for centuries, in which its own temporal dimension is not acting in a linear way in practically nothing. It is incredible that such a crucial sector, in a country like ours, is not updated or fostered as an institution, application and operation. It is also clear that it is not possible to analyze this issue without the political and economical artifacts underpinning the induced maintenance of such *status quo* we still face today; and in not having significant goals and interest towards a fair and balanced development in Brazil, it is in the Education (or in the lack of it) where we can assure having an ignorant country.

If we analyze some data from Brazilian ranking and population rates from Programme for International Student Assessment (PISA) in the last 3 years we can prove how much we have a dichotomy between the reality and what should be. Can we continue assessing Education with the latest years' or centuries' eyes? We do not hold the *chronos* or Cartesian time to solve such a high level problem as a folk's Education. Not knowing math does not merely mean not having education, when seen in a ranking, but it means not knowing how to compute, in other words, is lacking the development of high impact cognitive skills, for "thinking". Our children and youth are not only out of classrooms, but also heading towards a defective rationality, which is even worse. Today's time is more a quantum dimension than a relative one; it is a probabilistic dimension with trends, interconnected variables we are immersed in, leaving us no merely linear options. A society who "does not compute, does not know how to think"

The Brazilian University nowadays is no longer "the academy" which has given its philosophical origin, at the same time it is not able to update itself, conceptually speaking, before such a plural and diversified society, being still kept as the greatest Higher Education entity.

The "knot" is not only conceptual, but it also concentrates the operation that balances between the regulation, the market and the sustainability. A perfect concept has been created and shared for many universities by the world, the opening universities, but in Brazil, this concept is not yet totally accepted, so how to do it?

In the latest years, precisely in the latest 8 years, we have been hearing business jargons like IPO (Initial Public Offering) (13), business going public or mergers and acquisitions, in the Higher Education sector. Universities like Estácio, Anhanguera, Laureate and Devry Grups spring stars in a competitive capital market, previously only present in the private business world, but not in the educational sector.

Within this new scenario, the idea of a purely Academic University does not sustain the concept of University anymore. However, every University must be academic, for its philosophical origin there is the objective of building knowledge.

Exploring these various scenarios and contexts of the higher education I believe we are very close to the University of the future, one that does not abandon its conceptual beliefs from the past, but one that learns how to reinvent itself to always ECHO the public it is indeed serving.

ILBES: AN INNOVATIVE ICT-ENABLED INTERGENERATIONAL LEARNING APPROACH IMPLEMENTED ACROSS EU

Gabriel Rissola, D-O-T Research and Consulting, Andrea Diaz Mattei, University of Barcelona & D-O-T Research and Consulting, Spain

Public libraries, educational, cultural or welfare centres, and other public spaces where digital services are embedded, hereby referred as Blended Environments and Spaces (BES), have become an important provider of free, public access to ICT, the internet and learning environments for socially-disadvantages target groups. They are a reference point for new technologies, non-formal learning, people empowerment and social integration. The clientele of BES largely include seniors and elders who are digitally illiterate, and youngsters volunteering as adult trainers on the basis of their own digital competences. At the same time, the current economic downturn is pushing the job-inexperienced youngsters to look for help at these and other centres with social vocation due to the reduced employment opportunities they found.

The Intergenerational Learning in Blended Environments and Spaces (ILBES) methodology was developed and is being exploited through a family of *eScouts* projects. It is inspired in two proven learning methodologies (Community-Service Learning and Participatory and Appreciative Action and Reflection) which were combined to design an intergenerational learning circle that facilitates the socio-digital inclusion of seniors and the entrance of youth to the labour market and adult life, while improving solidarity between generations and local community cohesion. A unique character of ILBES is that it secures a two-way intergenerational exchange, where youngsters train seniors to become digitally competent while the seniors mentor youngsters to improve their employability prospects.

Research and piloting activities involved so far 250 seniors and 250 youngsters recruited with help of local stakeholder organisations like telecentres, welfare centres, schools, etc. in two different rounds, the first one in Spain, Italy, United Kingdom, Germany, Poland and Bulgaria (2011-2012) and a later one in Croatia, Latvia and Lithuania (2014-2015). The participant seniors needed to be aged between 55 and 75 years old, were willing to acquire digital competences taught by young people and in return be interested to give advice to young people with a view to ameliorate their preparation for the labour market and adult life. The candidate youths needed to be aged between 16 and 25 years old, and were willing to make social work taking advantage of their digital knowledge, with a view to ameliorate their preparation for the labour market and adult life.

Based on these experiences, a twofold strategy for the further development of community and educational centres offering digital services and training as "**eInclusion catalysts for intergenerational learning**" is proposed (where eInclusion refers to both digital inclusion and the use of ICT to achieve wider inclusion objectives). Firstly, the need to professionalize BES staff by supplying them with methods and practical know-how to facilitate intergenerational learning. Secondly, the embedding of eInclusion as a transversal field of activities into lifelong learning policies – including the promotion of digital literacy on the European and regional policy agendas as a means to strengthen social cohesion.

The ultimate shared goal is to multiple the digital skills of European citizens in order to enable them to find better employment opportunities and to participate meaningfully in society. Intergenerational learning facilitated by community-based social innovation and eInclusion centres and supported by ICT means seems to be a worthy approach to reach this aim.

TECHNOLOGY AS A VEHICLE FOR INCLUSION OF LEARNERS WITH ATTENTION DEFICITS IN MAINSTREAM SCHOOLS

Hanne Voldborg & Elsebeth K. Sorensen, Aalborg University, Denmark

The potential of technology for supporting educational processes of participation, collaboration and creation is widely accepted. Likewise have digital tools proved to enhance learning processes for disabled learners. A currently topical group, politically and educationally, in the discourse of inclusion is learners with extensive developmental and attention deficit disorders. This paper investigates the potential of technology for supporting the inclusion of this group in the general school system, i.e. into mainstream classes, using technology as a tool to join, participate and contribute - and as a vehicle for general human growth in their learning community. The paper presents the primer results and describes and discusses the challenges of both teachers' and learners', involved in the inclusion process. Finally, on the basis of findings, a typology of tools is suggested, which may support inclusive teaching and learning for the target group in question.

In 2012 the Danish Government passed a law on inclusion, which requested public schools in Denmark to include 97% of all learners in the mainstream education system. As a consequence, many learners, who earlier visited special schools and had Special Educational Needs (SEN) teachers, now had to be included in mainstream classes with mainstream teachers. This is a challenge for the schools, for the SEN learners, for the mainstream learners and for the teachers involved. While pointing to the lack of specific tools as well as competences in teachers for handling inclusion of children with extensive developmental and attention deficit disorders, school leaders and teachers are looking for new ways to handle this challenge. It's a very broad group of SEN learners, who appears to have learning problems and struggling with problems such as: Lack of attention, selective and continuing attention and response inhibition as well as lacking ability for planning, promoting, strategic thinking, change in attention, flexibility in working memory, self-regulation and self-monitoring.The investigation, on which this present piece of research is based, is part of a work package in a wider research project, ididact, which employs ICT as a vehicle in the challenge of inclusion of learners with extensive developmental and attention deficit disorders (focus learners) in mainstream schools.

In sum, our research on ICT as a vehicle for inclusions indicates: i) interventions with ICT have high impact on physical and academic inclusion, while less so on social inclusion; ii) using ICT for shielding, focusing, structuring and overviewing helps focus learners to join, participate, and maintain attention, while to some extent avoiding conflicts; iii) specific planning and strict time schedules for lessons and activities, supported by digital assignments in LMS/VLE systems enhance participation, attention and self-monitoring in task solving; iv) use of ICT enhance comprehension, differentiation, production, dissemination and compensation and promote the learners' abilities to participate and contribute; v) the teacher's knowledge of the learners' special needs, and the teachers' use of the five types of interventions did have a positive effect in terms of supporting focus learners' to participate more equally in the classroom. While our pre/post test showed no significant progress in the learner's social and pro-social behaviour, no indication was found of ICT interventions having an impact on social inclusion.

This paper finalizes by suggesting an ICT-pedagogical strategy containing a typology of tools and interventions: Structure & Overview, Shielding & Focus, Comprehension & Differentiation, Production & Dissemination, Collaboration & Knowledge Building. Utilizing this typology in the pedagogical strategy is likely to enhance the process of inclusion in classrooms of learners with extensive developmental and attention disorders.

EDUCOMMUNICATION PRACTICES: HOW TO PLAN AND IMPLEMENT COMMUNICATION MANAGEMENT PROCESSES FOR EDUCATIONAL PROJECTS MEDIATED BY COMMUNICATION TECHNOLOGIES

Luci Ferraz de Mello, Universidade de São Paulo, Brazil, Universal Learning Systems, Ireland

This paper argues about the basis of communication management for education studied from the Educommunication field which researches the interrelation Communication – Education. It presents the importance of knowing and understanding how communication management shall be handled at educational projects to reach the objectives aimed. So first of all we present a background of this highly technological society we live in and we talk about how communication technologies affect the way we interact to other people and present some considerations about the importance of having that really focuses attention on the importance of communication for education.

We also present what is this new field to which the NCE´s (ECA/USP) members call the Educommunication. Then we explain the project EDUCOM.Jt and present how we developed this planning scheme to prepare and implement Educommunicative dynamics.

THE INFLUENCE OF THE SEX VARIABLE ON HOW PARTICIPANTS IN A MOOC PERCEIVE EMOTIONS

Urtza Garay Ruiz, Inmaculada Maiz Olazabalaga, Carlos Castaño Garrido, Universidad del País Vasco, Spain

The analysis of how emotions influence the teaching-learning process is an instrument which, in recent years, has helped open new avenues for educational research and has also yielded interesting results. One notable example of the analysis of emotions or affordance in MOOCs is Cheng's exploratory study of the emotional potentiality of a MOOC (2014). The author's conclusion was that emotion such as excitement and a desire to help other students play an essential role in the MOOC participants' learning process, which was defined as constructivist and focused on the interaction between the participants.

In line with this area of research, which is centred around the influence of emotions on different aspects of the learning process in MOOCs (e. g. active and continued participation), we are presenting a study about the perception of emotions during a MOOC organised in 2014 at the University of the Basque Country. The course structure was based on the cooperation between the participants through social networks.

The main goal of this study is to describe the variety of emotions felt by participants over the course of a MOOC. More specifically, we intend to carry out an emotional assessment of what the MOOC students felt. The pillar of this approach will be an independent variable: the participants' sex. The study sample included the 392 people (264 women and 128men) who registered for and completed the MOOC.

In general, the participants perceived a positive emotional development throughout the learning process in the MOOC. The emotions defined as positive have been assessed as positive or very positive by all participants, both women and men. On the other hand, the emotions defined as negative have been assessed by the participants as negative. So the first conclusion that may be drawn from this is that doing a cooperation-based MOOC appears to be an emotionally positive experience for the participants.

The second important conclusion is that, despite the positive emotional experience, there are different degrees of positive or negative among men and women emotions. We were able to establish that emotional experience of women, whether positive or negative, is much more polarized than men, which I would describe as "neutral" or "moderate". This polarization is particularly evident in some of the positive emotions, which also reveal significant differences in the perceptions of men. That distinctive polarization between the participating women can also be found in two of the negative emotions defined as irritability and frustration. Therefore, we conclude that the sex variable appears to have a significant influence on the emotions provoked by the process of learning a MOOC. With this in mind, it may be interesting to conduct further research to analyze the causes of these differences.

"I AM DIFFERENT FROM OTHER WOMEN IN THE WORLD" THE EXPERIENCES OF SAUDI ARABIAN WOMEN STUDYING ONLINE IN INTERNATIONAL MASTER PROGRAMMES

Anna Szilagyi, Laureate Online Education, Netherlands

This paper presents findings from a qualitative study that investigated seven female Saudi Arabian students of the University of Liverpool's online Masters programmes.

Qualitative, first-person research methods and hermeneutic phenomenology were chosen for the analysis and interpretation of transcripts. The principles of cultural anthropology were used to take a snapshot of the interviewees' particular world to provide an overview of the Saudi Arabian culture where the role of women is at the centre of academic, political, religious and social debate.

These findings reflect the participants' everyday lives, identities, values and beliefs, presented in a self-reflective, personal 'life-world' story of one single Saudi Arabian woman. The findings demonstrate that the primary motivators in choosing online international education to further study are existing limitations of travelling to a university campus and customary gender-segregated education in Saudi Arabia.

As a contrast, international online education offers the opportunity to gain up-to-date research-based knowledge in their chosen profession, learn critical thinking and problem solving skills and communicate with male and female students from different cultures.

A CASE STUDY OF POLYSYNCHRONOUS LEARNING IN UNIVERSITY BIOSCIENCE EDUCATION

Barney Dalgarno, Lucy Webster, Charles Sturt University, Australia

Contemporary university students are engaging in new ways with teachers, peers and content in and out of class capitalizing on the affordances of mobile devices and new kinds of synchronous and asynchronous online learning tools. The multiple ever-present communication streams that are emerging through these new tools and devices are leading to learning scenarios incorporating interaction patterns that have the potential to transform the learning process. The term 'polysynchronous learning' has been co-opted and adapted to capture these new learning scenarios.

Traditionally interactions between learners and teachers or between learners and learners have occurred either synchronously (participants communicating at the same time), or asynchronously (communication occurring over a period of elapsed time). Moore (1989) also described three categories of interaction, learner-instructor, learner-learner and learner-content. In traditional face to face learning contexts, for example, learner-instructor and learner-learner interaction would occur synchronously through verbal communication, while learner-content interaction would occur both synchronously in class and in follow up asynchronous private study. In traditional online learning contexts, learner-teacher and learner-learner interaction would normally occur asynchronously through, for example, a discussion forum, while learner-content interaction might occur asynchronously through engagement with online learning resources.

Recent developments, however, are questioning the rigid association of synchronous communication with face to face contexts and asynchronous communication with online contexts. For example, face to face contexts often provide asynchronous communication streams for use during or after class in the form of discussion forums and social media tools. In online contexts it is becoming clear that there are potential benefits from synchronous real-time communication alongside asynchronous communication. Additionally, the gradual introduction of blended learning options and the need to cater for students physically present, students participating synchronously from a remote location, and students participating asynchronously at a later time, is leading to new thinking about ways of blending synchronous and asynchronous learning.

The term polysynchronous learning has been used to capture the distinct type of learning experience afforded by these emerging learning scenarios. Dalgarno (2014, p.4) defines polysynchronous learning as "the integration of learner-learner, learner-content and learner-teacher interaction through a blending of multiple channels of face to face, asynchronous online and synchronous online communication". Figure 1 (see in the electronic Proceeding) helps to illustrate the way in which polysynchronous learning differs from traditional face to face and online learning by representing the differences in patterns of interaction across modalities in face to face, traditional online and polysynchronous learning environments.

In the study, 'Blended synchronicity: Uniting on-campus and distributed learners using media-rich real-time collaboration tools' (an Australian Office of Learning and Teaching Innovation and Development Grant funded project) seven case studies involving blended learning designs were explored (see Bower et al., 2014). This paper draws on the findings from one of these case studies to illustrate the notion of polysynchronous learning within a university Histology subject.

DEFINING A PEDAGOGICAL MODEL: THE TU DELFT ONLINE LEARNING EXPERIENCE

Nelson Jorge, Sofia Dopper, Willem van Valkenburg, Delft University of Technology, The Netherlands

In early 2014, the Delft University of Technology (TU Delft) started an innovation program with the aim to respond even more effectively to recent developments in open and online education. Drawing on the fields of Distance Education research and the university's vision of the "engineer of the future", TU Delft's Extension School created a unified pedagogical model – the Online Learning Experience (OLE) – contributing to greater consistency in the development of online courses.

TU Delft's Online Learning Experience

The OLE is a student-centred, online learning model that holds eight interrelated principles:

- Flexible – not only being able to study independent of time restraints or location, we offer students the possibility to choose the educational resource format that will help them learn in a more effective way.
- Diverse – students will be able to choose between different content formats and challenged with different types of learning activities, which can be collaborative or individual, depending on their learning goals, in order to improve retention and performance, while motivating to learn.
- Inclusive – requires preparing tools and technologies to ensure accessible and user-friendly courses, offering different types of learning activities, content in multiple formats and flexible choices to maximize learning.
- Supportive – our courses are designed to promote the development of a learning community where students can share experiences and learn from others, supported by an e-teacher with expertise in the field that guides, promotes peer interaction, answers questions and gives feedback.
- Interactive – grows from the simplest learner-interface interaction to higher-levels of learning, when learners can apply what they learn in real life and develop meaningful knowledge from information – learner-context interaction. Learner-support and learner-content are essential interactions to achieve this.
- Active – students will be able to actively engage with the learning community and course content, embedded in the TU Delft's spirit to think critically, to take the initiative, to operate independently and to work in teams.
- Authentic – our courses are designed to promote learner-context interactions to reach high-level learning, enabling students to apply technical and scientific know-how into their own context.
- Innovative – increases in the available amount of quantitative and qualitative educational data offer us new opportunities to observe, analyse, and ultimately improve learning processes.

Implementing and evaluating the model

In order to create a structured model, the steps implemented include the development of an online course proposal, teachers' training workshops, instruments and regular meetings to give pedagogical and technical support. The evaluation process includes the collection of learners' feedback through questionnaires and preparing a report with recommendations for improvements.

Challenges and further developments

Wrapping up in a single model different learning strategies that coexist among TU Delft's eight Faculties can be seen as challenging, since it needs to take into account different didactical approaches. In this sense, the OLE can also be an opportunity to think about the changing need in educating engineers, leading to positive changes in pedagogical practices and learner experiences. Creating and implementing the OLE is an important step to ensure high quality online courses. The model will continue to develop based on new research, evaluation and experience that we gather at TU Delft.

AUGMENTED REALITY IN ONLINE EDUCATIONAL CONTEXTS: THE UOC CASE STUDY

Ivan Alsina-Jurnet, Lourdes Guàrdia-Ortiz, Universitat Oberta de Catalunya, Spain

Introduction

The implementation of the European Space for Higher Education (ESHE) has entailed a process of a deep renewal of the European Universities. The new model encourages the adoption of constructivist methodological approaches to learning, in which the learner should become a proactive agent in his/her own learning process. There is also a need to provide conditions to engage students in more authentic learning activities. Within this framework, Augmented Reality (AR) has become increasingly recognized as a new medium that could help educational institutions to meet some of the requirements of the ESHE. This technology allows for new ways to access information and to interact with the environments that can be used to design better learning experiences. Thereby, AR provides unique features, which enable the development of situated, experiential, contextualized, and authentic teaching and learning activities. However, beyond the current proliferation of AR applications in education, the use of this technology in eLearning contexts is still in an undeveloped stage and its potential is just now beginning to be explored.

Objectives

The present study aims to explore when and under what circumstances it could be useful to incorporate AR in the context of an online university. It is important to note that this research is part of a broader project in which AR technologies will be implemented within the UOC University.

Methodology

A mixed methods approach was used to collect data from fixed-choice and open-ended questions using an on-line survey. The survey was primarily adapted from the Virtual Worlds Faculty Survey. Additionally, new Likert-scaled items and open-ended questions were included based on the objectives of the study and the review of the relevant literature.

Discussion and Conclusions

The study was designed to gain insights into UOC's faculty perception on using AR technology within online educational contexts. To reach this purpose, 15 teachers from the UOC's Master's Degree in Education and ICT (eLearning) were included.

Results revealed that most of the faculty already knew the advantages of AR and its potentialities for educational purposes. In addition, almost half of them had used it in his/her educational practices. Besides that, the number of teachers considering that they have good knowledge about the benefits, costs and AR educative applications was very low. A concern over the need for faculty development in learning how to use AR technology in online education emerged in this study. The study also suggested the feasibility of introducing AR technology within the UOC educational model. It was highlighted the potentiality of AR to promote an immersive, constructivist and user-centred learning. In particular, it was recommended to use the Geo-based AR to promote discover-based learning, enhance collaboration processes and engage on-line students in authentic activities. Regarding the use of markers, faculty stressed its potential to facilitate the understanding of complex and abstract phenomena.

The findings obtained in the present research will guide in the development of the next phases of the project, in which we will design, develop, implement and evaluate AR learning and teaching strategies within the UOC's educational context. This project aims to evaluate the efficacy of AR technology to improve students' learning experience and enhance traditional ways of delivering on-line education.

BAZAAR: INFORMAL LANGUAGE LEARNING AND EXCHANGE AT MARKET PLACES

Thomas Fischer, Walter F. Kugemann, Ulrike Mangwa, New Technologies and Learning in Europe, Germany; Corinna Bartoletti, Elena Zecchetto, Borgorete, Italy; Julide Inozu, Cem Can, Cukurova University, Turkey; Roy Smith, The MRS Consultancy, United Kingdom; Raffaela Pascucci, Claudio Crispoltoni, Commune di Perugia, Italy; José Luiz Fernandes, E-VIA / Palco de Sombras, Portugal; Tatiana Velitchkova, DIA-SPORT Association, Bulgaria

The main aim of the European Research & Development project 'Bazaar: Learning and Exchange at the Market Place' (http://www.bazaarproject.eu) is to promote language learning and at the same time the exchange of experiences, knowledge and ideas amongst adult learners with a migrant background in daily settings. The educational approach is based on the key concepts of learner centricity; life-relevant learning; learning embedded in everyday contexts; social inclusion, community and citizenship. By these means Bazaar tries:

- To empower individuals, to promote social interaction and enhance intercultural dialogue at community level;
- To relate to societal needs, to promote social dialogue and social inclusion of migrants and to encourage their civic engagement;
- To trigger the motivation to learn amongst the migrant population, especially those often excluded from education e.g. older men and women;
- To design and to test learning activities, methods and materials that are sustainable and replicable.

Bazaar uses the term 'Market Place' in both ways, literally and metaphorically:

- As a concrete space where people naturally meet and interact;
- As a place used to facilitate communication, cooperation, intercultural awareness and a ground of mediation to resolve possible resolve conflicts;
- As a concrete learning environment that sustains the integrity of all learners as they attain relevant educational success;
- As a place of ideas and as a place to apply creative thinking;
- As a learning facilitator.

Bazaar resides within the changing dynamics of learning of nowadays and is based on the concept 'Life-Relevant Learning' (LRL). The almost ubiquitous availability of learning resources 'at your fingertips' puts the focus on the motivation of the individual. When expected learning outcomes are sufficiently relevant for an individual, it is assumed that she or he will find adequate and accessible ways to achieve these outcomes.

The language learning programme proposed by Bazaar therefore comprises four dimensions:

- Global – introducing the participants to all competence areas of the target language, namely, linguistic competence, socio-linguistic competence and pragmatic competence leading to general communicative competence;
- Modular – improving learners' language competences in a bazaar / market space setting for particular purposes;
- Weighted – focusing on acquiring language skills in certain directions and proficiency levels;
- Partial – taking a teaching responsibility only for certain activities and skills in line with the particular existing and available settings existing.

The concepts of Bazaar have been tested and evaluated in diverse learning environments in Bulgaria, Germany, Italy, Portugal and the United Kingdom.

ONLINE TRAINING OF TRAINERS FROM THE OPEN UNIVERSITY, PORTUGAL

Susana Henriques, Jose Antonio Moreira, Maria de Fatime Goulão, Daniela Melare Vieira Barros, Universidade Aberta, Portugal

This paper describes an online training course for trainers in the perspective of new trends in online learning processes. Online training of trainers is based on training as part of online pedagogical and teaching models and not only on support and interfaces; discussions about teaching and learning in new scenarios; and online scenarios having the new trends on the development of e-learning in mind.

The main purpose of this paper is to characterize the online teacher training course and its innovations within a paradigm referenced by networks, pedagogy of participation and the use of informal spaces in an innovative co-learning design.

We conducted a brief descriptive analysis supported by bibliographic references, reflections and discussions previously held about the proposal of the course. This paper is part of the work done by the course research team, who is developing a research project for improving innovation in e-learning.

EMBEDDING DIGITAL COMPETENCES IN THE CURRICULUM A CASE STUDY ON STUDENT-EXPERIENCE OF AN ONLINE TECHNOLOGY-ENHANCED, ACTIVITY-BASED LEARNING DESIGN

George Evangelinos, Debbie Holley, Anglia Ruskin University, United Kingdom

Eight online study activities that included elements of digital competences identified by the European Union Digital Competence (DIGCOMP) framework were delivered via an institutional Virtual Learning Environment (VLE) to examine whether the participants possessed the digital skills necessary for their studies and check whether the needed skills should be offered as a separated training course or be embedded in the normal curriculum. Designed along Gilly Salmon's 'e-Tivity' model the activities were offered to 102 first-year Midwifery students as a part of their first-year study module taught by a number of tutors under the co-ordination of the module leader in two different campuses; the eight sessions comprised of: i) a pre-course bespoke, self-assessment questionnaire to establish the digital-competence potential across the groups and identify areas of interest, ii) six technology-enhanced e-tivities representing short problem-based tasks on midwifery-related content aimed at revealing different aspects of digital competences and iii) the final activity focussed on reviewing the student experience through short reflective diaries.

The majority of the participants reported that they gained or refreshed skills, characterised the tasks as 'interesting', 'enjoyable and motivating their learning', and declared their preference for the use of multimedia. Some of them liked the honing of self-directed learning skills and only a small number reported that the activities did not stretch enough to enhance the already possessed skills. A few reported distracted by non-facilitated online delivery of the activities and required clarification about the depth and the breadth of the needed detail. The same participants often expressed positive and negative experiences deriving from technology-use, appreciation for the increase of communication channels on offer, referred to self-awareness, to the impact of new technological developments, the social media, and the impact of challenging tasks; however, others thought that technological skills could be time-consuming to manage and that the availability of technology did not necessarily result in its increased use in demanding situations. It was extensively agreed that training and support for the use of technology were very important. As to the provision of feedback positive experiences summarised the need for meaningful and timely feedback, while others complained about the lack of direct communication with the tutors and requested examples to enable their better understanding on the nature of the work that had to be done. Group work was appreciated as it allowed acquaintance with the peers, the sharing of knowledge and skills, the exchanging of ideas and other. Networking and socialising with colleagues were well received, group-work tasks were seen as an ice-breaker and team-formation dynamics were identified when people were asked to work together; difficulties in participation were reported only by those who lived far from the university campus. From a pedagogic perspective comments were positive for information and research literacies, information dissemination and critical evaluation of the sources; only few stated preference for a standardised list of resources. Although the VLE was found easy to use, some problems reported when dealing with video files. The utilisation of various digital devices mainly concerned the participants' needed technological skills and at the beginning some felt discouraged by the quality of work their more technically able peers presented.

In conclusion two factors should be carefully examined: a) the lack of protected time within the curriculum delivery to undertake the activities and b) the lack of an accreditation scheme.

METHODS FOR E-EVALUATION OF BULGARIAN DISTANCE STUDENTS IN LIBRARY AND INFORMATION SCIENCES

Marina Encheva, State University of Library Studies and Information Technologies, Bulgaria

Introduction

During the period 2013-2014 with the financial support of the Operational programme "Human Resources Development" the State University of Library Studies and Information Technologies in Sofia implemented a project on the introduction of Internet-based distance learning at master's level at the Faculty of Library Sciences and Cultural Heritage. Since inauguration of the project, a special attention has been paid on the methods for electronic evaluation of the students' achievements that would be applied in the master's distance-learning programmes of the faculty. The current paper presents the results of the analysis made in relation to the defining of the electronic evaluation approach and the type of the test questions, applicable by means of the platform for e-learning ILIAS used at the university.

Determining the evaluation approach

When planning electronic test it is important to be determined what exactly will be measured with it as well as to reconsider the purposes of the training according to the exact part of the learning material which will be used as a base for the evaluation. It is necessary that the trainer defines for himself what exactly he or she is teaching the students – knowledge, skills or way of thinking as well as what facts, knowledge and skills he/she expects to be mastered by them. The attitude of the university teacher towards the knowledge that will be evaluated by the test must be determined also by the fact whether the students study consecutively the learning material of the course or skip certain parts of it. Another important aspect of the process of elaboration of a strategy for examining the success of the students is the decision about how the mid-term test will be treated and to what extend it will influence the final grade.

Defining the types of questions in the electronic test

After the approach in e-assessment is defined the type of questions and the method used by students for answering them is important to be specified. There are different variants of test questions as each of them stresses on specific knowledge and qualities to be assessed: e.g. the knowledge of facts or the visual memory of the examinee. When the test questions are chosen it is necessary the aim of the test to be taken into account by the trainer.

Among the most widespread types of test questions are those with structured answer. The following kind of questions can be outlined here: with alternative answer (yes/no; true/false), multiple choice questions and matching questions. Through the closed type of assignments the learner operates with an entirely defined structured situation in which the evaluation is objectified to a maximum, the learning content can be fully covered and accordance with the aims of measurement can be achieved

The questions which require text input are in the category of the open questions. The e-tests based on this type of questions are used for examining whether the students have learned the names of different things (abbreviation, technical or business terms, foreign words, commands and rules in languages for programming, parts of numbers, etc.). The greatest difficulty in the creation of such tests is formulating the question in such a way that would permit an automatic evaluation of the answer by the computer.

Simulation based tests involve accomplishment of highly interactive tasks. The simulators used enable the implementation of definite procedures. Rather than assessing the students' abstract knowledge on a given subject, the simulations estimate the student' skills for performing complex activities

Conclusion

The electronic assessment tests help not only students, but also teachers, for reaching a higher level of development and realization into the training process. They improve the training's effectiveness, while contributing for gaining more complete and sound knowledge, by stimulating of a creative and scientific active work process, by contributing to the streamlining of the training process, and turning it into a process which is truly pleasant for the trainees.

TEACHERS' IT TRAINING AS AN IMPORTANT ELEMENT IN EDUCATIONAL PROCESS

Olga Grishina, Marina Melamud, Elena Sidorova, Plekhanov Russian University of Economics, Russia

The Faculty of Distance Learning (FDL) of Plekhanov Russian University of Economics has been involved in providing different programmes, based on ICT, for more than a decade. This ranges from the fully-fledged Bachelor and Specialist Degree distance education to short-term vocational training and upgrading courses, and consequently great experience in designing and developing educational digital resources has been accumulated. However, today's full-time 'digital' students also expect their education to include technology, as they have become inseparable with their gadgets and devices. So the need to adapt and integrate ICT into the traditional education has become increasingly apparent. But blended learning requires new competences from the teachers and also their close cooperation with programmers and other technical staff. That leads to changes in traditionally individualistic academic culture bringing about the necessity to work in teams, allocate roles and responsibilities for the courses design, teaching and assessment.

Different e-learning environments provide students with enriched learning opportunities, extending learning beyond the classroom and helping to personalise the educational process. However, the survey conducted by FDL has identified that only a small number of teachers use the full capacity of the e-learning platforms for the interactive communication with students. Teachers mainly use them to deliver information, such as manuals, lectures, presentations, etc. The next most-spread activity is to supply students with references for additional sources on the Internet, electronic libraries and so on. Also only few use forums, webinars and wiki. In our opinion, the main reason for this is the low competence of the teachers in the field of e-learning technologies.

Project

To solve this problem, a new course 'Design and Development of E-learning Resources' to upgrade university teachers' competence in IT has been elaborated at Plekhanov University.

The first group, consisting of Plekhanov teachers was formed in the beginning of 2014: 11 people had been selected from the volunteers, who mainly represented the 'economic block', as economics is the core competence of the University. The course puts forward 2 main tasks:

- to familiarise the listeners with the theoretical basis, systems and technologies of e-learning;
- to help them acquire the basic competences of an e-learning resource developer and elaborate ready to use software tools to support the learning process.

Consequently, the course can be roughly divided into 2 parts – theoretical and practical. As webinars are particularly convenient for the interactive learning especially for courses with a lot of charts and graphs, the next practical step is devoted to the software tools used for webinars and online conferences. Different e-learning platforms are being investigated, ranging from 'box' services to SaaS-solutions. They include Moodle, Webinar.ru, Comdi, iMind, Acrobat Connect Pro, Mirapolis Virtual Room, Virtual class, Webtutor, eLearning Server, iWebinar, , Competetum ONLINE, Teachbase.ru). However, only the platforms supporting the Russian language have been deliberately chosen, in order to involve all students, not only those practising the English language.

At the final stage, the participants are supposed to design and develop certain parts of their courses. They are taught to compile and upload educational resources on LMS server, adjust monitoring environment and estimation of the students' progress. The project 'The design of the electronic educational resource for the learning process' is the climatic finish of the course.

All 11 teachers of the first group completed the training courses successfully. Their feedback expressed high degree of satisfaction with it and demonstrated their willingness to integrate interactive activities such as simulators, short videos in their classes and extend their teaching process beyond the classroom for example, in webinars and conferences. Though most of the participants still do not feel completely secure with IT, they overcome their resentment against the new methods of teaching. Now they clearly understand the possibilities of modern technologies, are able to formulate their needs and objectives to the programmers and work in close collaboration with them. They can customize the created courses to the needs of particular groups or individuals and choose to use multimedia tools to make the learning process more attractive for students. Since then the training for the teachers has been organized on the permanent basis.

USING SMARTPHONES IN ACTIVE LEARNING: ENTREPRENEURSHIP BEHAVIOR TAUGHT DIFFERENTLY

Isabella Chinelato Sacramento, Sandra Regina Holanda Mariano, Universidade Federal Fluminense, Brazil

Introduction

This poster presents the results of a 60-minute live undergraduate activity using smartphones used as a method to teach entrepreneurial behavior skills. We share the experiences of the implementation of a class dynamic aimed at Brazilian graduate students in Entrepreneurship. The activity is detailed to offer potentially valuable contributions to the development of other learning tools aimed at graduate students using active learning concepts and cell phones in class in an educative way. The conference themes addressed are tools and resources for learning through mobile devices, innovative uses of smartphones and mixing formal and informal learning.

Background

Human capital theory says that those who have more knowledge, skills, and other competencies will achieve more and perform better. Entrepreneurial orientation can have a mediating role in the environment-performance relationship, important in governance patterns that generate opportunities for their organizations to attract resources. In Brazil, studies by Sebrae (Regional São Paulo Brazilian service of assistance to micro and small enterprises), an institution supporting the development of small and micro companies in Brazil, show that the absence of previous planning and inadequate business processes are on of the main bankruptcy causes among micro and small enterprises (2008). Fluminense Federal University has created the first Brazilian Entrepreneurship department. A graduation in management and entrepreneurship is offered to 100 students a year contributing to generate perceptions of the desirability and feasibility of starting a business and gives practical knowledge as how to conduct all main business operations.

Mobile phones reach almost the entire Brazilian population. Almost 300 million mobile phone lines were already active in 2013 with 136.45 accesses per 100 inhabitants. Prepaid services amount to 78.05% of this total reaching 211.58 million phone lines. Mobile broadband had 103.11 million accesses, 1.31 million of them from 4G terminals. (ANATEL – Brazilian National Telecom Agency, 2014). Smartphones add a lot more teaching and connecting possibilities mainly due to the Internet. Although good quality broadband access is still not available throughout the country, some universities, including Fluminense Federal University provide free access to the students at a reasonable speed, allowing the activity to take place.

Findings

The search activity yields the educational results it was designed to provide. The undergraduates are very excited to be asked to do an activity using their smartphones. They marvel at particular searches using specific formats. The majority of the learners notice that difficulties in searching prevent them from using readily available open educational resources (OER) and programs. Having to do searches at the main available OER databases, establishing contact with enterprises and educational resources through their own smartphones open their minds to the enormous capabilities of being connected.

The active learning approach presented helps students to make contact with their own behavior when faced with an unexpected challenge. Allowing for many different proposed behavioral learning outcomes, depending on the subject taught, this very fast dynamic can be done in virtually any classroom space and has a powerful appeal for the learners because of its ludic aspect. They experience the method practically using their own cell phones, are guided through the discussions to reflect about the theoretical background and about the applicability to their own realities.

PERICLES OR HOW TO ASSESS AND TO IMPROVE QUALITY IN HIGHER EDUCATION

Anne Boyer Loria, Gerard Casanova, Azim Roussalany, Florence Ducreau, Université de Lorraine, France

The PIA project called PERICLES is a French project with two main objectives.

The first one is to offer to Higher Education (HE) institutions a methodology and a digital tool to evaluate the quality of the formation they provide.

The second objective is

1. the development of a recommender system able to suggest open educational resources to learners and
2. to identify learning paths based on actual practices in order to compare them to those designed by the trainers.

The paper is organized as follows: a first section aims at giving an overview of the project. A second section describes the methodology and the digital tool dedicated to the quality evaluation. A third section is devoted to the recommender system and the paper ends by drawing some perspectives.

THE MANAGER IS BLOGGING: BLOG MAKING AS A TEACHING/LEARNING METHOD

Sidinei Rocha-de-Oliveira, Bibiana Volkmer, Universidade Federal do Rio Grande do Sul , Sandra R.H Mariano, Universidade Federal Fluminense, Brazil

The development of new technological resources and the popularization of access to online content, for the most part free, such as textbooks, articles, blogs, videos, games and simulations, have modified the ways learning take place. These resources enable students to take an active approach to learning, in the performance of tasks related to pre-existing content, as well as in the creation of new materials.

In Brazil, the Administration course is designed around three subjects: basics, vocational training, and technologies. Basic training includes anthropology, politics, sociology, philosophy, psychology, ethics, human behaviour, economics, accounting, communication and information technologies, and legal sciences. The sociology course explores the aspects of culture, control, social stratification, rationality and power, and the studies of the classical sociologists (Marx, Weber, Durkheim) all in the context of organization and work processes.

Since it includes a plethora of theoretical content, the students find it difficult to assimilate the subject with the actual practice of Administration, making it necessary to seek new tools to assist in the relationship between the theory and its application. The purpose of this article is to present the experience of designing blogs, carried out by four groups of students in Sociology Applied to Administration from UFRGS (Brazil).

Although new technologies have always been used in management education, it has increased recently, both through the emergence of new technologies and experimentation and use of them in the classroom. Faster processors, faster download, better image quality and cheaper computers and screens have helped make it possible to use video and audio in real time. As a result, websites such as iTunes U, YouTube, and Academic Earth are becoming global repositories for sharing teaching materials.

Advances in technology permit two major changes in management education. First, technology reduces passive learning, where the student only partakes of the content presented by the professor. Second, it allows for the building of active learning, both face-to-face and virtual, enabling students to broaden their participation as actors in the process. Thus, as can be seen, different technological resources may be used to encourage learning in management, where presentation of these experiences is relevant for greater popularization of these practices.

The primary objective of making a blog, which entails a website in which it is possible to post quickly and that may contain text, photos, videos and animations, is to reinforce the content studied during the course and make students reflect on it. In addition, the choice to produce a blog as one of the course assignments was for the purpose of building a closer link between classical content and the virtual world that is part of most young people's lives. The assignment was carried out in groups of four or five students and was comprised of four main stages: i) creation of the blog and giving it a name; ii) weekly posts related to the course content; iii) preparation of a 5-10 minute video on one of the themes studied; and iv) presentation of the blog and its evaluation by co-students.

The creation and development of blogs by students yielded a number of benefits in the learning process. The main ones include: greater student interaction through weekly group activities; – stimulating creativity in the creation of the blog and posting challenges; monitor weekly how the content studied was being understood by the students, making it possible to correct any misunderstanding of concepts and to delve deeper into topics of greatest interest; expand study time beyond the realm of the classroom; involvement of students in the assessment process; development of new skills such as designing a blog and creating videos.

GAMIFICATION OF A SOCIAL LEARNING NETWORK IN A VIRTUAL UNIVERSITY: IMPLEMENTATION PROPOSAL, AN ACADEMIC NETWORK

Fernando Bacelar, Lina Morgado, Universidade Aberta, Portugal

This paper is a doctoral research project, concerning the implementation of Gamification in an Academic Social Network (*SOL- Socializing Online Learning*) at a virtual university. Gamification is the use of the Elements derived from Games in *non-game* contexts, to promote the interaction, engagement and resilience of users, in several types of activities. These Elements can be isolated and used in many different configurations. Almost any activity can be *Gamified and Gamification* is already being used in several universities in the United States and the United Kingdom, from small courses to postgraduate studies.

We want to verify the way Gamification (and the Gamification Elements) can influence social interaction and Social Learning inside this Network. We are using a Mixed-Methods approach and a Design Based Research methodology.

We support our proposal within the Web 2.0 paradigm, taking into account the Community of Inquiry Framework (COI), Connectivism, Heutagogy and the Pedagogy of Nearness. To help defining the focus of analysis, we look at the Social Forms for Education. This way the COI framework, though with a Socio-constructivist approach, is also a good framework to understand the Social Form *Group.*

For our implementation we take support on theories of use and acceptance of technology, motivation and Computer Human Interaction: Fogg's Behaviour Model, Self Determination Theory, Flow Theory, Unified Theory of Acceptance and Use of Technology, Collective Effort Model and Goal Setting Theory.

The research will take several phases:

Phase 1

So far, we made a literature review following our topics, and conduct some semi structured interviews.

- Incoming work:
- The analysis of the Interviews will inform the construction of a *Gamified* prototype of SOL.
- Usability Tests will be conducted with some users (n>=6); opinions will be collected using a Focus Group.

Phase 2

- With the results of the Focus Group the Gamification Elements will be incorporated in the SOL.
- Data will be gathered using Observation (posts, and comments), Social Analysis and the Analytics of the ELGG platform.
- In the end of the second phase a Survey will be deployed.

Phase 3

- All the data will be integrated and analysed.
- All adjustments will be needed made to the platform.
- A new Survey will be deployed after these adjustments.
- All data will be integrated, triangulated, analysed, presented and discussed.

Some preliminary results indicate salient design characteristics of the SOL Network that should be considered to the implementation: students feel there is little interaction between them, and feel that there is some lack of control over the SOL functionalities. Hopefully, after the implementation of Gamification our research will inform the theory and will give guidelines to the instructional design of a *Gamified* educational environment.

STUDENT OWNED E-PORTFOLIO P3 (PORTFOLIO – PROCESS – PRODUCT) EMPOWERING STUDENTS FOR PROFESSIONAL AND PERSONAL DEVELOPMENT USING SYSTEMATIC REFLECTION AS A PEDAGOGICAL METHOD, IN THE HEALTH GUIDANCE PROGRAM, LULEÅ UNIVERSITY OF TECHNOLOGY

Martin Karlsson, Lotta Berglund, Institution of Health Science, Sweden

The demands from society increase and students need to be able to adjust and continue learning after they have finished their studies. This means that they need to be made aware of their learning strategies and their competencies. The aim of this project were to create a student owned e-portfolio that could develop and enhance their reflection skills to build self-awareness to highlight their skill- and generic competence progression and to give them a tool that connected to their lifelong learning process. An additional goal was to make the e-portfolio free, outside of the university domain, and available on almost any computer or mobile phone operative system.

What we have done

LTU defined in 2012 a basic pedagogical idea, to enhance the student´s learning and to support educational constructive alignment. From that idea we developed an educational system linked to our initial idea of an e-portfolio. In September 2014 we introduced an e-portfolio made in the cloud service "Box" to approximately 30 students in their first year of the Bachelor Programme in Health Guidance, Major Health Promotion at Luleå University of Technology (LTU). The e-portfolio consisted of seven main folders: 1) Archive – Health Guidance Program; 2) Reflection portfolio; 3) Competency portfolio; 4) Career Center; 5) Contact portfolio; 6) Share folder; 7) Archive – Lifelong learning.

During the introduction we emphasised that the e-portfolio is student owned, and that we only gain access to their share folder (6) when invited by the student. The e-portfolio focused on systematic reflection throughout the program. It includes two levels: course- and program level. On the course level, reflection is integrated in the teaching by teachers in the course. The program level reflections consist of two reflections carried out during the last week of every semester. The first reflection is about their generic skill progression during the semester and the second one is about the progression toward the graduation goals for the program. The students are also asked to file material in their archive (1) for later use in the program.

Results and implications for the students

The project, at the time of writing this abstract, has progressed half way into the first year. After some initial technical barriers, the students have become comfortable and fluent in using the portfolio. During this first period we focused on the reflection portfolio (2) and the archive (1). Students report that they now appreciate the reflection portfolio and using reflection as a method for learning and personal development. The reflection towards the graduation goals is designed to give us data to future studies.

In the future

During the second year we will continue to work with the archive (1) and the reflection portfolio (2) both on course- and program levels. But we will reduce our control of them, and shift our resources and work more with the competency portfolio (3). We will invite students to find products from their work stored in their archive (1) or their reflection portfolio (2) to showcase competencies and different generic skills, like problem solving, written/spoken communication, creativity, etc. in their competency portfolio (3). Future development work on the e-portfolio will focus on the competency portfolio (3) and to find ways to integrate the reflection portfolio (2) even more closely in the courses. We will also seek funding to elevate this project into research studies.

LEARNING TO LEARN COMPETENCY DEVELOPMENT WITH INFORMATION AND COMMUNICATIONS TECHNOLOGY USE: MULTIPLE CASE STUDY AT SECONDARY SCHOOLS

Balbina Rocosa, Albert Sangrà, Nati Cabrera, Universitat Oberta de Catalunya, Spain

The PhD project research wants to be an approach to the learning to learn (L2L) competency by focusing on how to deploy this competency with an intensive use of information and communications technology (ICT); identify what practices of L2L are being developed with the ICT support and define improvement proposals and specific guidelines that help the development of L2L with the ICT use.

The research project was designed based on current interest and need to move towards the personalized learning. Regarding that, we have been identified two main areas to promote its implementation: the L2L competency and ICT uses in learning.

Today personalized learning is a tendency as a pedagogical practice. L2L is considered key to move towards the personalized learning and is the guide of all other basic skills. Is the competency core between the basics.

The research is based on social, economic and pedagogical reasons for the introduction of L2L competency at schools as well as the ICT transformer potential in educational practices. Moreover, the need for research from the practical point of view in this field is observed.

Different sources claim investigation on L2L practices considering this aspects: the need for research on L2L competency and others skills to improve its development; the challenge to develop a shared thought of L2L in practice; the need to develop holistic ways to easy understand and promote L2L; the promotion of L2L as transversal skill otherwise its application will be diluted.

We want to analyse the processes that enable the development of L2L competency, both from a strategic and methodological perspectives. The research also aims to identify what practices are being developed with the support of ICT, and show from students and teachers perceptions, specific practices which promote the L2L competency.

To achieve that we propose a multiple case study carried out in contexts with a holistic and intensive use of ICT selected in Catalonia secondary schools.

The research results will provide an analysis of the challenges, problems and lessons learned from the L2L competency development and the role played by ICT in relation to that and the practices that are being arisen. It will also specify improvement proposals, recommendations and guidelines that facilitate this development considering the ICT use.

The contributions of the research will be related to give an empirical analysis of the development of L2L competency in a school context with an intensive ICT use. Another added value will be to raise awareness and disseminate the ICT uses and benefits, in a cross and transversal overview beyond a specific discipline.

The research will be more focused on learning rather than teaching, gathering teacher perceptions but also emphasizing students' perceptions.

The first research phase will have as a result a report with the cases study analysis of the development of the L2L at strategic, methodological and curricular integration levels, with the ICT use, and compared with L2L models. The second research phase will provide a report with the L2L practices developed with ICT support at schools.

A final report will be produced with the guidelines and indicators to engage the development of L2L competency with the ICT use and support.

RAPID DEVELOPMENT OF AN ELECTRONIC LOGBOOK TO SATISFY STUDENT PRACTICUM ON PLACEMENT IN AUDIOLOGY

Pearse Murphy, Athlone Institute of Technology, Ireland

Problem Background and Identification

The use of technology by academics in teaching, learning and assessing in higher education has become increasingly important in the early part of the 21st century. In this paper the author traces the literature in the area of electronic logbooks (ELBs) also referred to as ePortfolios and presents a case study on how the deployment of an electronic logbook was achieved in a short timeframe for audiology students at Athlone Institute of Technology using iCloud technology. Audiology training involves the acquisition of practical competencies and knowledge in the use of equipment and technique's in the diagnosis of issues with the human auditory system. Audiology students develop these competencies in college first and then progressively improve them on their placement practicum. For the undergraduate audiologist this involves mastering skills in up to 35 different competencies. The audiology student has three levels in which to perform a competency. These levels are observation, participation and fully demonstrated. The size of each student's record may be up to 6000 data fields. Practice tutors and practice educators on placement support, assist and monitor audiology students' progress while mastering these competencies by maintaining and signing off on a logbook. Paper based logbooks may restrict collaborative feedback between practice tutors, placement module leaders and students due to the lack of visibility to all stakeholders concurrently. Collaborative internet based networks are extremely flexible and amenable to all stakeholders in the management of the student learning continuum where placements are spread over a wide geographical area. This was the scenario in this case study.

Problem Resolution and Deployment

The author decided a web based / cloud database platform which could be deployed rapidly with varying levels of user security might fit the fundamental requirements of this problem. The timeframe for this project was 6-8 weeks. After about a week's research, Caspio © was chosen as the platform to use. Caspio © is an unconventional Silicon Valley technology company specialising in cloud based platforms. Development and testing took 3 weeks. When the author was happy with the functional testing of a prototype of the ELB, he utilised a training day in the college for practice tutors and practice educators in order to facilitate user acceptance testing. With the green light from the user acceptance testing the system was deployed. Total project rollout time was 4 weeks. Some minor customisation using Javascript were made to speed up data entry after rollout.

Conclusion

Much of the literature outlines the increasing use of ELBs as part of clinical competency training for healthcare professionals. The question of quality control in training in competencies is coming increasingly under the microscope from various stakeholders such as funders, the professions themselves and service users. The sample papers perused in the literature review, in general espouse the positive attributes of ELBs over paper base systems. Deficits in areas such as data analysis and traceability in paper based system were traced through and highlighted in the discourse. In addition it was shown that paper based systems are extremely cumbersome when it comes to stakeholder visibility in the clinical competency training process. Advances in information and communications technology (ICT) in recent years, particularly in the domains of infrastructure, relational databases, web technologies and cloud based computing solutions have enabled platforms to emerge which can allow rapid deployment of solutions such as ELBs. This paper is an example of a case study of a rapidly deployed ELB for audiology students undertaking a yearlong clinical practicum. This case study clearly delineates the use of a rapidly deployed cloud based technology solution into a clinical education setting. The platform identified and used in this case study is Caspio ©. This paper also found that the use of ELBs is not only beneficial in the initial competency based training of healthcare professionals, but the literature advises that ELBs have a very significant role to play in CPD for the entire career of the health care professional.

EXPANDING THE ENVIRONMENT OF ADULT HIGHER EDUCATION BY PROMOTING WORKPLACE/UNIVERSITY PARTNERSHIPS AND THE USE OF INFORMATION AND COMMUNICATION TECHNOLOGIES AND SOCIAL MEDIA

Judith O. Brown, Pamela Luckett, Barry University School of Professional and Career Education, United States of America

Introduction

Colleges and universities in the USA face criticism of their increased cost of tuition, lack of connection between academic learning and the workplace ,and the need to provide students with 21st communication and information technology access (online courses) and materials (tablets, e-books). This is especially true for adult learners whose family, work, and societal responsibilities place additional burdens on how to complete their degrees in a timely and cost effective manner with practical outcomes as well as theoretical concepts.

One way to address these concerns is through University/workplace partnerships that save all constituencies (workplace, university, and student) time and money to degree completion and have the potential to produce learning-outcomes advocated by all parties. As Ylikoski and Kortelainen pointed out (2012): "University workplace partnerships are becoming increasingly important as the demands for authentic learning are growing." (p.i).

These joint ventures have the potential to mitigate the cost of a university education through the use of ICT resources and tuition discounts and provide the type of applicable learning adult learners are seeking. As andragogy guru Malcom Knowles (1989) pointed out, adult students are goal oriented and relevancy oriented. They are concerned with practical, problem solving and bring significant life and work experiences to the higher education classroom., Moreover, they possess a degree of self-autonomy and self-direction (Blackmore, 1996) not shared by their tech-savvy traditional age counterparts (Berge & Collins, 1995). While the use of ICTs in the classroom and beyond is increasingly important to them, our observations indicate adult learners embrace a more hybrid learning model in which knowledge is co-constructed with guidance from the instructor-facilitator in distance and face-to-face interactions.

Method

This paper explores the experience-over a five month period- with one partnership agreement in a single case study format as delineated by Creswell (2012). It begins with a brief discussion of the background of PACE's partnership agreements including legal and access concerns. This is followed by a more in-depth study of one of the school's partnership agreements with the Miami Police Department highlighting both the advantages and challenges of university/workplace school's partnerships and the use of ICT's and social media in learning environments.

Findings

Two major themes resulted from the study. First, it underscored the opportunities and challenges of education/work partnerships. The study supported the importance of University/workplace partnerships for adult learners, however, the uncertainty of long-term partnerships due to limited student access (closed site-organization employees only) and the time spent over the changing legal aspects of such agreements often rendered these associations less stable than hoped for by both parties. The study's second theme concerned the role of ICTs and social media in teaching and learning for adult students. Yet, this study indicated ICTs and social and digital media in education and the workplace environment did not resonate with all learners. In the case of adult learners they are generally more comfortable with a hybrid learning environment. A hybrid model approach provides them with additional learning opportunities while maintaining interpersonal communication. The study found that face to face sessions interspersed with synchronous or asynchronous sessions using a variety of technologies, including audio, video, computer or correspondence better suited this group of learners.

ASSURING GRADUATE CAPABILITIES: A UNIVERSITY-WIDE STRATEGY TO EXPLOIT TECHNOLOGIES FOR GRADUATE EMPLOYABILITY

Beverley Oliver, Deakin University, Australia

This paper presents a case study on the quest find new ways to assure graduate employability by using the most effective digital technologies: paradoxically, employability challenges are increasing at the same time that emerging technologies provide individuals with greater opportunity to 'be their own brand'.

Deakin University, 40 years old, was founded as a distance education provider. Today, it has 50,000 enrolled students (about 80% elect to study in a traditional on campus mode – with extensive digital resources; and 20% elect to study completely online). Today's 'distance' learners may live around the corner, or in very remote Australian communities. Deakin's promise to its students is to "offer a brilliant education where students are [academically, geographically] and where they want to go [in their lives and careers]. In particular, Deakin set itself the challenge to use the technologies at the digital frontier to offer education that assures graduate employability, meaning that students and new graduates are supported and prompted to acquire "the skills, understandings and personal attributes that make [them] more likely to secure employment and be successful in their chosen occupations to the benefit of themselves, the workforce, the community and the economy" (Yorke, 2006). In brief, the task was to refresh the curriculum and the digital spaces to assure engaging learning experiences for all students, and equip them with the capabilities to find either traditional positions and create new modes of employment in a digitally enhanced world. This work has been underway since mid-2012 and centres on student achievement of the **Deakin Graduate Learning Outcomes**:

- Discipline knowledge;
- Communication;
- Digital literacy;
- Critical thinking;
- Problem solving;
- Self-management;
- Teamwork;
- Global citizenship.

Strategies include:

1. **Institution-wide curriculum framework**: devising and implementing the curriculum framework and the institution's agreed 21C graduate capabilities, expressed as the Deakin Graduate Learning Outcomes;
2. **Curriculum renewal:** Embedding the Graduate Learning Outcomes in every degree, expressed as Course Learning Outcomes and Standards, ensuring assessment is redesigned to prompt students to create digital artefacts that evidence their achievements;
3. **Reconfigure the learning management system** (LMS): to meet minimum standards to enable achievement of the Graduate Learning Outcomes in every degree;
4. **DeakinSync:** Overlaying the LMS with an overarching digital hub that enables students to access all services as well as have direct entry to the units in the learning management system, and self-enabling tools such as portfolio and connectivity tools;
5. **Me in a Minute** providing all students with a free service to showcase their achievement of capabilities and make their one-minute video pitch to prospective employers, encouraging networking through LinkedIn and other professional networks.

Deakin Hallmarks, piloting 2015, using digital badging technologies to credential and warrant outstanding achievement of the **Graduate Learning Outcomes.**

THE EUROPEAN CAREER DEVELOPMENT PROGRAMME: SUPPORTING HIGHER EDUCATION STUDENTS TO ACQUIRE PROFESSIONAL AWARENESS AND CAREER MANAGEMENT SKILLS

Gigliola Paviotti, Melius Srl, Gilda Rota, University of Padua, Italy

Background

In Europe, 74% of education providers are confident that their graduates were prepared for work, but only 38% of youth and 35% of employers agreed. Furthermore, it has been pointed out the fact that often universities believe that when the university is successful in making students meet or exceed standards in the chosen field, then education has done its job. Higher education institutions, instead, are in charge also to prepare students to face the today's world of work, which requires flexibility and adaptability, capacity of graduates of being independent in managing and enhancing their skills, to "think on their feet", and be able to make decisions and to generate ideas.

By definition, "career guidance refers to services intended to assist people, of any age and at any point throughout their lives to make educational, training and occupational choices and to manage their careers. Career guidance helps people to reflect on their ambitions, interests, qualifications and abilities. It helps them understand the labour market and education system, and relate this to what they know about themselves". To do so, guidance and career offices at the university usually offer support at the access moment, as educational guidance in the choice of studies, and at the exit moment, supporting transition to the world of work. To support the development of career development skills, however, the process cannot be limited at the transition moments.

The ICARD project

ICARD aims at developing a European Career Development Programme addressed to promote acquisition of professional understanding and career management skills for students. The programme will take into consideration present practices and programmes in universities,, particularly the Queensland University of Technology's Career Development Programs, which introduce career development in the curriculum, adopted by many Australian universities.

ICARD funded by the European Commission under the Erasmus+ programme will provide:

- an updated state of the art of the available programmes, modules or practices fostering self-understanding and self-learning on professional development, including education guidance and career guidance, covering the entire study cycle at the university;
- an online repository of running practices in European and International universities;
- the European Career Development Programme, a transversal learning programme aimed at fostering acquisition of professional awareness and career management skills in higher education students
- guidelines and recommendations for adoption of the programme, made available as Open Educational Resources.

ICARD Methodology

Having investigated the practices: how universities promote the acquisition of career development skills, the ICARD working group will develop the European Career Development programme, compliant with the following principles:

- the programme will cover the three phases of the study cycle at the university, namely entry-ongoing-exit, and accorded to the related career development skills;
- the programme will be composed by independent modules, linked in order to offer complete learning pathway;
- active learning and situational learning techniques will be preferred;
- the pathway will be ICT based (e-learning);
- the learning materials will have different formats, such as texts, video, audio, but will be in any case accessible from a computer and from wearable devices (such as tablets and/or smartphones);
- self-assessment will be made available at the end of each module.

21ST CENTURY CITIZEN SKILLS: DIGITAL COMPETENCES IN EDUCATION. CASES IN CATALONIA

Azucena Vázquez Gutiérrez, Montse Guitert Catasús, Universitat Oberta de Catalunya, Spain

Among the skills that every citizen should have acquired in the 21st Century, you have digital competences, which allow them to develop fully in a digital society that requires higher-order learning (Fields, 2011). In this proposal, the analysis of the strategies used in three different schools to promote the acquisition of digital skills of their students will be discussed. Through three case studies framed in the doctoral thesis "Classrooms 2.0 teacher's Vision, uses and development of the digital skills of students. Cases in Catalonia" conclusions will be presented on the proposed topic.

The inclusion of skills in the curriculum has several purposes:

- First, integrate different learning, both formal, incorporated in different areas or subjects, such as informal and non-formal.
- Second, allow all students to integrate their learning to relate them to different types of content and use them effectively when it is necessary in different situations and contexts.
- Thirdly and finally, guide teaching, to help identify the contents and evaluation criteria that are essential character and generally inspire the individual decisions on the process of teaching and learning.
- Several conclusions where derive from the analysis of the data pertaining to this investigation, among which are the following:
- The proposal of the schools regarding the treatment that is giving to ICT as well as the position of the management team regarding these, has a great influence on competency dimensions for work in the classroom.
- Perceived differences in classroom practices when dealing with different dimensions of competence, being those related to classical office which are more present (specially competence 2: Use the text editing applications, multimedia presentations and numeric data processing for the production of digital documents).
- The teacher shows a tendency to always work the same digital competencies within their classrooms (especially related generic applications), while there are others who rarely work (especially those relating to healthy habits in the use of ICT).

DEVELOPING PROFESSIONAL IDENTITY IN AN ONLINE LEARNING ENVIRONMENT: PERSPECTIVES OF PEER INTERACTION

Line Helverskov Horn, Aalborg University, Denmark

From a socio-cultural perspective, the development of a professional identity is an on-going process that is social in nature and negotiated in communities of practice. Internship placements in higher education function as such communities of practice, with an improved sense of professional identity as the outcome for the intern.

This paper describes the interactions in an online learning environment. The online platform sought to enable peer interaction between younger and older students in a discussion of the professional identity of Natural and Cultural Heritage Management (NCHM) professionals. By analysing user data and through a qualitative data analysis approach inspired by Creswell, defining themes of NCHM professional identity are identified. Thus suggesting that a discussion of professional identity can be facilitated in the current setting and indicating a need for designing educational activities with this purpose.

PERCEPTIONS REGARDING STUDENT WORKLOAD FOR LIFELONG LEARNING SKILLS IN A RANDOM ONLINE SHORT TERM ENVIRONMENT (ROSE)

Keren Levy, Elaine Hoter, David Burg, Ohalo College of Education, Israel

An intensive online environment over a limited period of time is a form of hybrid b-learning that could be a solution for situations when it is impossible to operate the educational system on a K-12 and a higher education level, in areas of conflict in which occasional outbreaks of tension disrupt normal routine, or in areas prone to extreme weather occurrences or outbreaks of disease. The 1989 Convention on the Rights of the Child stipulates that children have a right to education, and indeed, children and young people living under such circumstances should not be deprived of their right to a continuity of learning during these periods (Sinclair, 2001). A continuation of studying can be achieved, at least partially, by utilizing technology, not only to bridge the spatial gap, but also because technology, when used well, has the potential to preserve and nurture a sense of community.

We coined the term Random Online Short-term Environment (ROSE) to designate an unplanned online learning environment that continues for a limited period and functions as a seamless continuation of routine face-to-face learning. During a ROSE, students study in a space which is not always suitable for learning, in which the technological resources could be limited and the learning process can potentially be interrupted, due to the fact that other members of the family share the same space. Although ensuring a continuity of learning during these periods is a challenge, it is important to conduct research and design for this kind of environment.

This paper presents the results of research carried out on an online week held in a teacher-training college in the north of Israel during 2013/2014 and 2014/2015 in which all face-to-face courses were substituted with an online venue for students and lecturers to learn and teach. The online week emulates a situation in which the routine of the academic year is disrupted for a limited period of time due to external factors. The event was purposely planned to take place during the "Hanukkah" week because pupils of elementary and high schools in Israel are at home on vacation. Activities were planned ahead, unlike an authentic ROSE which is unplanned for by definition. We believe that it is important that teacher-trainees gain experience in such an environment from a pupil's perspective, while at the same time understand the pedagogical challenges associated with distance learning in a ROSE.

This paper concentrates on student workload as it appeared to be one of the most prominent issues during the event. We used a sequential mixed method design when planning our research (Creswell, 2009). We collected quantitative data, analyzed it, and then collected and analyzed qualitative data in a second phase that was built on the results of the initial quantitative results. We finally interpreted the entire analysis by comparing and juxtaposing the data collected in both phases. Means, standard deviations and independent samples t-tests were calculated (SPSS, version 21). Textual responses and transcripts of interviews were analyzed qualitatively (ATLAS.TI, version 7).

General student satisfaction was low (mean: 4.1 ± 1.2). The majority of students (78%) felt that there was a heavy workload during the online week. Concomitantly, this was the most frequently mentioned factor in the textual responses of students regarding recommendations for the future. In order to understand what contributed to this sense of workload, we subsequently conducted a series of semi-structured interviews after the event of 2014/2015 with faculty members (N=5) and students (N=7) with the objective of elucidating their perceptions of the issue of workload. Analysis of the data revealed that there were 3 main themes that contributed to the sense of workload: The nature of the activities, i.e. the number of activities, their complexity and the amount of time required to complete them, the challenging study environment and a misconception of the online week ("A holiday should be a holiday", or "Let us enjoy the holiday" etc.).

The implication for the future is that faculty need guidance not only regarding pedagogy and technology, but also as to the nature of the specific learning environment of the ROSE. From the students' point of view it seems that time management skills training could possibly be of help in dealing with workload (Romero, 2011).

Although the research focused on a ROSE it has implications for e-learning and blended hybrid learning environments planned for lifelong learning (LLL). Awareness of the issue of workload and responding to the need of having to balance work, study and family demands is a key to a successful and competitive online program in higher education.

THE INTEGRATION OF INFORMATION LITERACY SKILLS INTO THE CURRICULUM

Luis Guadarrama, Marc Cels, Cindy Ives, Corinne Bosse, Athabasca University, Canada

The project (Evaluation in progress): Exploratory Evaluation Survey

This poster summarizes the aims of the student evaluation for the Information Literacy Skills Modules that were integrated into the curriculum of several Early European History undergraduate courses in the humanities. The Skills Modules were incorporated with the view of improving students' research skills and their awareness of the rigorous principles of academic integrity. The focus for this exploratory survey is to collect information about students' perceptions about how the Skills Modules assist them to complete their written assignments and their research. The results of the evaluation are expected to inform course design practices at AU and beyond where teachers seek to improve students' information literacy skills. This survey will remain open until December 2015.

The Problem

For a long time, professors and tutors have been complaining about students that don't bring to their university studies the Information Literacy (IL) skills needed to conduct their university studies satisfactorily. As in other humanities and social science courses, many students in history-type courses tend to perform poorly because they have not sufficiently mastered the IL skills needed to complete assignments satisfactorily. There is strong indication that the lack of IL skills not only limits students' performance but also results in academic misconduct, like cheating and plagiarism.

Purpose and Significance of the Study

The purpose of the evaluation is to inform course design practices at Athabasca University. It is expected that findings could shed light on how to enhance the Skills Modules strategy to make the support more suitable for students who may need to enhance their IL skills. Secondly, this evaluation is intended to inform course design practices across AU.

The survey

The survey is available online and it takes 5-10 minutes for students. The survey was reviewed by other AU learning designers, the course coordinator, by tutors in the course, and other AU researchers.

Evaluation Core Questions

To what extent do students perceive their performance improve because of the IL skills standards integrated into the curriculum of history courses?

- What are students' perceptions of the Skills Modules?
- To what extent students think the IL skills modules inform them on using the library efficiently?
- To what extent students think the IL skills modules improve their understanding to complete their assignments?
- To what extent students consider the ISLs modules guide them to adhere to principles of intellectual integrity?

Preliminary findings (Evaluation is in progress)

Preliminary findings show a strong indication that students perceive the Skills modules as a useful help to complete their assignments. Figures show that students think the skills modules are helping them to master the skills required to write their research papers. Overall students perceive that the Skills Modules help them to complete assignments successfully, reward their efforts to learn the course material, help them to improve their overall performance and least but not last, they also think they could transfer the information literacy skills acquired in their courses in their future university courses. The study will conclude on December 2015.

CITIZEN INVOLVEMENT VIA SMARTPHONE A DEVELOPMENT PROJECT BY STUDENTS IN PUBLIC ADMINISTRATION

Jakob Djurhuus Albrechtsen, Linda Hauschildt Nielsen, University College Lillebaelt, Denmark

Introduction

As part of their education in Public Administration (PA), a group of students at University College Lillebaelt (UCL), Denmark has been working to uncover the need for developing simple apps for Smartphones, which can give elderly and disabled citizens a feeling of security in their daily lives and help them have an effective contact with the public authorities.

The project has been conducted in close cooperation with the students in PA, representatives from the groups of citizens the apps are meant for and students who have the technical skills to develop prototypes of the apps.

Project phases

The project progressed in three phases: The Clarification phase, The Development phase, The Testing and Selling phase.

In the Clarification phase it was important for the students to communicate closely with the representatives from the groups of citizens the apps were meant for. Therefore, user surveys were carried out and an idea-generating seminar was arranged with representatives from the groups.

The result of the process was that two concrete needs were identified, which the citizens wanted a digital solution for in the form of two apps, one which would improve elderly people's feeling of safety in daily life, and one that would improve the elderly and disabled persons' opportunity to give easy and speedy responses to questions from the state and municipality.

In the Development phase the students of PA were meant to give concrete, precise and detailed descriptions of the structures and contents of the two apps. It was a great challenge and learning process to transform the wanted functionality of the two apps into a simple, visual and well-structured design without losing some of the requirements that the apps were meant to fulfil. The results of the students' hard work were two prototypes for the wanted apps which were ready for testing.

In the Testing phase the apps were tested by the target groups in order to see if any modifications were needed. At the same time the students were engaged in the Selling phase, where the aim was to find a partner who would undertake the apps for further development and commercializing.

The Output of the Project for the Students in Public Administration

The students in Public Administration have gathered and worked up information from the surveys and interviews with elderly and disabled citizen and made descriptions of the design and content of the apps. They have handled the communication of wishes and needs to the technical development group and supervised the development of the prototype.

Through the work with the development of apps matching the needs articulated by the target group the students of PA at UCL have experienced an intense, innovative and active learning process in which the students find that the need to transform theoretical knowledge to concrete practice in direct contact with the citizens contribute in a very positive way to their processional skills and understanding.

UISEL – UBIQUITOUS INFORMATION FOR SENIORS LIFE THROUGH MOBILE DEVICES

Licia Boccaletti, Serena D'Angelo, Anziani e Non Solo Soc. Coop., Italy; Pedro Cano, José Maria Roa, APFA, Spain; L'Ubica Gasilova, FPPS, Slovakia, Denisa Lombrea, Maria Toia, IREA, Romania; Carlos Carvalho, Claudia Azevedo, Virtual Campus, Portugal, Oldrich Stanek, Zivot90, Czech Republic

UISEL Project

Life expectancy is growing. So there is an equally growing need to fully integrate senior citizens in the Knowledge Society where ICT tools play a crucial role. Their current exclusion, due to technological illiteracy, prevents them from fully exercising their rights but also prevents the society from benefitting from their large experience, life-wisdom and know-how. Furthermore, with the advent of mobile devices (smartphones and tablets), this problem was aggravated, as more and more information, communication and formal duties are being designed and processed for that context. Info-exclusion in adult citizens aged 50 and above relates partially to some reluctance towards change and, particularly, towards new technologies but also to the lack of attention given to the specific needs of this people category.

The UISEL project (under the GRUNDTVIG Lifelong Learning Programme (LLP) of the European Commission, Education and Culture DG) is conceived as a way of integrating senior citizen into the Knowledge Society, by improving their access to ICT tools and by enhancing the content and quality of training courses for teachers and staff that work with this particular target group. This is achieved by developing i) an e-learning multilingual training course addressed to trainers and caregivers based on an open sources platform; ii) an APP containing the multilingual training course targeting senior citizens which focuses on the use of mobile devices, for instance, in regard to fiscal obligations, social security issues, emergency situations, medical monitoring, preventing isolation, and even leisure and time occupation and iii) a serious game App articulated in mini-games that contained a set of exercises to support seniors to learn and practice the basic gestures of touch technology.

The training material has been developed on the basis of a pedagogical approach which derived from the analysis of the specific learning needs and motivations of the elderly taking into consideration variances in group-specific learning competences. This needs analysis has been conducted through desk and field researches carried out in each involved country.

The project will involve more than 35 experts in the field of adult education, ICT learning and more than 140 senior citizens living in Italy, Portugal, Spain, Austria, Czech Republic, Slovakia and Romania.

The project involves the following seven partner organizations: Anziani e Non Solo Soc. Coop – Italy; Aula Permanente de Formaciòn Abierta, Granada University – Spain; University of Vienna – Austria; Virtual Campus Lda – Portugal; Forum Pre pomoc Starsim – Slovakia; Zivot90 – Czech Republic; Romanian Institute for Adult Education – Romania.

UISEL at the EDEN Annual Conference 2015

UISEL' s goal, as foresaid, is to enhance the quality of life and facilitate the integration to the Knowledge Society of senior citizens, by improving their access to ICT tools and by enhancing the content and quality of training courses for teachers and staff that work with this particular target group. It aims to help such vulnerable groups to avoid isolation and social exclusion and to benefit from ICT, by providing distance learning in a new educational way: oriented learning and training. This as a result adapts to the *Expanded learning scenarios* conference theme "Tools and resources for learning through mobile" and the "New generation of methodologies for older generation of people.

A MODEL FOR BUILDING TRUST IN ONLINE ENVIRONMENTS

Elaine Hoter, Ohalo College of Education and the Mofet Institute, Israel

Introduction

The Internet allows us to learn about other cultures and people who are different to ourselves by actually meeting people from other cultures. However, in order to make these exchanges fruitful we must be able to build trust between the teachers collaborating on the project, between the teachers and the students, as well as between the students from the different cultures. We need to build a non-threatening environment where students collaborate with each other using the tools of the internet.

This poster will present research on building trust between cultures in conflict using the TEC model (Hoter, Shonfeld & Ganayem 2012) developed form Allport's Contact Hypothesis (1954).

The Contact Hypothesis

Allport claimed that given the right conditions positive contact with people in conflict or people from different social and cultural groups – the "out-group" could lead to a positive change in not only how the person in the out-group is viewed but also towards the out-group itself. The conditions included meeting over a period of time, equality between the participants and institutional support. Over the years the Contact Hypothesis has undergone revisions with different conditions added or deleted particularly noticeable is the work of Pettigrew & Tropp in this field (Pettigrew & Tropp, 2008).

With the potential of the Internet to form a meeting place for those who would never normally meet, the contact hypothesis has been adapted to the Internet. There are many advantages to learning and meeting online particularly for groups in conflict, for example there are no longer restrictions as to place or time and the participants can meet online and in virtual environments. (Amichai-Hamburger & McKennan 2006, Hoter, Shonfeld & Ganayem 2009). Meeting face to face (F2F) carries with it all the stigmas connected with the out-group, but meeting "the other" online before meeting face to face allows the participants to gradually get to know one another and build rapport and respect.

The TEC Model

The TEC Model developed by the TEC Center in Israel, provides the stages to build trust in online environments. Israel is a very segregated society where Jewish religious and secular students as well as Arab students study within different educational frameworks. This segregation coupled with the political situation leads to fear and prejudice between the groups. The TEC model brings the students from the different groups together for the first time. The students study for a year together in small multicultural groups and only meet F2F at the end of the year. Collaboration is the key to all the classes and projects. The collaboration is on all levels from management, coordinators, teachers and students. Each of the small group assignments requires a higher level of collaboration thus building trust gradually between the group members and group cohesion.

The class teachers experience online collaboration prior to the course through participation in an online collaborative learning course. They are then divided into groups of 3 teachers, each representing a different culture, sect, or nationality (for example a Jewish school/college a Christian school/college and a Moslem school/college, a special education class or a class from a school/college in another country). The teachers or lecturers spend three intensive days together where they get to know one another and plan the joint year course they will teach together. Throughout the year the teachers meet in their small groups online on a weekly basis and also attend online sessions with lecturers and other teacher/lecturers in the projects. In addition to the weekly asynchronous assignments, the students meet asynchronously for virtual conferencing and in virtual environments. The students and teachers/lecturers all meet together at the end of the year to celebrate their achievements.

The subject matter can be almost anything and the idea is not to speak about politics but areas we have in common. Courses this year given in the TEC Center include courses for students training to be teachers in Science and Environment studies, Technology in Education and English literature concentrating on literature of minorities written in English in particular Palestinian and Jewish women's literature. Courses given within the schools include the subject of civics, learning about other cultures and traditions, our environment, mathematics, and courses in English on various topics.

Research

The poster will present both the model and research carried out to examine if the participants change their views towards the out-group(s). Students filled in online questionnaires before during and at the end of the course. The research results show a lessening in stereotyping and prejudice between the participants (Walthers, Hoter, Ganayem & Shonfeld in press).

ICT FOR LIFELONG LEARNING IN ARMENIA AND GEORGIA

Arusyak Abrahamyan, Harutyun Gzraryan, State Engineering University of Armenia, Armenia, Eva Szalma, European Distance and E-Learning Network, United Kingdom, Tamar Lominadze, Georgian Technical University, Georgia, Paata Gogishvili, St. Andrew the First-Called Georgian University, Georgia, Edita Gzoyan, Aram Mirzoyan, Institute for Informatics and Automation Problems, Armenia

The ARMAZEG – Developing tools for lifelong learning in Transcaucasus region: e-Learning project (financed by the European Commission within the TEMPUS program) aims to stimulate educational reform in Armenian and Georgian universities by developing lifelong learning methodologies, implementation strategy, teacher training and setting up of e-learning centres.

The project involves twelve partners from Europe and Transcaucasia with a clear vision to establish new links in the educational sphere between the two regions. With the assistance of four European partners ARMAZEG's Armenian and Georgian institutions import and adapt e-Learning practices in their educational agenda to realise a flexible organisation of higher and adult education locally. A thorough needs analysis accompanied by study visits to the state of the art European universities helps the Transcaucasian partners improve learning by supporting student-centred methodologies, research-based higher education and enabling the internationalisation of their higher education services.

The first outcome of the project is a state-of-the-art report about the assessment of the current situation with regard to the level of development and the use of tools of e-learning and lifelong learning in Armenia and Georgia, with detailed analyses of e-learning readiness on the institutional level of the involved universities.

THE APPLICATION AND PRACTICE OF INFORMATION TECHNOLOGY IN DISTANCE EDUCATION OF SHANGHAI OPEN UNIVERSITY

Hong Wang, Jianfeng Hong, Shanghai Open University, Shanghai, China

Shanghai Open University (SOU) is a new higher institute with use of information technology in education. After years of development and integration, a fundamental framework of information-based system has been set up in SOU. The system is composed of three parts - one network, two application platforms, and three centers.

One network

To establish one network for all learners, teachers, managers from all branches, and provide a unified, safe and reliable network service.

Two applications

The digital campus system is a digital space based on the digital information and network, in order to expand the time and space of campus, to enhance the efficiency of teaching, research, management, service, to realize the comprehensive information of the education process, and to improve the management quality and efficiency.

The learning and teaching management system is a learning platform with full function, high performance, and friendly interface to learners, teachers and managers, providing supports throughout the whole online education process, with a variety of interaction between teachers and students, and a variety of terminal access.

Three centers

The **data center** is established with use of cloud computing technology, and acts as a secure and reliable data center for storage and management of the data and digital resources.

The **management center** is to strengthen the management of the information of the 42 branches, and evaluate the construction and application of information technology.

The **research center** is to carry out researches on application of new technologies in education with use of the big data technology, statistics and analyze the data of the learning platform and data center.

And focusing on the network, platforms, resources, applications and service for daily teaching management administrative management, learning support service, etc, it plays an important role in upgrading of the quality of distance education. In the process of the construction of the information system, the strategic guideline for teaching platform development is 'holistic in plan, sustainable in development, step-by-step in implementation, and innovative whenever possible'.

In addition, Shanghai Open University plays an important role in the process of building a learning society in the city of Shanghai. With establishment of the Shanghai Learning Network, Shanghai Education Resources Center, Shanghai Academic Credit Bank, Shanghai Elderly Distance Education Network, etc., the university has greatly promoted the development of the learning society where anyone could learn anytime and anywhere.

With extensive use of information technology, the applicability has become the indispensable core development capability in boosting distance education and achieving strategic targets of the university. In other words, strong information technology applicability is an important symbol that differentiates SOU from other educational institutions. Not only the applicability enhances university's existing capability to better adapt to the fast development of distance education, but also directly support and enhance university's integrated development capability. Therefore, all stakeholders should be fully mobilized to actively participate in application and boost applicability to become the core development capability so as to ensure the sustainable development of distance education cause of the university.

CROSS-BORDER COLLABORATIVE E-LEARNING: THE ESCART GROUP WORK

M. Zolfo, C. Kiyan, L. Jiang, B. Ingelbeen, L. Lynen ,Institute of Tropical Medicine, Belgium

Being able to access educational material, as well as accurate and up-to date information, is essential to health care workers based in resource limited settings (RLS): by bringing knowledge through distance learning courses and continuing medical education modules the Institute of Tropical Medicine (ITM) in Antwerp has contributed in the last decade in solving the challenge of the scientific isolation of these colleagues deployed *in the front line*.

We hereby describe the collaborative learning project embedded in the ITM Electronic Short Course on Antiretroviral Therapy (eSCART) distance learning training. The eSCART is a tutor-guided distance learning course on anti-retroviral therapy (ART) targeting physicians working in RLS. It is articulated in 13 modules, grouped into 5 blocks lasting each 1 week and with a student investment time of 8-10 hours per week. A 14th module, "Search of biomedical literature and formulation of evidence-based recommendations through Internet", runs all over the 18-weeks of the with the aim of having students applying concepts of Evidence-Based Medicine (EBM) while searching literature about a specific HIV/AIDS-related topic, assessing the strength of evidence found and formulating recommendations, within an international students' team. During the Group work, the asynchronous online discussion is articulated around 4 stages, where students are asked to fulfil the following learning objectives:

1. Formulate the PICO question (an important clinical research question is chosen and enquired according the "PICO approach": Population/Problem, Intervention, Comparator, and Outcome);
2. Look and make a list of MeSH Keywords that are appropriate for the selected PICO question;
3. Search articles in PubMed combining MeSH terms;
4. Select and retrieve the "most important" citations and articles related to the topic from the search results;
5. Evaluate the level of evidence of the studies;
6. Give strength of evidence; and
7. Formulate recommendations.

The groups, composed of max 8 students, are guided in their process by facilitators familiar with the scientific topic and trained in facilitating, who encourage the collaborative discussion, keep tracks of the time schedule and deliverables, ascertain the quality of the discussion and make sure that the requested products for each stage (Stage I, II and III) are submitted in time by the group.

Students in eSCART Group work collaborate in gaining new knowledge and in completing a collaborative project. They need to be assesses: i) for an individual component (individual assessment: personal contribution to collaborative work); and ii) in a collective manner (collective assessment: group dynamic, product outcomes).

Besides the personal assessment done counting items such as the number, regularity and length of contribution, on the Group work discussion forum, the individual performance is assessed on the basis of the quality of the contributions. A grading rubrics has been developed for this reason, with a well specified hierarchical level of performance. Online asynchronous discussion is to be considered a valid and mindful tool for collaborative learning. The feeling of belonging to a group might be a successful key in attending educational learning goals, moreover if individual and collective assessments are shared in advance and clear instructions are given in order to encourage individual achievements while supporting and fostering a group. This increases the quality of the assessment in terms of *transparency* (students receive the rubric in advance to know how their performance will be assessed). Moreover training facilitators/teachers in using rubrics as online assessment tools has been key to provide timely constructive feedback to the groups in order to direct the group dynamic in line with the criteria and standards described in the rubrics.

EDUCATIONAL APPS FOR HIGH SCHOOL EDUCATION AT NATIONAL AUTONOMOUS UNIVERSITY OF MEXICO

León Martínez Jorge, Tapia Rangel Edith, National Autonomous University of Mexico, Mexico

Introduction

The incursion of apps into the educational field is in its initial stages. There is a long way to go, this is why it is necessary to develop and use innovative educational resources that effectively support the students' learning and teaching processes. Under such premise, National Autonomous University of Mexico (UNAM) has developed an integral formation project for high school students through a number of apps that support learning within different knowledge areas such as Mathematics, History, Geography and Spanish. This paper will present a theoretical framework for educational apps, their use and a short account of this experience.

Apps in Mexico, Educational apps and Educational apps at UNAM

A mobile app is software which has been designed to run on smartphones, tablets and other mobile devices. Apps ubiquity, usability and usefulness in everyday activities have placed them in a prominent position among smartphone users. The key features for a successful app include easy operation, that meet needs and requirements and interoperability. The use of mobile devices has grown in Mexico and today 84% of Mexicans use some of them. On the other hand, 60,000 apps are downloaded in Mexico every day. It is still a low percentage of those apps that correspond to education category. Additional to key features, the apps possess some features that favour its inclusion in education as: a specific purpose, intuitive, can integrate all the other features available in mobile devices including cloud capacities, can be carried inside students' pockets. For this reason the apps are powerful educational tools inside and outside school. In UNAM, a pilot project was developed for the use of tablets tablets in formal, face-to-face education at secondary level in the Escuela Nacional Preparatoria of UNAM. The project has considered in its activities the compilation and developing of educational applications for mobile devices in different operating systems, suited to the curriculum of Escuela Nacional Preparatoria. Dirección General de Cómputo y de Tecnologías de Información y Comunicación (DGTIC) and Coordinación de Universidad Abierta y Educación a Distancia (CUAED) partook of this activity, establishing guidelines for app development and a methodology. The guidelines for app development deal with two main aspects. The first is related to the "Guide for identity, style and human interface". The second aspect is represented by the instructional script developed by teachers and pedagogical consultants, which is later translated into an app by graphic designers and visual communicators. Furthermore, the methodology for developing apps attended the following phases: Definition of the project's profile, content analysis, pedagogical consulting and proof reading, visual communication and integration, pilot testing and release. Attending these guidelines, the CUAED has produced twenty-six educational apps available at https://apps.unam.mx. These apps are grouped into 3 categories: Math, Spanish and Geography. To access the apps it is necessary to be part of UNAM, either as a teacher or a student, and to register for installation in mobile devices.

Conclusions

The experience has allowed the consolidation of a group of specialists who have been enriching a development methodology focused on the creation of digital educational resources in different formats that allows UNAM to compile and promote the knowledge produced by its academics, and to carry forward its purpose of "forming professionals who are useful to society" by developing new ways of teaching and learning through currently available technologies. In addition, it will be important to measure the impact of the apps during a second phase in order to update and improve them. Even though the goal when providing youth with learning experiences through apps was to support their learning processes, it is also possible for them to acquire digital competences, which are elementary and necessary in the context of professional and personal development in the age of the knowledge society. Once the apps have been consolidated, it will be necessary to expand their availability in such a way as to become learning tools for the general public throughout their lives.

ROLE OF THE RESEARCH IN EDUCATIONAL POLICIES AND PRACTICES IN DISTANCE EDUCATION AND E-LEARNING AT HIGH EDUCATION LEVEL IN PORTUGAL

Angelina Costa, Lina Morgado, Universidade Aberta, Portugal

Higher education is, by its nature, a place of innovation in relation to knowledge and its construction and dissemination. Scientific development, in this case in education and technology, has produced emerging needs analysis, evaluation and reflection of the scientific production, making them important tasks among the academic community. This demonstrated the need to better understand the state of the art research on distance education and e-learning, higher education in Portugal, and see forward, anticipating different scenarios.

The last aim of this study is to outline scenarios of future in distance education and e-learning, in higher education, looking at Portugal's condition within the European context. Accordingly, we've decided to investigate the role of research results in educational policies and practices, since they could ground decisions in the present and become a framework for the future.

Three stages of investigation have been defined. The first step was to map the state of the art of research on distance education and e-learning, in higher education, but go beyond, in a second moment, summoning discussion and reflection of the protagonists in the process. Thirdly, the prospects of national and European perspectives of specialists in this field will be faced up.

Phase 1 – Documentary analysis of scientific production in the area concerning a ten year period

This phase involves an unconventional meta-analysis, a "qualitative meta-analysis", from the perspective of Cardoso (e. g. Cardoso, 2007; 2008; 2012; Cardoso, Alarcão & Celorico, 2010; 2013). Following the objectives of the investigation, such a study will be used but with a qualitative approach in what it is intended to embrace, record and analyze all types of studies produced within a given time frame, within a comprehensive theme, subjecting the data to content analysis and descriptive statistical procedures. The corpus of analysis consists of all documents that report research conducted in distance education and e-learning in higher education, produced in Portugal, in a period of ten years, from 2004 to 2013, inclusive, under the form of master dissertations and PhD theses, publications in journals, conference proceedings/seminars, books and chapters' books.

Phase 2 – Analysis of the prospects of the academic community about scientific production in this field and identifying future scenarios through discussion groups

The sample consists of three groups of university researchers with a maximum of twelve elements. The criteria for selecting the sample are: a) researchers in higher education; b) heterogeneity in terms of gender, age, academic education and institution; c) willingness to participate in the study. Content analysis of the transcript of the speech produced in discussion groups through appropriate software will be held.

Phase 3 – Analysis of the prospects of European experts about future scenarios in Portugal and in Europe through the methodology Delphi study

The sample consists of ten academic researchers from EU countries with recognized academic work in the field of distance education and e-learning. The criteria for selecting the sample are the same as phase sample 2. The list of participants in phase 2 and 3 will be built by the inquiry, at least three researchers.

Still in the research process, we present here the global design of the study and preliminary and partial results of phase 1 research.

LANGUAGES FOR SPECIFIC PURPOSES – LANGUAGE CENTRES FOR CULTURAL HERITAGE PRESERVATION

Walter Zeller, astyle, linguistic competence, Austria, Evangelia Varella, Aristotle University of Thessaloniki, Greece

General Framework and the Preparation of Course Materials

Promoting to learn more than one language is central to the European Union language policy. Everyone within the European Union is encouraged to do so in the interests of mutual understanding and communication.

Preparing material for courses on Languages for Specific Purposes, such as law, economics, health sciences or – as in our case – cultural heritage preservation bears an intermediary status between philology and the various specific fields of knowledge. Thus, material concentrates more on language in context than on grammar and language structures, an approach that greatly enhances the relevance of what students are learning.

Project Outcomes

Generally, the project aimed to achieve efficient communication among those active in cultural heritage preservation in the multilingual European environment by offering complete and easily accessible possibilities for learning and assessing the language skills in several European languages (French, Greek, Italian, Slovene, and Spanish). The project has reached the following targets:

- Face-to-face and online courses and examinations on the agreed level (in general, Level B2 of the Common European Framework)
- Covering major and less spoken languages such as French, Greek, Italian, Slovene, and Spanish (in alphabetical order)
- Training courses and testing implements for tutors and teachers for enabling them to deal with all aspects of these focused, personalised learning activities.
- Certification of every type of knowledge and skills acquired
- Integration and operation of all activities within accredited LSP Language Centres
- Implementation of the Language Centres Network in the Southern Mediterranean basin

Interactivity of the Project Partners

The project was realised by the close co-operation of

- Institutions teaching cultural heritage preservation and valorisation
- University language teaching units
- University or professional ICT experts
- Professional partners dealing with cultural heritage preservation and valorisation

EDMONDO: IMMERSIVE TEACHING//LEARNING EXPERIENCES IN ITALY

Andrea Benassi, Letizia Cinganotto, INDIRE, Italy

This paper presents the state of art of an ongoing immersive training experience based on Virtual Reality currently held at INDIRE, the National Institute for Documentation, Innovation, Educational Research of the Italian Ministry of Education and Research. The Institute has been dealing with a number of issues in recent years, mainly related to educational research, innovation and training. The immersive world created by INDIRE is called "Edmondo" and is used for different learning and training projects both for students and teachers.

This paper illustrates an Action-Research project planned and carried out in Italy with a group of teachers engaged in training paths to improve their language competences in English and their methodological competences related to the use of immersive technologies at school.

The virtual approach to the educational area is found in the combination of media and has been commonly recognized over the last few years as a very effective and powerful tool to enhance the learning/teaching dimension. According to the social-cultural and constructivist approach, meanings and understandings grow out of social encounters, which represent the starting point of the learning experience.

In particular, the focus of this research is on EFL (English as a Foreign Language) and on CLIL (Content and Language Integrated Learning) that can get a significant added value from the use of immersive technologies.

The research project stems from the following research question: *"Can immersive technologies enhance the teaching/learning process with particular attention to English language teaching (EFL) and to the learning of curricular subjects through a foreign language (CLIL)?"*

The steps of the project:

Step 1

Literature review about immersive technologies in EFL and CLIL, through a recognition of the main national and international contributions to this field.

Step 2

Planning training paths for teachers developing two different pathways:

- English language course for teachers in "Edmondo", aimed at B1/B2 level of CEFR;
- methodological course for teachers in "Edmondo", aimed at developing skills related to the teaching of English and the teaching of subject contents through English in an immersive world.

Step 3

Assessment of the training paths carried out in "Edmondo", through the use of different tools, such as self-assessment questionnaires, portfolios, diaries, narrative tools etc. aimed at fostering reflective practices within a virtual community of teachers, also with the use of social networks such as Facebook.

Step 4

- Planning and experimenting lessons in "Edmondo" with students of different school levels, according to guidelines, hints, prompts and suggestions given to the teachers by experts and trainers.
- Through quantitative and qualitative research tools, the different phases and aspects of the lessons will be recorded, explored and analysed.

Step 5

A final report will include the outcomes of the research, with guidelines, suggestions and hints to the teachers, also taking into account a wide range of scenarios and technical features that may suit the different teaching strategies and learning styles.

MATH FORMULA EDITION IN LMS, PRESENT AND FUTURE

Ramon Eixarch, Albert Creus, Carles Aguiló, WIRIS team, Spain

Learning platforms (LMS) typically pay very little attention to STEM tools. Teachers or content creators in the fields of science, technology, engineering and mathematics face serious difficulties when creating materials for their students, often having to deal with scripting languages and poor WYSIWYG math formula editors, poor both in functionality and in supported devices.

If the students are required to type in themselves the math formulas, for example as the answer to an exercise, or in a forum, these limitations can become insurmountable.

When it comes to formula edition, as with any other content type, there are two key moments involved in the communication act that educational content implies: the moment of creation and the moment of reception, which is the moment when the user views the created content.

Relevant benchmarking will address both moments. More precisely, at edition time, technology and usability will be addressed, whereas at view time, we will focus on quality and accessibility of the output.

The selected solutions for this benchmarking cover the major industry and open-source LMS solutions at the time of writing. We will discuss three solutions provided by Moodle, Canvas and WIRIS, which has been adopted by some other big actors like Blackboard Learn, LearningStudio by Pearson, Itslearning and Desire2Learn, among others.

We will finally present some probable future developments in this field.

TEACHER EXPENDING PEN: ICT INTEGRATION IN TEACHER EDUCATION PROGRAMS

Davoud Masoumi, University of Gävle; Maryam Bourbour, University of Gothenburg, Sweden

Despite increasing investments in provision of ICT technologies (e.g. provision of government-funded laptops to students and teachers, interactive electronic whiteboards, introducing social media and applications, etc.), it is probably true that the widespread and routine use of new technology in teaching remains a goal still to be achieved. In spite of massive investment and increased presence of ICT-based technologies in schools, these technologies have not a significant lasting impact on teaching and learning practices. Why ICT technologies have found such a small place in teaching and learning practices or have been used to sustain existing practices has been a very puzzling problem. There can be unquestionably a large number of possible factors that may affect the complexity of ICT integration in education.

A review of the evidence suggests that provision of a ICT- supported technologies on its own cannot lead to changes in teaching and learning, but teachers' beliefs, knowledge and expertise with these technologies can transform educational practices. In other words, ICT technologies will not be used in school unless teachers have the skills, knowledge, and attitudes necessary to infuse it into the teaching and learning practices. Thus, it can be argued that "the teacher" is the key to understanding the ICT integration in education as the most crucial mediating factor in educational settings.

For the most part, teachers use ICT-based technologies as an adjunct or add-on, and for supplemental purposes e.g. drill and practice activities, word processing, etc. but "have not yet applied these technologies in their classroom teaching and learning". Concerns about slow integration of ICT in schools' educational practices, similarly, have led leaders and policy makers at educational institutions and governmental levels to place a greater emphasis on providing more opportunities for pre-service teachers to use ICT in their educational practices. The challenge for teacher education institutions, then, is to prepare teachers who know how to integrate effective use of ICT in their pedagogical practices.

This study, accordingly, looks at the integration of ICT in teacher training in the wider perspective of school development. To prepare teacher trainees for work in a rapidly changing, information rich and technology based society, more specifically, it analyses the key strategies in integration of ICT in teacher training programs and provides implications and directions for future analyses of ICT integration efforts. In order to analyse and synthesize the studies and examples of best practice to integrate ICT in education particularly in teacher education, a meta-synthesis exercise was undertaken. In other words, a systematic review method was employed to identify, critically appraise, and synthesize studies and examples of ICT integration in education generally and in teacher education programs in particular.

The met-analysis outlines the key strategies that have been taken to incorporate and promote ICT in teacher-education programs. A part of the addressed strategies, which addresses the institutions policies, infrastructure and approaches, can be considered as macro strategies. Such strategies is often in alignment with the regional and national polices and stearic plans. The other part of strategies addresses the practices that teacher education programs embed to integrate ICT in their programs. By exemplifying and providing ways to employ ICT in different learning situations, these practices reflect examples of different ways of embedding ICT in teacher training programs. Mention should be made that the addressed strategies are complementary, thus a combination of the given strategies may be more efficient way in integrating ICT in teacher education programs.

EXPANDING LEARNING SPACES IN HIGHER EDUCATION – UNDERSTANDING A HYFLEX MODEL

Marie Leijon, Björn Lundgren, Malmo University, Sweden

In this paper, we seek to investigate the interplay between space, interaction and learning sequences in a higher education HyFlex learning environment. HyFlex is a model where the course design combines physical and virtual spaces and face-to-face with online learning. Hy stands for hybrid and Flex for flexibility. This certain HyFlex model has been developed at Malmo University during a couple of years, first and foremost within the master program "Communiation for Development" (http://wpmu.mah.se/comdev). In Teacher Education 90 credits, students can, in some courses, choose if they want to attend lectures and seminars on campus or online. Here we use the HyFlex Model as a more specific conceptualization of blended learning. It focuses on flexibility, design and agency.

The paper presents an on-going research project and aim to discuss some tentative findings focusing on different aspects of spaces and interaction in a HyFlex learning environment using the theoretical perspective Designs for learning. This perspective offers a way to understand space with the concepts designs for learning and designs in learning. Designs for learning highlight the conditions for learning as institutional framing, norms, curricula, learning resources and didactic design. Designs in learning focus on how both teacher and students design their learning path during a learning sequence. In relation to a HyFlex learning environment, designs for learning helps us to understand how different spaces, both in the physical and virtual room, constitutes essential elements in communication and interaction. With designs in learning we could deepen our understanding of how different spaces become resources in a meaning-making process. Research on blended/HyFlex learning environments in higher education concerns several different aspects, like course design and student choices. Our focus in this paper is the interplay between different kinds of spaces and interaction i a HyFlex design. This area, especially with focus on higher education, is somewhat under researched.The aim with our study is to investigate the interplay between space, interaction and learning sequences in a higher education HyFlex learning environment. The following research questions are asked: What kinds of different spaces are connected in a HyFlex model? How are the spaces designed? And how do the participants interact in the different spaces?

The case study combines video observation with interviews. The tentative results in this paper, however, stems from observations of the streamed material. The material is analysed from a multimodal perspective focusing on both visual and auditory information and connects as well as the participants use a variety of semiotic resources, including space in their communication.

In the results we identify five (or more) different kinds of spaces that are designed in this model; the physical setting at campus, the space the facilitator designs for the streaming, the virtual space that the remote students meet when they connect with their laptop, the connection between several different space outside campus and a parallel chat space. The results show how a HyFlex learning environment in higher education offers flexibility in time and space for students. Especially from a teacher perspective this flexibility comes with a hybridization of spaces. A hybrid and flexible pedagogic environment includes complex settings and demands collaboration between the lecturing teacher and the facilitator. This HyFlex model points towards team teaching but also raises questions about power, design and agency.

BLENDED LEARNING DESIGN – THE POTENTIALS AND PITFALLS DESIGNING BLENDED LEARNING COURSES IN A PROFESSIONAL BACHELOR CONTEXT

Lise Lau Pedersen, University College Lillebaelt, Denmark

University College Lillebaelt has decided that 30 percent of all educational elements must be generated as blended learning by the end of the year 2015 as part of a modernization addressing following educational needs:

- Blended learning can help match the expectations of the future students who have grown up in digitized homes and schools.
- Blended learning helps **individualization** and **differentiation**. The students can organize their own learning paths – decide for themselves where and when to study, which paths to follow and in what tempo.
- Blended learning helps provide resources for the individual subjects (for instance subjects with a high degree of complexity or difficulty) or groups of students (those in danger of dropping out for instance) without necessarily increasing face to face teaching, but by developing asynchronous study activities and learning resources for digital distance learning.
- Blended learning can contribute to supporting and improving efficiency of educational efforts. This can for instance be done through programmes for several classes by using video conferencing, allocating traditional face to face teaching to synchronous and asynchronous study activities produce digital materials which can be employed didactically and reused by the teachers. This can also mean that the particular competencies which teaches have in Svendborg can be used at other locations in UCL and disseminated to a larger group of students without further costs.

Educational Innovation and Learning Resources (EILR) was asked to develop and support the blended learning implementation strategy. EILR is an inter-faculty unit in UCL, which develops and supports digitization and learning approaches in the professional bachelor programme.

The paper addresses the potentials and the pitfalls in the blended learning implementation strategy.

The blended learning implementation strategy contains phases for preparation, development, implementation and evaluation.

The preparation phase addresses the importance of goal-setting and includes the winnings and the purpose.

The developmental phase looks into the challenges identifying needs & designing and building prototypes and the implementation phase identifies the potentials and pitfalls in testing and adjusting the blended learning courses.

Finally the evaluation phase questions how to ensure useful data.

DESIGNING AND DEVELOPING COURSES ON LITERACY AND COMPUTER INFORMATION LITERACY SKILLS

Valeria Damiani, Francesco Agrusti, Università Roma Tre, Italy

This contribution is built on an ongoing research carried out by Rome Tre University during the first year of the LIBE project (Supporting Lifelong Learning with Inquiry Based Education). The project has been funded, within the Lifelong Learning Programme, by the Education, Audio-visual and Culture Executive Agency of the European Commission (project reference number 543058-LLP-1-2013-1-IT-KA3-KA3MP).

The consortium involved in LIBE is led by Rome Tre University and is composed by Lillehammer University College (Norway), University of Twente (The Netherlands), Birkbeck University of London (UK), Faculdade de Psicologìa e de Ciências da Educação Universidade do Porto (Portugal).

LIBE project aims at offering young adults with low levels of education (16-24 years old) a set of personalized e-learning courses on transversal competences, i.e. literacy, numeracy and problem solving in technology-rich environments, in four languages (English, Italian, Norwegian, Portuguese).

The aim is to engage young and young adults in short-term, adaptive, open access e-learning modules, in anonymity. Despite it can be hard to engage low educational achievers to learn without the direct personal contact with teachers and educators, the benefits of using distance education are several. Other than the flexibility guaranteed from asynchronous learning, there is the possibility of taking advantage from an individualized, non-competitive and highly differentiated formative assessment feedback, which will allow end-users to make the most from their learning experience. LIBE courses are composed of 32 Multimedia Presentations (MPs) and 125 Learning Objects (LOs). All the learning materials produced in English were translated in the target groups' native languages (Italian, Norwegian, and Portuguese).

The present contribution concerns the development of the 63 learning objects related to literacy and computer information literacy by Rome Tre University. These LOs, that will be inserted in the LIBE Virtual Learning Environment (VLE) by fall 2015, are divided into two Learning Units (LUs). The first LU is exclusively focused on literacy, and the second one mainly concerns computer information literacy but also encompasses some activities related to literacy. The core of the development stage was related to the implementation of LU inside Moodle creating a specific sequencing pattern to obtain a mandatory learning path in order to guide the student during the course.

INTERNATIONAL VIRTUAL MOBILITIES FOR OPENING UP EDUCATION

Diana Andone, Politehnica University of Timisoara, Romania, Mark Frydenberg, Bentley University, United States of America

As new technologies are introduced into educational environments, they influence educational paradigms, methods and delivery. When free and open source software effects these disruptive technologies, there is an impact on higher education systems, resulting in a profound impact on how students learn. The Internet, the Web, and Web 2.0 technologies are the biggest examples of recent disruptive technologies. The Internet has changed the way people communicate and share information. The Web has made knowledge become omnipresent. Web 2.0 technologies enabled users to create knowledge which becomes ubiquitous.

Many of the online tools that students use in their daily lives are making their way into the classroom to foster the development of digital literacy skills. Several innovative ideas to foster the use of ICT and the development of digital literacy skills. The concept of virtual mobility can be defined as a set of ICT supported activities that realise or facilitate international, collaborative experiences in a context of teaching and/or learning it. Since 2008, the authors have offered TalkTech, an online collaboration enabling students from their universities to research technology trends, share their experiences, and create multimedia objects to present their findings. As members of international teams, they must produce a viable digital media product created working with international partners located on another continent. Throughout the six-week project they must select appropriate digital tools to support with their communication and collaboration efforts, manage time zones and technologies, and track their progress. The purpose of this collaborative project is to create a controlled work environment which models the global enterprise, where the use of web-based collaboration and communication tools are commonplace. The analysis in this paper will show how this project supports Wheeler's characteristics of digital literacy.

FLIPPED CLASSROOM: ADVANTATGES AND DISADVANTAGES OF APPLICATION

Ramon Palau, Josep G. Rovira, Universitat Rovira i Virgili, F. Seritjol, Escola l'Agulla, X. Sune, Departament d'Ensenyament, Spain

The present work falls within the network group ALEN (Active Learning Educational Networking) formed by different members of the educational community with long professional experience. This research focuses on understanding and evaluating the point of view of the students regarding the Flipped Classroom in order to be able to assess how the learning, and also the strengths and weaknesses of this methodology are perceived by them. This network is within the research group ARGET of educational technology at the University Rovira and Virgili.

ALEN group has as main objective to create a network of national and international professionals with the world of education, with the aim of introducing new active methodologies and disseminate them, and to spread the experience of the project of research and experimentation.

Concerning research the focus are on three points. Firstly, improvement of the results by comparing with other subjects or topics made with different methodology. Secondly observation of what happens during the process. Thirdly the point of view of the student as perceived learning, the strong and weak points with respect to other methodologies.

The research focuses on the experience of the student. Once you have carried out FC sessions with the students, they complete a questionnaire to evaluate the items on which the Flipped Classrooms are based: the materials proposed by the teacher, the classroom activity, the role between classmates and finally, the role with the professor. Participating teachers in the Sessions Flip or not Flip are trained in this methodology through lectures and presentations of experiences, in addition to training workshops. Once they have done these sessions, the teachers put the methodology into practice with their students, and then give their pupils the questionnaire so that they can assess the experience. By collecting data from the questionnaire created by researchers and belonging to the ALEN Working Group, the methodology can be valued and conclusions extracted in order to be able to identify those positive and negative aspects for students from its implementation, as well as the evaluation and analysis of the items discussed above.

Different research about FC found improving the academic performance of students, their motivation and their involvement, improving student critical thinking, collaboration and cooperation between equals and how to learn. This methodology, not only shows benefits in the acquisition of learning, but that they also promote a more committed, emotional learning and behaviour, the cognitive challenges, enjoying the learning process, showing a greater involvement in interventions in the classroom, thanks to increased interest from students by the teaching material proposed by the teacher.

Teaching based on this improvement, by the FC, is based on the use of time in the classroom with students, work more practical than theoretical, which favour the acquisition of knowledge in a more meaningful way. In this way one can move the passive reception of the content by the student, in order to be able to work with them in the classroom, through small groups, discussions or practical tasks, concepts that have assimilated through materials submitted by the teacher, thanks to the new technologies. As detailed in a recent study collaborative spaces, where classrooms and student desks are organized in such way that facilitate discussions in small groups, and that students have the chance to explore their own ideas promotes learning and the improvement of results. This theory also rests with the cone of Dale (1968), where he says that students remember 20% of things that explain them but can remember 90% of the things that can be done.

CAPACITY DEVELOPMENT FOR E-LEARNING – EDUCATIONAL STRATEGIES AT MID SWEDEN UNIVERSITIES

Laura Brander, J. Ola Lindberg, Mid Sweden University, Sweden

This paper aims to explore the capacity development for e-learning at Mid Sweden University since launching an educational strategy in 2011, in which e-learning was one of two priority areas for development. The goal was that Mid Sweden University would be recognized as successful in e-learning in comparison with other Swedish universities and that e-learning should be included at all levels of education, both online and on campus. According to the strategy, Mid Sweden University would be active in developing forms and methods for e-learning. As a part of this process, several academic departments started innovative e-learning projects of a model character. In the end, these projects would be implemented on a whole university scale. Four years have passed since the strategy was introduced, and five "model projects" have been implemented during that time. In which ways have these five projects helped to shape the capacity development for e-learning at Mid Sweden University?

Capacity development is understood as a process in which individuals, groups and organizations strengthen their ability to cope development towards a particular goal. In this context, capacity development may thus be seen as the process by which individual employees and departments at Mid Sweden University develop their ability to manage and improve a learning environment that is permeated by e-learning. The development aims at the strategic objectives in the educational strategy.

The empirical data consist of project documentation (project reports and conference papers) and interviews with key persons of the projects. A method of content analysis of qualitative data, where the content is coded and grouped under specific themes, was used. Here, the content analysis had a deductive approach and focused on four aspects/themes that are considered important for capacity development for e-learning, namely *pedagogy, communication, technology* and *organizational systems*. How are these aspects highlighted in the project reports and the interviews? What new e-learning tools, methods, communication tools, and organizational models have been introduced at the Mid Sweden University since 2011 and how has this contributed to the capacity development for e-learning at individual, group, and organizational levels?

The analysis shows that the educational strategy for e-learning and the five model projects have contributed to both cultural and structural change at Mid Sweden University. The capacity development for e-learning has been stimulated and the preconditions for achieving educational objectives of the strategy have been strengthened by the introduction of new technologies, pedagogical methods, communicational, and organizational systems. Capacity development has occurred on several levels within the organization and the four studied themes are highly integrated with each other. Individual employees and departments at Mid Sweden University have developed their ability to manage and enhance a learning environment that is permeated by e-learning, for example by introducing blended learning and mobile learning as teaching methods. The most obvious changes have occurred within the departments that participated in the projects, and the administration, where the front desk function (case management system) was introduced.

However, this study also implies that the management of the university should increase its efforts, to change the organization so that teachers would get more space for their individual capacity development and course development, which in turn can enhance the quality and sustainability of university education in whole. It remains to be found out whether and to what extent four of these model projects will be applied to other parts of the university. University management's role will be crucial in this matter.

EFFECTIVE LEARNING STRATEGIES: MAKING SENSE OF AND WITH LEARNING BY MEANS OF $B^2R^2SDL^3$ AND S2S*

Ignatius G.P. Gous, Univeristy of South Africa, South Africa

The goal of teaching any subject or course is not merely to get students to master current content and skills, but to assist students to become self-directed lifelong learners who can continue to grow in and even lead the field they choose to navigate. The reality is, however, that students do not know how to study properly, or they use study strategies that are ineffective, such as rote learning, underlining, rereading and massed practice. This is the case, in spite of current and reliable research indicating how to learn effectively. Therefore the following research questions have been posed.

1. What does neuro-educational research say about study strategies – which strategies are effective and which are not?
2. How do students study – what strategies do they use, how effective are they, how aware and how satisfied are the students about their own study strategies?
3. What is the effect of the S2S study strategy intervention program on the awareness about, use of and performance as the result of study strategies used by students?

The presentation is an interim report on the process, outcomes and findings of an action-based research process where ten Medical, Dentistry and Veterinary students followed the 6 week *Study 2 Succeed* (S2S) program on Self-knowledge, Focus, Listening, Reading, Memorising, Performing and Application skills. At the end of the intervention the participants evaluated the usefulness of the strategies taught in the program, and their performance was compared to their previous results in tests and exams. All the students reported positively about the program, and rated their study strategies, skills and habits as being more effective than before. All the students also reported higher marks – as much as 20% – than in previous years (granting the difficulty to attribute better performance to the intervention in the light of so many variables involved).

The results point in the direction that learning (and teaching) should heed the formula **$B^2R^2SDL^3$**: it should be Brain-based, Reality Related, Self-Directed Life-Long Learning. Each of these aspects is discussed. The results have implications for how lecturers should teach subject content in ways that also develop the ability to master content, both in face-to-face and in distance education settings.

* **$B^2R^2SDL^3$** = Brain-based, Reality Related, Self-Directed Life-Long Learning.
S2S = a project called *Study 2 Succeed*

COMPETENCE FRAMEWORKS IN AGRICULTURE – PACT

Thomas Kretschmer, Christian M. Stracke, University of Duisburg-Essen, German, Cleo Sgouropoulou, Elisa Ninou, Technical Educational Institute of Athens, Greece, Carmen Müller, DLG-Academy, Germany

Background

Agriculture is suffering from a lack in qualified employees as well as appropriate, tailored-made and modularised VET opportunities. The demand for qualified farm workers and managers is not satisfied by an adequate supply of properly trained staff or training opportunities. Thus, Competence Modelling is raising the awareness and interest of all stakeholders in lifelong learning in the agricultural sector. It is gaining importance for organisations and their human resource development, for employees and individual learners, for education and training providers as well as for political decision maker.

In this context, the following can be observed:

- Many VET providers offer trainings for the agricultural sectors, which do already address the needs of a changing agricultural labour market or current EU/national policies, training opportunities of the ACT consortium members;
- Some VET providers have modularised their trainings, introduced the learning outcomes approach which in fact facilitates the update with units from "peer institutions" which address labour market needs to a certain extend.

The "Pathways for Agricultural Competence and skills based Training" (PACT) framework

On the basis of desk research and focus groups/interviews in several European countries, the PACT framework was derived. It contributes to making definitions of competences reusable and accessible across learning and recruitment systems, thus facilitating the development of additional services related to the generation of personal profiles, achieved learning outcomes and competences. The PACT framework - matching emerging job profiles and existing training opportunities - links training opportunities and units of training to learning outcomes, the expression of job profiles through the use of competence descriptions and the generation of personal profiles of achieved learning outcomes and competences. Thematically, PACT is limited to competences concerning innovation and management.

Competences and skills in PACT:

- Systemic, holistic thinking and sustainability
- Self-management
- The capacity for interaction
- Organic farming
- Technical and scientific innovation
- Further agriculturally related sources of income (incl. renewable energies)
- Business administration/management.

The seven thematic dimensions in combination with five competence levels (in alignment with the level descriptions of the European Qualifications Framework – EQF) also allow a quantitative comparison to match profiles with requirements.

Due to its generic approach, PACT can also be used to describe overlapping professional fields or can easily be adapted to other thematic fields.

For further info, please go to http://www.act-now.eu

A VALUE CREATION FRAMEWORK FOR AN ONLINE PROFESSIONAL LEARNING COMMUNITY

Gaëlle Le Bot, Lina Xue, Wim Van Petegem, Astrid Van Wieringen· KU Leuven, Belgium

As economic constraints leave fewer resources available for professional development, researchers and practitioners have become increasingly interested in the interplay between learning, community and technology. They are examining the potential of online communities of practice (CoP) to enhance and extend traditional professional development opportunities. They support the idea that participation in a learning community leads to change practice behaviours. According to Booth and Kellogg (2014), in online CoP, practitioners "co-construct new forms of meaning and understanding in ways that are individually and collectively valuable, and apply that knowledge in their professional practice".

In addition, for supporting professional development opportunities and continuing education, e-learning technology revolutionise learning and life-long learning for example, in supporting resources and guidelines for participation that are appealing and valuable for busy practitioners. The potential of e-learning technology is to extend professional development opportunities in terms of information and community resources available with the benefits of connectivity, flexibility and interactivity. E-learning technology should be seen as an interactive tool to support the active involvement of the learner with peers in sharing and creating new knowledge.

Our project is to combine learning, community and e-learning technology in the health sector. This project is part of an European FP7 training network, iCARE (**i**mproving **C**hildren's **A**uditory **Re**habilitation), which aims at training a community of people with different approaches and expertise in different fields and specializations. This community of people includes researchers, audiologists, educators, teachers, speech therapists, caregivers, parents and deaf children who are part of the same professional network. For the inclusion of children with hearing impairment in the oral society, they pursue – with different levels of expertise and experience – a common goal: the development of communication and social skills in these children.

In that context, we aim to develop an online professional learning community (PLC) which will permit all members of that community – individually and collectively – to extend their professional and personal development opportunities through different types of e-learning activities, tools and interactions. This PLC, as a CoP will be characterized by the creation and sharing of user-generated materials, improving the auditory rehabilitation of children with hearing impairment. This PLC involving parents and other caregivers into the children's learning experience will enable sustained mutual engagement of all professionals, allowing them to explore good practice, articulate perspectives, accumulate knowledge and create a shared context for ongoing exchanges.

TRANSFORMING, EXPANDING AND ENRICHING LEARNING SCENARIOS WITH COOPERATIVE LEARNING IN SELF-PACED COURSES

Luis Guadarrama, Josh Evans, Cindy Ives, Corinne Bosse, Athabasca University, Canada

The Project (Evaluation in progress): Exploratory Evaluation Survey

The poster summarizes the work-in-progress for the evaluation of the redesigned online self-paced course Human Geography 302: The Canadian North. With the goal of enhancing students' performance, expanding the learning scenarios and enriching students' learning scope, the course was fully redesigned using cooperative learning strategies. Learning design with a critical-thinking approach was adopted. An exploratory evaluation survey was designed to learn about how much students think the new learning design facilitates and enriches their learning.

The Problem – Concerns before Redesigning the Course:

- Students were complaining about isolation - Students-students interaction did not exist in any way
- Students' engagement was low and drop-outs and failure was somehow high
- Students were not making sense of the cultural, geographical, and economic richness of the Canadian North,
- Limited learning scope: students limited their learning scope to their own particular experience
- Despite students had no contact, they limited the topics for their assignments to the same traditional topics

Purpose and Significance of the Study

This study is intended to determine the views of students on cooperative learning. The study intends to inform and persuade professors and subject matter experts in Athabasca University (and beyond our community) about the positive implications and benefits that cooperative learning has for students in self-paced courses. The outcome of the study could form the basis for further research that could potentially determine whether or not cooperative learning strategies should be promoted for designing undergrad self-paced courses.

The Survey

The survey is available online and takes 5-10 minutes for students. The survey was reviewed by AU learning designers, the course coordinator, by tutors and other AU researchers with a wide experience in educational research.

Evaluation Core Questions

- What are students' attitudes towards cooperative learning in individualized online self-paced courses?
- To what degree cooperative learning fosters students' deeper understanding of the subject matter?
- To what extent cooperative learning enriches students learning experience? To what degree cooperative learning fosters students' engagement?
- To what extent do students think cooperative learning enriches their learning scope in the course?
- To what extent students perceive that cooperative learning strategies foster positive attitudes towards learning?
- To what extent sequenced assignments give students a better sense of developing disciplinary skills?
- To what extent formative assessment gives students better opportunities to meet learning goals successfully?

Preliminary Findings (Evaluation is in Progress)

Preliminary findings show a modest improvement on students' performance after GEOG 302 was fully redesigned (January 2014). The percentage of students getting better grades seems to be increasing whereas students getting lower grades seem to be diminishing, indicating greater students' engagement. Failure and dropouts seem to be decreasing too. The study will conclude on December 2015.

DISTANCE LEARNING FOR ADULT LEARNERS – NEEDS AND CONSIDERATIONS

Khalil Alsaadat, King Saud University Saudia Arabia

The number of nontraditional students has grown more rapidly than the number of traditional students (U.S. Department of Education, 2001). The growth of nontraditional adult enrollment in higher education demands a different and more flexible delivery system to meet students' needs. Distance learning is designed to ensure compatibility with the characteristics and needs of the adult learner. By retaining their jobs while attending school, adult learners are able to continue to gain in work experience while pursuing educational goals. Kuhlmann provided some considerations when building e learning courses for adults they are as follows:

- **Set clear expectations and objectives**. Let them know why they are taking the course and what they should be learning. People like to get oriented and know what's expected of them.
- **Adult learners don't like to fail** and they don't like to fail publicly. Make it clear when they are being tested and when they aren't.
- **Create an environment where they have as much freedom as possible**. Let them click around and explore. I know that many customers want to lock navigation so that they "get all of the information." This is faulty thinking. If they need to confirm their grasp of the information, then give them exercises to practice applying it so they can demonstrate their understanding in a real way.
- **Give them ways to collect information**. This is a great way to counter the locked navigation issue. Create situations where they need to make decisions and then free up the navigation to collect the information needed to make decisions. This is a much better way to assess understanding than viewing a screen full of text.
- **Focus on relevance**. I've worked on plenty of projects where the learners are never considered. I recall one company I worked for that wouldn't let me talk to any potential learners, even though we were rolling the training out to 3500 people across the country. If your content isn't relevant to the learners, they'll just tune out and you're wasting time and money. You can guarantee that little learning will happen.
- **Create a visual design that is friendly and inviting**. This helps with the initial engagement and sets the tone of the course. I've had customers tell me that they can't do that because the subject matter was real important and serious. So they needed to have a very serious tone (read boring). If it's important, than it makes sense to create a course that's as visually inviting as possible.
- **E-learning is a multimedia experience** so it makes sense to leverage as much of the multimedia as you can (in context though). You don't want to add multimedia for the sake of it, but you do want to use all of your resources to create the best course possible.
- **Free Willy!** People are like orcas with floppy dorsal fins. They yearn to be free. One of the worst experiences in e learning is when the course navigation is locked. There are better ways to help people learn. Focus on relevant, decision-making scenarios. And if you're building compliance, click-and-read course with no performance expectations, then make the course as simple as possible so that the learners can get in and out. Don't frustrate them or waste their time with a bunch of extra branched scenarios. Tell them what they need to know and let them go.

Do you need to test everything? Every day we take in all sorts of information that is critical to meeting our goals. When my boss sends an email detailing new plans, he doesn't follow it up with a quiz. Assessing a person's understanding is an important part of learning, but do we need to always have a test? In many ways it retards the learning process. As soon as people find out they're being tested, they quit learning and focus on how to pass the test. If you don't need a test, don't include one. If you do need to assess their understanding, perhaps there's a better way to do so.

BUILDING A LEADERSHIP CULTURE

Bruce Chaloux, Southern Region Education Board, Lawrence C. Ragan, Penn State World Campus, United States of America, Brian Mulligan, Sligo Institute of Technology, Ireland

The worldwide growth of online learning has created significant opportunities for higher education institutions globally, bringing many new institutions into the distance education community and transforming the role of distance education in other institutions. We are now well into the second decade of e-learning. Many of the pioneering e-learning leaders in our institutions are nearing retirement or moving on to broader leadership roles. To ensure effective succession planning, we need at this time to develop the next generation of leaders, preparing them as change agents and managers in the field.

The Sloan Consortium and the Penn State World Campus are proposing to offer at the 2011 EDEN conference a workshop focused on emerging leaders in e-learning programs. This 90-minute workshop will feature senior U.S. and European leaders in the field, using a tested model of working with professionals on leadership issues areas related to unit operations, institutional policy, and personal leadership style.

"Building a Leadership Culture" is an outgrowth of the Institute for Emerging Leaders in Online Learning (IELOL), a collaboration between the Sloan Consortium and the Penn State World Campus in the United States. Since 2009, the Institute has brought together an international community of more than 60 educators designated by their institution as emerging leaders who, along with senior leaders from the Sloan Consortium, have worked to create change leaders for the future. This effort built on the success of the Administrative Leadership Institute, a workshop held for several years by the two organizations as part of the annual Sloan Consortium Worldwide Conference.

The proposed workshop is modeled after those successful programs and will use the Sloan Consortium's five "pillars of quality" to illustrate the different operational and policy dimensions involved in building a leadership culture in a university-based e-learning operation. These quality pillars embody the ideals of online education in a quick, holistic view of continuous quality improvement and provide a helpful framework for the challenges of leadership. The pillars include:

1. **Access** – All learners who wish to learn online have the opportunity and can achieve success.
2. **Learning Effectiveness** – The provider demonstrates that online learning outcomes meet or exceed institutional, industry, and/or community standards.
3. **Student Satisfaction** – Students are successful in learning online and are typically pleased with their experiences.
4. **Faculty Satisfaction** – Faculty achieve success with teaching online, citing appreciation and happiness.
5. **Scale (Cost Effectiveness and Commitment)** – Institutions continuously improve services while reducing cost to achieve capacity enrollment.

Around this framework, three strategic leadership areas will be addressed:

- **Operational Leadership** –This section of the workshop with identify leadership issues, challenges and strategies in each of the five quality pillars.
- **Policy Leadership** – This section of the workshop will focus on leadership strategies needed to address both institutional and external policy issues related to creating a transformative innovation in the mainstream of a higher education institution. In many institutions, e-learning began as an innovation that operated outside the institutional mainstream. Today, e-learning is becoming recognized as a transformative innovation that will help institutions adapt to changing societal and individual learner needs. Increasingly, emerging leaders need to work within the mainstream to achieve sustainable success.
- **Personal Leadership Style** – This section of the workshop will explore several dimensions of personal leadership style needed to create change in this kind of institutional culture. Many leadership development programs grow out of corporate management experience. However, higher education is a unique social institution, regardless of how it is funded. Leading change in this unique environment requires personal and professional skills that are better suited to a large and often decentralized community.

AN INTRODUCTION TO MOOC DESIGN BY THE EMMA TEAM

Deborah Arnold, Université de Bourgogne, France, Sally Reynolds, ATiT, Belgium

Introduction

MOOCs continue to be a hot topic and knowledge of MOOC design practice is evolving constantly, as we analyse the shortcomings of some of the early MOOCs (transmissive approach, lack of engagement, learner isolation, etc.). This workshop brings together experts from the EMMA project, with experience in pedagogical design, production and MOOC facilitation to engage participants in questioning their own design approaches for an optimal learner experience. In order to get the most out of this workshop, participants should have at least an idea for a MOOC they plan to create, either as a teacher or as a media producer or learning technologist.

Workshop concept and aims

In this practical workshop we will take you through the different types of popular MOOCs currently available, cMOOCs, xMOOCs, sMOOCs etc and help you to understand the pedagogical and design implications of each. Part of this workshop will include a review of your ideas and current state of planning with known experts in the field of MOOC design and delivery. We will also share with you the general experiences of some of the EMMA MOOC providers where they will explain why they made certain choices in relation to MOOC design. By the end of the workshop we expect that you will have decided on the basic design features of your own MOOC.

In order to get the most out of this workshop, participants should have at least initial ideas for a MOOC they plan to create, either as a teacher or as a media producer or learning technologist.

The aim of the workshop is to give participants insights into MOOC design and to enable them to draft an initial outline of design for a MOOC of their choice (or to work on an example provided by the facilitators).

Working methods

Participants will have the opportunity to work collaboratively on their own MOOC design issues, or on examples provided by the facilitators. They will work in small groups (ideally 5 people max). The optimal number of face to face participants is thus 15. For the online group, we suggest a maximum of 10.

Each group will be expected to produce a concrete outcome, in the form of a poster, summarising and illustrating their design choices. Large sheets of paper, coloured pens and post-its will be made available. These posters will be photographed for publication on social media and for further use.

Facilities for an online group to participate via web conference will be provided. A specific task will be suggested to the online group (for example Q&A with an expert or a collaborative design activity) who will also have time to present their outcomes to the face to face group.

Workshop structure

1. Quick introductions of participants: who I am, my previous experience of MOOCs (as learner, teacher producer), what I expect to get out of the workshop.
2. Basic characteristics of xMOOCs / cMOOCs / sMOOCs
3. Design principles
4. Practical activity in small groups
5. According to the needs and interests expressed in the round the table introduction, participants will form small groups around a common topic. Each group will be facilitated by a member of the EMMA team.
6. The following themes are examples of what each group might focus on:
   - General principles of MOOC design
   - Designing and producing engaging videos
   - Designing individual and collaborative learning activities
7. Feedback – each group has 5' to present their outcomes (3 groups from the face to face session + a possible online group)

LEARNING ANALYTICS – WHAT DATA COULD TELL IF WE WERE WILLING TO SHARE INFORMATION. EXPLORING BENEFITSAAND BARRIERS TO THE USE OF ANALYTICS IN SCHOOLS AND UNIVERSITIES

Tore Hoel, Oslo and Akershus University College of Applied Sciences, Norway, Sally Reynolds, ATiT, Belgium, Dai Griffiths, CETIS, University of Bolton, United Kingdom

The increasing amount of data generated in digital learning contexts provides opportunities to benefit from learning analytics as well as challenges related to interoperability, privacy, and pedagogical and organizational models. When translating learning into numbers all kinds of discourse emerge, especially when the promise is that learners, teachers, local authorities, companies and others soon will have tools that make the churning and interpretation of these numbers available for all with a device. Enthusiasts and sceptics form positions, and the battle to come is less exciting for the many stakeholders that are oriented towards step-by-step improvements of learning based on sound evidence, within ethical boundaries.

Design of learning analytics applications must be based on requirements from the learners and teachers that will use the tools. Therefore, there is a need to engage these stakeholders in a discourse on benefits and constraints, ensuring that the conversation is documented and made available as input to design.

EDEN15 Workshop organised by the LACE project

New learning technologies using learning analytics have a great potential to optimise educational planning, personalise the learning experiences, and enhance teaching. Learning analytics (LA) is not possible without access to data, emanating from the different activities of the learners and their support. The large-scale production, collection, aggregation, and processing of information from various learning platforms and online environments have led to ethical and privacy concerns regarding potential harm to individuals and society.

Objectives of the workshop

Concerns about privacy, control of data, and trust are identified as a major barrier to benefit from new learning analytics tools. If we are to put to good use the new tools we, as learners and teachers need to share our data to make them available for analysis. This interactive workshop will

- give a short introduction to the current state of art in learning analytics,
- map the concerns participants have about getting access to and sharing data for learning analytics,
- discuss and agree upon feasible solutions for data sharing following a structured approach.

This workshop will give an update on the development of LA applications in schools and higher education and explore the concerns about data sharing and privacy, control of data and trust. We aim to understand the issues with greater clarity, and to find ways of overcoming the issues and research challenges related to ethical and privacy aspects of learning analytics practice. The workshop is highly interactive and will through a simple, but structured and well-tested process engage the participants in finding solutions that could be accepted in European schools and universities.

The workshop is organised by the LACE project, the Learning Analytics Community Exchange instrument funded by EU's 7th Framework Programme to integrate communities working on LA and Educational Data Mining from schools, workplace and universities. LACE has organised a series of workshops on ethics and privacy helping to build an awareness in Europe and internationally on these issues; code of practice for learning analytics; and a taxonomy of ethical, legal and logistical issues of learning analytics. The workshop series and results are documented at the LACE project website: www.laceproject.eu.

EMPOWERING UNIVERSITIES: THE TRANSITION OF EUROPEAN HIGHER EDUCATION TO NEW MODES OF TEACHING AND LEARNING

George Ubachs, European Association of Distance Teaching Universities, the Netherlands

Workshop organizing committee

EMPOWER is initiated by EADTU, the European Association of Distance Teaching Universities. The objective of the EMPOWER project is to support policy reform in European higher education with regard to the transition of European higher education to new modes of teaching and learning. The project is supporting innovation in practices of new modes of teaching and learning. New modes of teaching and learning will have an impact on the reform of mainstream higher education for 18-25 students, open and flexible education for 25+ students (incl. CPD) and the emerging area of open education (OERs, MOOCs). However, European universities still face problems with regard to the implementation of new modes of teaching and learning. Main issues are that traditional formats are often copied into ICT based formats without the added value of new pedagogies; missing strategies and frameworks and staff has to overcome a resistance against change.

The objectives of the EMPOWER programme are:

- to better exploit the potential of ICTs to enhance the quality of teaching and learning;
- to develop new institutional strategies, organisational and business models for different application areas;
- to involve and commit national/regional governments and stakeholders to promote and stimulate implementation.

EMPOWER covers 12 fully operational pools of expertise on all relevant fields of new modes of teaching and learning. The initiative involves more than a hundred experts from all over Europe.

The European Association of Distance Teaching Universities (EADTU) is Europe's leading institutional association in online, open and flexible higher education, and is at the heart of the modernisation agenda of European universities. Growing from its eleven founding members in ten European nations, EADTU now has a membership of fifteen institutions and fourteen national associations across 25 nations. Its membership covers over 200 universities and around 3 million students.

Workshop format

The EMPOWER Workshop will be a combination of presentation, discussion and hands-on practice. The workshop attendees will be introduced to the concept of EMPOWERing Universities – the 12 pools of expertise linked to new modes of teaching and learning, the approach by expert pools, associate universities and visiting experts.

The workshop will be divided into two groups, who separately are assigned to the discussion of the following topics: i) Curriculum development and course design ii) Institutional policy development for new modes of teaching. The first group will be chaired by Lourdes Guàrdia, Professor and researcher of the eLearn Center at Universidade Oberta de Catalunia (UOC). The second group will be chaired by Mark Brown, Director at the National Institute for Digital Learning, Ireland.

Afterwards, all group results and experiences will be discussed. Also feedback on the EMPOWER initiative will be collected.

For more information, please visit the EMPOWER website: http://empower.eadtu.eu

TOWARDS LOW-COST PRODUCTION OF MOOCS

Brian Mulligan, Institute of Technology Sligo, Ireland, Miquel Duran, Silvia Simon, University of Girona, Spain, Jörn Loviscach, Fachhochschule Bielefeld, Germany, Gráinne Conole, Bath Spa University, United Kingdom

Are MOOCs financially viable? How can MOOCs be developed where projected audiences are relatively small? Would this be less of an issue if MOOCs could be developed at lower cost? The aim of LoCoMoTion, an Erasmus+ funded project, is to investigate and disseminate low-cost MOOC development techniques. The highly experienced team, from five higher education institutions across Europe, will present on various techniques, both before and during the workshop, to a local and distributed audience. They will facilitate discussion before, during and after the event through electronic and face-to-face methods. The workshop will be presented under four topic headings. Each of the four topics will be delivered as a short (6-minute) presentation directly to the audience and simultaneously as a webinar using Google Hangouts on Air. These presentations will also be pre-recorded and published online before the event to initiate reflection and discussion before the conference delivery. (Access to the Hangout will be published shortly before the start of the workshop and the link, along with links to the pre-recorded presentations can be found at moocs4all.eu) Each of the four short presentations will be followed by a moderated discussion among local and online participants.

1. Content development, sourcing and hosting of MOOCs
   The production of videos and interactive material such as quizzes is a major cost factor. Lean approaches focus on the value for learning rather than on production value. Staying with "good enough" rather than "looks like a professional TV show" also helps to produce much more material (e.g. lots of worked examples) and limits the loss when material has to be updated and redone. Using freehand sketches done live also relieves one of obtaining permissions for existing photographs or diagrams. This topic will cover practices that can be used to minimise the workload in producing content such as videos and quizzes, while maximising the quality. It will also cover the use of openly available materials from other sources.
2. Pedagogical Approaches, Communication and Support of MOOCs
   This topic will explore the pedagogical options available to developers for free large scale courses. As well as addressing the xMOOC/cMOOC debate, it will address how peer-to-peer communication and support can be both used to facilitate deeper learning without generating an excessive workload. Indeed one of the key issues is maximizing registration in the course and minimizing dropout rates. Thus, the convenience of a well-balanced team (and time scheduling) will be considered. Furthermore the connection between MOOCs and actual openness will be addressed (closed forums vs internet forums, internal vs external social networks, etc.)
3. Institutional Services
   Institutions may wish to use experts within their own organisations to create MOOCs that may not have high levels of technical skills or knowledge. This topic will explore the types of facilities and services that can be provided to subject matter experts to facilitate the creation of MOOCs at reasonable cost.
4. Assessment and Accreditation
   This topic will cover scalable assessment methods used in MOOCs such as objective tests, automated essay grading and peer assessment. In addition, it will address the relationship of assessment to the awarding of certificates of completion through to the awarding of accredited college awards. This will include financial models being proposed to make such approaches viable and will include the concepts of "disaggregation" and Competency Based Education.

SMOOCS FOR ALL, ALL IN SMOOCS: DISCUSSING THE SOCIAL SIDE OF MASSIVE OPEN LEARNING EXPERIENCES WITH THE ECO PARTNERSHIP

Divina Frau-Meigs, University Sorbonne Nouvelle, France

The emergence of the MOOC phenomena in Europe has been dominated by a concern of the research community towards the over dominance of course design models which are inadequate both pedagogically and culturally. As such, there is a quest for alternative approaches that can meet high pedagogical quality standards and represent traditional European educational values, as social equity and multiculturalism. In the framework of the European-funded project ECO (Elearning, Communication and Open-data: Massive Mobile, Ubiquitous and Open Learning – http://ecolearning.eu/our-project) a new pedagogical model was developed, called the sMOOC. This model is an alternative model to existent approaches, namely the xMOOC and the cMOOC. The ECO sMOOC pedagogical model and its additional conceptual tool – pedagogical framework – make possible a flexible implementation adjusting its features to diverse institutional scenarios and personas.

In this workshop, 16 of these European sMOOCs (social massive open online courses) will be presented and the results of its development and implementation discussed. Participants will be invited to take part in an interactive session sharing ideas and experiences. Critical aspects of MOOC development and delivery will be analyzed, as instructional design, pedagogical design, learning scenarios, technical requirements (platform and mobile devices), interaction, resources, performances, assessment, gamification, eQuality, accessibility, juridical aspects, scalability, virtual mobility in heterogeneous teams for creation, business plan, factors of resistance, and sMOOC management.

Members from the ECO project will animate the workshop, which is divided in 4 different moments:

1. Presentation of the European sMOOCs experience carried out in the framework of the ECO Project, including 16 sMOOCs selected practices;
2. Interactive group work focusing on two selected aspects from the ones mentioned above;
3. Each group will report on the work done, presenting the main streams of discussion;
4. The group reports will be commented by ECO project experts and then discussed by all participants;
5. Conclusions will be drawn regarding the contribution of the sMOOCs experience for the establishment of a new concept for European MOOCs.

LOST IN TRANSITION? D-TRANSFORM AS A COMPASS FOR THE USE OF ICT TO TRANSFORM THE HIGHER EDUCATION SYSTEM

Paul Bacsich, Sero Consulting, United Kingdom

Many universities at last have a reasonable grasp of the learning technology and pedagogic aspects of e-learning and have installed adequate IT systems and staff development to deliver e-learning. However, as universities move from incremental change involving early adopters to step-change and then massification in e-learning, the role and skill set of leaders becomes increasingly important – in fact an increasingly important barrier. Thus it becomes important to hear from leaders with knowledge and experience of how to overcome these barriers.

The aim of the workshop is to demonstrate to participants how senior staff have navigated through the problems of change management in institutions and from their experiences and those of the audience draw lessons on what are the crucial barriers and how to surmount them.

The invited senior staffs are drawn from various countries and types of higher education institution: Belinda Tynan, Pro vice-chancellor Learning and Teaching in the Open University UK; Jim Devine, consultant to the EU modernisation agenda for schools and higher education; former President, Dun Laoghaire Institute of Art, Design and Technology; András Benedek, former secretary of state of education in Hungary, director of the Institute of Applied Pedagogy and Psychology at the Budapest University of Technology and Economics; Clive Mulholland, Principal and Vice-Chancellor of the University of the Highlands and Islands.

The workshop is the first public event of the D-TRANSFORM project. The project aims to set up a "University Leader Program" at the European level, addressed to university presidents and vice-presidents on the role of e-Education in shaping University strategies. It gathers together specialists of e-Education from various institutions (University, higher education ministries, consultancy in learning innovation, e-Education networks) and primarily considers that digital technologies, like Massive Open Online Courses, (MOOCs) and Open Educational Resources are an essential lever for transforming the higher education systems and adapting them to the new needs of youth and requirements of work-market (lifelong training).

D-TRANSFORM intends to produce recommendations on various aspects of a university strategy on the use of digital tools. Based on these recommendations two "leadership schools" will be set up, dedicated, for the 1st time in Europe, to the university governances. Through leadership schools, the project's goal is to help university governing bodies to define their own digital strategies and coordinate them with public policies defined at the European/national level; and finally, to plan e-education according to the university needs and profile.

CULTURAL GAPS AND SOLUTIONS FOR EDUCATION IN INTERNATIONAL SETTINGS

Thomas Richter, Thomas Kretschmer, University of Duisburg-Essen, Germany

Increasing globalisation and mobility of learners and faculty is inevitably reflected in a wider range of cultural diversity in educational scenarios. On the one hand, increased cultural diversity presents itself as a very positive development: It helps learners to achieve competences in intercultural communication and collaboration. On the other hand, if the learners' experiences are not accordingly reflected, frustration through perceived intercultural conflicts could emerge. Loss of motivation could be a consequence, which is directly related to higher dropout rates. We consider education as a process in which learners are guided on their way to transform experiences into knowledge. Thus, we are looking for ways to support both students and educators, to better understand and deal with socio-cultural diversity in education.

With the 2008 started and on-going "Learning Culture Survey", we aim to foster the implementation of culture-sensitive education. The motivation of this study is based on the need for better understanding of the reasons for intercultural conflicts in education. When aiming at the reduction of (unintended) cultural conflicts in educational scenarios and support of students to keep their motivation on the highest possible level, these issues are particularly pertinent to international learning scenarios, such as in Internet-based Technology Enhanced Learning (TEL), or urban education. In order to investigate and contrast a vast number of national contexts, our standardized questionnaire has been translated into a multitude of languages. We already were able to collect and analyse data in/from several countries, such as Bulgaria, Cameroon, Germany, Ghana, South Korea, Turkey, and Ukraine. While some of the studies were not fully representative, we achieved a good impression of what to expect in future studies. In 2014, we started investigations in France, and prepared environments for China, Greece, Japan, and Portugal.

Our hitherto accumulated insights led to a higher awareness regarding the character and possible impact of cultural diversity in education. As for practical scenarios, the results are being used to:

- Improve the preparative work of students and faculty members in terms of mobility;
- Support the students' and instructors' development of intercultural competences;
- Determine preventive activities to avoid cultural conflicts;
- Design culture-sensitive learning contents;
- Sensitise moderators of international learning groups regarding cultural conflict potential;
- Define conflict potential for learning resources that are to be adapted to new contexts.

The latter issue is eminent for the reuse of educational material, which is defined as one of the major advantages of TEL and is particularly relevant for the further exploitation of Open Educational Resources.

The Workshop

The workshop follows an action-research design, will take 90 minutes, and focuses on the following three goals:

- raising the awareness of and sensitising the participants for culture-related issues in education;
- providing a structured and facilitated environment for the participants to share intercultural experiences amongst each other in order to better understand other countries' educational contexts and jointly finding tailor-made solutions for already arisen issues;
- inviting the participants to join forces for the further exploitation of the Learning Culture Survey.

Virtual attendance of participants is welcome and possible.

"A JOURNEY TO THE 'OPEN DISCOVERY SPACE': PLEASE FASTEN YOUR SEAT BELTS!" – IMPACT AND SUSTAINABILITY OF INNOVATIVE E-LEARNING PORTALS – USER PERSPECTIVES ON PORTALS' VALUE PROPOSITIONS

Lampros Stergioulas, Munir Abbasi, Georgios Xydopoulos, Maria Fragkaki, University of Surrey, United Kingdom, Marlies Bitter-Rijpkema, Open University of the Netherlands, The Netherlands, Alan Bruce, Universal Learning Systems, Ireland, Christian M. Stracke, University of Duisburg-Essen, Germany

This workshop demonstrates the best practices and lessons learnt from the Open Discovery Space (ODS) project. The ODS project has developed an innovative eLearning portal and a large variety of community services and tools that enable teachers to better respond to open innovation digital disruptions in classroom creativity and to adapt learning materials, resources, scenarios, tools, and technologies to individual student's learning needs, and thus to revolutionise the communities of practice in eLearning.

A journey to the "Open Discovery Space" will drive you to an innovative eLearning planet. ODS caters for individual student's learning needs and communities of practice needs as well, paving the way for a pedagogical revolution in the educational space. ODS offers a unified infrastructure that connects the schools and other educational institutions, and the teachers Globally as well as facilitating collaborative innovation and the exchange of experiences, policies and educational materials and resources.

Most importantly, this community-oriented social learning platform goes beyond the existing OER practices by enabling and facilitating its stakeholders to actively collaborate, innovative, create and co-create new ideas and open resources tailor-made to best reflect their interests and requirements. Moreover, we will interact through activities from teachers' best practices, discovering some of the challenges of utilizing an eLearning portal that will offer a great value to the educational community. The main topics under discussion will be: integrating community building options for learning in the school, ODS innovation model, resources, best practices and new digital learning and teaching technologies/tools for the teachers to enhance their skills, competence, networks building, innovation, creativity, and impact assessment of learning interventions and usability.

OPEN EDUCATION AND INTERNATIONALISATION: ARE YOU UP TO THE CHALLENGE

Fabio Nascimbeni, Universidad Internacional de la Rioja, Brazil

The workshop aims at discussing, starting from the findings of the eMundus project, the potential of OER, MOOCs and Virtual Mobility to support long-term, balanced and inter-cultural academic partnership.

During the workshop, participants will be engaged in a number of reflections on how international collaboration in the Higher Education sector is changing due – among other issue – to the Open Education revolution. A number of cases from the eMundus Atlas will be presented and discussed that are implementing "transformative partnerships" by using Open Education solutions, exploring with the audience how these can be replicated internationally.

HANDS-ON COLLABORATION FOR OPEN EDUCATION: SHARE YOUR EXPERTISE AND IDEAS ON OPEN COURSES, TEXTBOOKS AND EDUCATIONAL SOFTWARE

Henri Pirkkalainen, University of Jyväskylä, Finland, Jan Pawlowski, Ruhr West University of Applied Sciences, Anne-Christin Tannhäuser, ESCP Europe Business School Berlin, Germany

The proposed workshop titled "Hands-On Collaboration for Open Education: Share your Expertise and Ideas on Open Courses, Textbooks and Educational Software" targets learning practitioners. This workshop will provide a networking opportunity to all those willing to support new initiatives in open education. The aim is to further sparkle collaborations on OER across the EDEN community starting from the very beginning of an idea creation and support with expertise at different stages of the OER life cycle.

Recent years have been marked by a strong movement towards Open Education, with the proliferation of educational material distributed under open licenses for anyone to use and/or re-purpose. At present, despite the vast amount of available resources, OER reuse is still not a common practice, and OER solutions are suffering either on low uptake or educators are merely passive users of knowledge. Underlying social inhibitors include absence of technical skills, unwillingness to share or use resources produced by someone else. Compared to the scale of opportunity that open contents hold, few educators currently possess either the skills to exploit it, or the confidence to create and innovate in a digital world. The OER re-use and adaptation to new contexts is also hampered by motivational barriers and the not-invented here-syndrome.

The approach of the "Open Educational Ideas" initiative addresses those issues by connecting educators and learners at the earliest stage of OER development through an online platform customized to support open course, material and textbook development.

The workshop will be facilitated by the **OEI2 project,** evolving around the promotion of innovative educational practices using open means, i.e. open learning resources and tools. In the first part, emerging approaches and methodologies will be shortly introduced and intensively discussed with the audience. The importance of engaging users at an early stage of the OER development process will be discussed. The presentation will focus on introducing an Idea Space that supports distributed idea development. The second part of the workshop will include hands-on working in two modes: Share your own idea and invite colleagues or Support initiatives of others: Adding, commenting, advice on further OER and potential collaborations. Group findings will be then discussed in plenum.

In addition to creating OER in a collaborative manner, the participants get to discuss and find out for themselves how open practices around idea generation and early planning of learning resources can assist their working.

The workshop will be opened for virtual participation. The session will be available online for distributed attendance and a chance to participate in the idea generation is offered. An idea sharing space will be offered by OEI2-project by the end of April. The participants will have to chance to share their ideas and collaboration through this portal when attending the workshop virtually. Before the workshop, potential participants can already start preparations by sharing their topics of discussion and requests for collaboration activities. This online (collaborative writing) document is currently in GoogleDocs: http://tinyurl.com/OEI2EDEN

The organizers will also arrange participation and online discussions for the event via the "Open Educational Ideas" Facebook community and Twitter live moderation (#openideas #EDEN15).

EXPANDED LEARNING SCENARIOS OF BEST PRACTICE IN THE UNITED STATES

Sharon Goldstein, Berkeley College, Dale Gomez, Florida International University, Susan Aldridge, Drexel Online University, United States of America

Each year the U.S. Distance Learning Association recognizes outstanding programs, individuals, and leaders in distance and eLearning through an international awards program. Award winning institutions Berkeley College, Florida International University and Drexel University Online provide an insight into their expanded learning scenarios.

A leader in providing career-focused education since 1931, Berkeley College is accredited by the Middle States Commission on Higher Education and enrolls approximately 8,000 students – including more than 900 international students – in its Baccalaureate and Associate degree and Certificate programs. Students can study in more than 20 career fields. Berkeley College is comprised of the Larry L. Luing School of Business, the School of Professional Studies, the School of Health Studies, the School of Liberal Arts, and the School of Graduate Studies, which offers a Master of Business Administration degree in Management.

Berkeley College has three New York locations – Midtown Manhattan, Brooklyn and White Plains. In New Jersey there are six locations – Clifton, Dover, Newark, Paramus, Woodbridge and Woodland Park. Berkeley College Online® serves a global population. In 2013, Berkeley College Online® was the first program in New York and New Jersey to receive certification for excellence from the United States Distance Learning Association Quality Standards (USDLA/QS). USDLA/QS certification places Berkeley College among an elite group of institutions worldwide that are recognized for excellence in distance learning. In January 2015, *U.S. News & World Report* named Berkeley College one of the Best Colleges for Online Bachelor's Degrees for the second consecutive year. The website address is www.BerkeleyCollege.edu.

Florida International University harnessed videoconferencing to create a one of a kind restaurant management lab. An advanced food production lab and a brewing science help bolster the school's research in food, wine, beer and spirits. The facility serves as a venue for faculty and students to incubate ideas and entrepreneurial ventures, and test new concepts. The restaurant management lab's new technology features the combination of an A/V system and fast web-streaming system, which will make the live streaming of events and lectures anywhere in the world possible. FIU's Chaplin School of Hospitality and Tourism Management use video conferencing and streaming to serve 1,200 students in China in addition to the 2,000 who take courses at the main campus in Florida. All courses are offered in English, and the Chinese students earn a U.S. degree. Utilizing video conferencing FIU plans expand globally. For more information regarding FIU's lab go to https://www.youtube.com/watch?v=cmkGipyDsK8&feature=youtu.be

Aside from its transactional value as a flexible medium for academic delivery, technology is also an extraordinary tool for connecting the dots between knowledge acquisition and knowledge application in a way that is active, authentic, and customized. Drexel University's College of Nursing and Health Professions employs the latest interactive technology to help online students in its RN-BSN degree sharpen their clinical assessment skills from a distance.

Although on-campus nursing students learn by doing in a high-tech, high-touch patient simulation laboratory, this arrangement is far from convenient for online students. So in moving the lab onto the laptop, the college has designed an innovative Health Assessment course that incorporates such technology enhancements as patient avatars, self-produced videos, and videoconferencing. Drexel's online nursing students are now actively and authentically engaged in perfecting their skills, while at the same time receiving real-time, in-person feedback from their professors.

ONLINE, OPEN AND FLEXIBLE HIGHER EDUCATION FOR THE FUTURE WE WANT: FROM STATEMENTS TO ACTION: POLICY CHALLENGES – THE EUROPEAN VOICE

Gard Titlestad, International Council for Open and Distance Education, Maxim Jean-Louis, Contact North | Contact Nord, Canada

From June 9-11, 2015, UNESCO, in partnership with ICDE, will be hosting a Global High Level Policy Forum at UNESCO's Paris headquarters on "Online, Open and Flexible Higher Education for the Future We Want. From Statements to Action: Equity, Access, and Quality Learning Outcomes." The Forum aims to develop a best practice framework for higher education, which highlights access, flexibility, affordability, engagement, student success and quality.

At the EDEN Conference, ICDE and EDEN invite to a workshop to engage on European level in the issues crucial for the future direction and actions expected for higher education and learning, to prepare for a European voice at the High Level Policy Forum 17 October in Pretoria, organized by ICDE in partnership with UNESCO and Commonwealth of Learning.

The focus is on possible policy responses, at the levels of governments, institutions, and in terms of innovation and research. Governments have three general types of public policy instruments they can use to enact their policies – regulations, economic means, and information – and the Forum responses may include any of these strategies. In addition, institutional, innovation, and research policy responses may highlight actions at those more specific levels.

The background carpet is colored by the comprehensive process for the revised millennium goals, for education to be set at the World Education Forum end May 2015 in Korea, the second ever since 2000. The Paris June-event, Barcelona June-event and Pretoria October-event are timely positioned to transfer statements into responses from highly motivated and qualified audiences developing the online, open and flexible higher education agenda.

Access, equity and quality learning are key features shaping a new vision of the post-2015 education agenda. Higher education is central to the future global sustainable agenda and to helping countries, particularly developing ones, achieve "equitable, quality education and lifelong learning for all by 2030", as stated in the Bali-message, issued by the ICDE-UNESCO Policy Forum end November 2014.

Some of the issues that are addressed at the Global Forum in Paris:

- It is estimated that 262 million students will be enrolled in higher education around the world by 2025 – an increase from 178 million in 2010.
- Who will these students be?
- What strategies are necessary to support their success?
- What do higher education institutions need to do to ensure that these students receive value from their education and that society values the education provided?
- How will the work of higher education contribute to promoting access, equity, and quality learning outcomes?
- To have quality education for all, in primary and secondary education, 5.2 million new teachers are needed by 2025, most of them in Sub-Saharan Africa.
- What capacities and skills do teachers need for the digital future? And how is the education system prepared to meet with those challenges?

How can faculty have a lead in creating the future higher education that we want?

EDUCAMPS IN EDUCATION: ENJOYABLE "OVER-THE-SHOULDER LEARNING" TO SHOW AND SHARE ICT PRACTICES

Sólveig Jakobsdóttir, University of Iceland, Iceland

Educamps provide unstructured collective learning experiences, where the possibilities of social software tools in learning and interaction processes are explored using face-to-face sessions that reflect social networked learning ideas (Leal Fonseca, 2011). At the University of Iceland – School of Education (UISE) the educamp model has been adapted and used in a variety of ways for different groups of teachers and teacher students to enhance technological knowhow, share practices and develop a social network. Educamps have for example been included in campus sessions for graduate and undergraduate students. During the last two school years, a series of educamp workshops at the UISE have been offered, linking teacher education staff and students with practicing teachers interested in ICT for teaching and learning at different school levels. During the first part of this workshop (15-20 minutes) the educamp model will be introduced briefly. Participants will then suggest interesting technology, digital resources etc. they would like to introduce to others (in a teacher role). The main part of the workshop will be divided into three periods (ca. 20 minutes x 3). Participants take turns being in a teacher or student role. In each period 1/3 of the group participants, spread around the room with their mobile devices and are in a teacher role while the others are in a student role. During the last part of the workshop participants will discuss their experiences of this type of workshop. Ideas will be collected about its relevance for participants' own practices and how this model could be used and developed further.

The objective of the workshop is to provide opportunities for networking and for participants to learn about the Educamp model by experiencing it first hand. There is a pressing need to develop low-cost ways for teachers to stay more current with new technologies. Teachers can also use this method with their own colleagues or students to harness the knowledge and technological knowhow which exists in the professional or learning community and/or can be developed through interest driven and connected learning.

Everyone who attends the workshop is required to participate, taking turns being in a student and a teacher role. An overview of presentations (e.g. on a Padlet, Mindmeister, Googledocs) will be provided as well as a summary of experiences, reactions and ideas for further use which will be e-mailed to participants after the workshop.

EMPOWERING LEARNERS AND EDUCATORS – VIDEO FEEDBACK TO WRITTEN ASSIGNMENTS

Ann-Sofie Karlsson, Tobias Ruhtenberg, University of Borås, Sweden

A challenge for teacher education in Sweden today is to find new ways of working in which the degree of media and information literacy of the teacher educators is high. Such renewal of teacher education is becoming more and more necessary to equip our students for the meeting with today's digitized school. As part of this we, on the teachers' education in Borås, have tried to provide students with visual feedback on written work.

The methods of feedback on written assignments in higher education, which normally take the form of handwritten comments or digital comment fields, are not always as effective as they should be. It is often difficult for students to understand the content of the comments while it is a challenge for the teacher to convey a clear message in writing. Students often need the teacher's help to decipher the feedback. It may mean that students who are in need of extended assessment do not receive the support they will need to develop and understand how to move forward with their learning. In order to examine ways to develop methods for feedback and assessment of students' examinations, higher education needs to develop and test new methods. Based on our own teaching experiences and practice oriented studies, we want to share our experiences of working with video feedback in higher education in order to improve communication between teacher and student in connection with feedback on written work.

We have tried video feedback as a method for assessing and supervising students the last three years. It started as an action research study for evaluating new ways of giving feedback to the students, inspired by Russell Stannard from the University of Warwick. Video feedback is now incorporated among one of the methods of giving feedback for some of us at the department of teacher education in Boras Sweden. The findings from the study showed that the students experienced a much higher understanding of the teacher's comments of their written assignments. Furthermore did the students feel that the feedback given was much more personal and they felt that the teacher had given them feedback that was pointing forward instead of only giving the results of the assignment. One option that the students really liked was the possibility of rewinding the video clip to repeat the comments from the teacher.

The technology is easy to adapt and it only takes a thirty-minute introduction to learn how to handle the tool. In addition to a computer, a headset improves sound quality. The software used on the computer will also record everything done on the screen so the result will be a video clip. For uploading the video file the user needs a YouTube account, Vimeo or an own streaming server. The link to the recording is sent to the student for viewing from any device and as many times preferred.

Video feedback technology can also be used by participants in online courses as a form of examination for example in foreign language teaching in which participants record screen casts where they read texts in the foreign language. The teacher can then get an idea of the student's linguistic ability in both text and pronunciation.

In summary, it is clear that video feedback leads to an increased understanding of the comments and feedback given to students. Students experienced the method as a well-functioning tool in their own learning process.

ENGINEERING PEDAGOGY AT UNIVERSITIES IN CHILE – A RESEARCH AND FURTHER EDUCATION PROJECT OF TU DRESDEN AND UNIVERSIDAD AUTÓNOMA DE CHILE

Steffen Kersten, Hartmut Simmert, Diego Gormaz, Technische Universität Dresden, Germany

Project "Engineering Pedagogy at Universities in Chile"

This article outlines an approach to a common project of the Technische Universität Dresden and the Universidad Autónoma de Chile for the development, implementation and testing of a postgraduate further education course with integrated e-learning components aiming at the development of competences in the field of arranging teaching and learning processes in academic university education. The starting point of the project is the relationship between teaching quality and student success. It is assumed that a systematic, demand-oriented further education in the field of higher education / engineering pedagogy for the teaching staff at Chilean universities will contribute to improving teaching in engineering sciences and therefore the rate of student success.

The goals of this engineering-pedagogical qualification are derived from an empirical demand analysis.

The development of postgraduate learning program is based on the modular structure of the curriculum "Engineering Educators" of the International Society for Engineering Education. Currently, various universities from all continents of the world are working to provide special modules for this curriculum for an online study.

The approach of learning organization for modules in engineering pedagogy at Chilean universities is directed to a concept of blended learning.

In the first stage of the project in 2014/2015 the development and implementation of four study modules each with two credit points are planned. For the correct decision regarding the modules an empirical demand analysis was realized.

About the modules

The different modules are systematically based on each other. The didactic concept of the training program provides teaching-learning arrangements in coordinated phases of classroom study, self-directed learning as well as individual coaching. In particular, the phases of self-directed learning and individual coaching are supported by internet-based learning scenarios. The selection of the tools of e-learning is determined exclusively by its didactic purpose and functions.

All modules are represented in a contemporary learning content management system. These are arranged similar to the course structure and include the multimedia-based learning materials. This includes the learning content, exercises of varying difficulties, examples of teaching and learning scenarios and tests. In addition, extensive tools for communication between learners and experts are available: chat, forum, wiki, email, podcasts and blogs. The managing of the course-content, the access control and the communication can be done by the teaching staff or by skilled management personnel. For the mobile learning is a special mobile version available.

THE E-HOOP LEARNING PLATFORM – AN INNOVATIVE APPROACH TO EXPAND LEARNING EXPERIENCES FOR PERSONS WITH SPECIAL NEEDS

Eleni Chatzidaki, Michalis Xenos, Lefteris Kozanidis, Hellenic Open University, Greece; Thomas Fischer, New Technologies and Learning in Europe, Germany; Aliki Economidou, Cyprus Neuroscience and Technology Institute, Cyprus

The European Research & Development project 'e-Hoop – Unified e-Hoop Approach to Learning Differences' (http://www.e-hoop.info) approaches the issue of different learning abilities and styles and adopts a collaborative approach between adults and children. e-Hoop is currently creating a universal, dynamic and adaptable e-Learning environment able to offer free personalised educational solutions to all learners regardless of their learning, cultural and social background.

The main target groups of e-Hoop are educators, primary school students and special educators with their students, schools and organisations working with people at risk of social exclusion. More specifically e-Hoop provides the appropriate e-Learning environment in order to address the following special needs of learners:

- Disabilities – visually impaired, blind, hearing impaired, deaf;
- Learning Preferences – visual, aural, read/write, kinaesthetic;
- Learning Disabilities;
- Dyslexia;
- Attention Deficit Hyperactivity Disorder (ADHD);
- Learning Styles – Activists, Reflectors, Theorists, and Pragmatists.

The educational material on the e-Learning environment can be created, used and modified by educators, while learners with diverse needs can easily use and benefit from the platform and the content. The e-Hoop learning environment is based on an Open Source (OS) platform that has been expanded in order to apply to different learning styles, and will allow the adaptation and presentation of educational content based on the individual learner characteristics and on the initial assessment of learners. The learning environment is exploiting broadband technologies and paradigms. The benefits of the learning environment comprise:

- Free personalised learning for all, especially for those with learning disabilities and who face the high risk of social exclusion;
- Easy upload of Learning Objects (LOs) to the platform and design of lesson plans through educators, thus supporting the concept of personalised learning;
- Provision of diagnostic tools enabling learners and educators to adapt the learning experience to individual needs;
- Creation of learning groups that are easy to track and manage;
- Immediate access to Open Educational Resources (OER);
- Fun learning user interface and environment that engages learners, thus decreasing dropout rates;
- Use of Open Source Software (OSS) allowing the future expansion of the e-Learning environment.

In order to achieve the above described aims and objectives, an e-Learning Platform that provides a dynamic and personalised learning environment has been developed by e-Hoop. The platform embeds tools that can evaluate learning abilities of each learner and support learners with special needs to expand, customise and enrich their learning experiences. The proposed educational approach is based on Distance Learning methodologies, exploits Information and Communication Technologies (ICTs) and the production of appropriately developed learning content in order to overcome the obstacles of a traditional classroom.

PERVASIVE GAMIFICATION WITH AUGMENTED REALITY AND REMOTE EXPERIENCES

Paula Carolei, UNIFESP, Eliane Schlmmer, UNISINOS, Brazil

This presentation will show a methodology to gamify any visit to museums or educative spaces transforming any experience in a pervasive game that combines augmented reality, visualization and remote agency.

The first part of this methodology involves a planning framework that helps anyone who wishes to build a gamified experience. This framework has fields to be filled as:

- a checklist that guides a previous mapping of the heritage or education place and that describes the important information about it.
- One that suggests competences, actions and storylines that will help to design the game play

The second part of the methodology helps in the recording and recovery of the gamified experience data for a later discussion.

We will demonstrate some experiments in which this methodology was applied. Also, we will describe how we use mobile and wearable platform (google glass or other glasses or another device with camera and data transmission) to step up and turn those experiences in a remote participation proposal.

These experiences supported by this methodology are relevant because they mean an attempt to solve some challenges of working with education in a hybrid format where technology can provide us with a deeper exploration of the physical space, especially when there is heritage and cultural interest, or even provide a type of differentiated experience and various environments. Also, they propose gamification strategies and the use of augmented reality technologies and remote agency that can expand our relationship with these spaces, transforming visits of inductive and instructional logic into investigative proposals with more deductive and exploratory logic creating challenges and playful actions, associating new layers of information to the physical spaces and deepening interaction and collaboration. The remote action provides a kind of living experience and even a telepresence in space, it means that those who are physically distant feel as if they were in the environment and can actively join the action.

REMOTE DESKTOP VIRTUALIZATION AS A MEANS OF CONVERGENCE OF STUDENT AND PROFESSIONAL WORKPLACES

Oleksandr Melnychenko, Kherson National Technical University, Ukraine

Introduction

Desktop as a Service (DaaS) is a powerful tool for E-learning purposes. But in addition DaaS can be used as an effective mechanism for workplaces convergence of professionals, educators, and students. Progress in this field can be achieved due to creation of a single virtual environment, which provides the interaction between all the main participants of the educational process on the basis of infrastructure consolidation, unification of operating functions together with gradual, purposeful enrichment and convergence of intellectual activity.

Methodology

The system implements the following basic principles. First, it is the principle of changing the role: all participants without exception may at different times and in different circumstances act in roles of student, specialist or educator. Secondly, it is the principle of changing the activity: all participants can shift the focus of their activities on gaming, professional or educational aspects. Thirdly, it is a principle of intellectual development as an interaction between systems of change: any intellectual change is realized through interaction of at least several systems, which provide changes. Each of them is formed from the elements such as an object of change, a means of change, and a subject of change. The object of change is the area of intellectual activity. The means are real or virtual ICT tools. Subjects perform participants of interaction with relevant to their current roles and primary activities goals, objectives, motivations, etc.

In general, an attempt to implement these principles in practical technologies is based on the methodological approach, proposed by the author, which is utilizing the concepts of the systems of change, and intellectual development as an interaction between such systems.

Practical results

The practical implementation is based on such open source and open architecture projects as Ulteo Open Virtual Desktop as a virtual desktop and application delivery platform (www.ulteo.com), OpenStack software for creating corporate cloud (www.openstack.org), Moodle as a learning platform (moodle.org) and some others.

We begin with a special section of syllabus which includes a software list and describes demands to the desktop for each discipline. Then we categorize this information for all disciplines onto groups of software and demands for each spatiality and each semester. At last, we get some sequence of evolving descriptions of workplaces which leads from the freshman's computerized working environment to professional. The final professional environment we are coordinating with local employers, such as software engineering companies and machine building plants. And finally, we include such workplaces – both as a means and as objects of change – into a network of complex interacting systems which provide change of knowledge and skills over education.

It is possible to emphasize the following novel characteristics of the present project:

1. An implementation of a new methodological approach, based on the decomposition of educational process into separate interplaying systems and their elements playing different roles in providing change.
2. The use of desktops as a means of interaction between the different roles that students, teachers and professionals play in the framework of educational coherent systems of change.

Conclusions

Presented results could be considered as having the great significance for creating a new powerful instrument for pushing complex changes within the ICT-supported educational systems. These methodological and practical means can be used to engage students in self-propelled intellectual activities and to accelerate their intellectual development through significant mutual impact of student and professional virtual workplaces due to their convergence.

TIME TO ASSESS LEARNING OUTCOMES IN E-LEARNING – TALOE WEB TOOL

Sandra Kučina Softić, University of Zagreb, Croatia, Inés Gil-Jaurena, Universidad Nacional de Educación a Distancia, Spain, Alfredo Soeiro, Rita Falcão, Universidade do Porto, Portugal, Jüri Lõssenko, Information Technology Foundation for Education, Estonia

TALOE -Time to Assess Learning Outcomes in E-learning (http://taloe.up.pt) is a two-year project co-funded under the European Commission's Lifelong Learning Programme, approaching the e-assessment concept by using technology for assessing students' learning.

TALOE's main goal is to develop a web-based platform to help teachers and trainers decide which e-assessment strategies to use in their online courses. This tool is aimed to raise teachers' awareness about the variety of e-assessment strategies in order to improve the quality of the learning process. The main idea is that teachers will describe the learning outcome of their course or module and the TALOE platform will analyse them and provide a suitable e-assessment strategy that is consistent with the intended learning.

For the alignment of learning outcomes and e-assessment, TALOE has adapted and developed another tool, the ALOA model. The ALOA conceptual model (Aligning Learning Outcomes and Assessment) highlights the connection between the intended learning outcomes and the assessment strategy used during a course. To ensure the validity of assessment in relation to what is intended from the course, it is necessary that the outcomes measured by the assessment tasks are the same as the ones expressed in the learning outcomes statements. After the definition of the extended ALOA model and setting of the matrix which is aligning the cognitive processes describing the learning outcomes and the categories of the e-assessment methods the next step was to develop the web-based platform that will help teachers and trainers decide on the e-assessment strategies to use in their online courses. The main idea for development of this web tool was that a teacher will describe one learning outcome of their course or module and the TALOE web tool will analyse it and offer the most appropriate e-assessment methods that are consistent with the intended learning.

The partnership has produced a first version of the web-tool at the beginning of the year 2015 and started with testing for the first functionalities of the intended platform. The first phase addresses only the simplest forms of knowledge. After initial testing of the matrix it has been confirmed that the matrix is working properly. The best (most appropriate) e-assessment methods are selected on the base of the absolute matches between input (learning outcome) and the e-assessment method. Further testing was done with collected case studies to see if the suggested e-assessment methods are closely related to defined learning outcome. The results showed that the majority of the teachers have planned assessment methods such as: forum discussions, written assignments and online tests, self-evaluation tests and some practical activities. The suggested e-assessment methods (by TALOE web tool) in some cases suggested additional possibilities of the assessment but in some cases indicated that the existing assessment methods should be revised. These results confirmed intended and planned task that the web tool also provides support and guidance to teachers to formulate the learning outcomes in accordance to Bloom taxonomy increasing this way the accuracy of the learning outcome received by tool.

At the moment in the process is testing by invited stakeholders to get their feedback on the relevance and usability of the tool. Based on their comments and information additional adjustments of the tool will be made.

The aim is to develop an interactive website that will provide a service to teachers and trainers of different learning context. It is intended that the TALOE web tool (http://taloe.innovate4future.eu) will be freely available to use publicly and will be of help to any person concerned in finding the solutions for assessment.

BOOK OF PROJECTS

Collection of “Synergy” Synopses

Thematic focus and relevance of the Synergy initiatives

	Acronym	POLICY	METHOD	RECOGN	TECHN	LANAL	ASSESS	OPEN	COMM	INFORM
	VM-Pass			X				X		
	Panorama e-learning PT	X								
	ECVET-STEP			X	X					
B5	SADE ICDE ON	X								
	OERup!	X	X					X		
	ARMAZEG		X							
	UAB System	X								
	UDLnet		X		X		X	X	X	X
	LeHo	X	X		X			X	X	
C5	Intergenerational Game Creation									X
	EHLSSA				X					
	SenApp				X					
	ProNursing			X	X		X			X
	P4G		X		X					
	EDUWORKS		X		X	X	X			X
	RIPE NCC Academy	X	X		X	X		X		X
D6	CCD FLITE		X		X				X	
	StartUP				X			X		
	iPro	X		X	X	X			X	X
	m-commerce				X					
	HOME	X						X		
	D-TRANSFORM	X								
E6	TALOE				X		X			
	EDUOPEN	X			X	X		X		
	Flexible Toolbox Project				X					
	MMSQC				X					
	BEU			X				X		
	eLene4work				X					
	MERIT				X			X	X	
F6	ADOERUP	X		X				X		X
	OntoTechnology			X	X		X			X
	ICARD				X			X		
	LACE					X				
	Digiskills									X
	SCORE2020		X		X		X			X
	SAILS						X			
	ODS							X		
	Hands-On ICT		X		X		X	X	X	X
G6	INUITEL		X		X					
	CAMELOT				X					
	JamToday				X					X
	SharedOER	X						X		
	OEI2							X		
	OpenProf							X	X	
	ECO							X		

Conference themes and their related tags

POLICY	Conceptual focus – policy observations and/or recommendations
METHOD	Methodology
RECOGN	Recognition of prior learning, competencies and soft skills
TECHN	Tools and technology
LANAL	Learning analytics
ASSESS	Assessment
OPEN	Open educational content, courses and practices
COMM	Working/learning with communities
INFORM	Informal learning and learner driven extracurricular activities

RECOGN OPEN

VM-Pass

Implementing Recognition of Virtual Mobility and OER Learning through a Learning Passport

Website: http://vmpass.eu

Runtime: October 2013 – June 2016

Supported / co-funded by: LLP Centralised – Erasmus MP

Partners: Associazione Sophia R&I, Italy, Universidad Internacional de La Rioja, S.A., ES, Vytautas Magnus University, LT, Baden-Wurttemberg Cooperative State University, DE, EDEN, UK, Katholieke Universiteit Leuven, BE, Knowledge Innovation Centre (KIC), Malta, European Association of Distance Teaching Universities (EADTU), Netherlands

Project representative to be contacted for further info: Francesco Fedele, Associazione Sophia R&I (f.fedele@sophiari.eu), Anthony F. Camilleri, KIC (anthony@camilleri.com)

Despite the rise of Virtual Mobility and OCW (Open Course Ware)-based opportunities for learning at institutions, around Europe – recognition remains uneven, and serves as a major barrier to uptake of these flexible forms of learning. In the past year, both UNESCO and the European Commission have called for this problem to be addressed through improved recognition tools. Thus, VM-Pass will aim to increase inter-institutional recognition of virtual mobility and OCW-based courses, by:

- Building on results from OER test project and piloting the use of a student-held learning passport to facilitate recognition & mobility
- Planning, testing and creating a recognition-clearinghouse to support the verification and investigation of learning passports
- Creating a typology of quality systems used in VM and OER systems, to support the learning passports and recognition-clearinghouse
- Engaging in dialogue with multiple institutions around Europe so as to mainstream use of the recognition tools created by the project

These activities together will provide recognition offices a tool which will reduce the bureaucracy involved in recognition processes, allow them to share experiences with peers and compare their recognition decisions' with other institutions – thus promoting harmonisation of recognition. All of this together, should make it easier for students to have their VM learning recognised, and thus increase the volume of students taking advantage of this flexible learning pathway, without increasing the administrative burden on their home institutions.

Main target groups of the project:

This project is squarely focused on Higher Education Institutions who intend to recognise learning experiences based on virtual mobility (including OER-based learning) or are already experimenting to do so. The project intends to involve these institutions in the two projects in two ways:

- A selection of HEIs will be involved directly in the project's activities through participation in the living laboratory on recognition of learning based on VM
- The wider HE community will be kept informed of the activities and successes of the project, with the hope that through continued information they will eventually join the project activities beyond the end of its life as part of its sustainability activities. This category activity will also indirectly target HE researchers, and the rest of the E&T Stakeholder Community.

RECOGN **OPEN**

Significant public results:

Series of info seminars for living lab members – a retrospective:

- http://vmpass.eu/news/seminars-in-retrospective/

13 March 2014: 1st online seminar in the frame of the Open Education Week:

- http://www.openeducationweek.org/ai1ec_event/join-the-vm-pass-living-lab/?instance_id=

25 April 2014: 1st face-to-face seminar in the frame of the 2014 OCWC Global Conference in Ljubljana

- http://conference.oeconsortium.org/2014/ai1ec_event/workshop-credits-for-learning-with-open-courseware-introducing-a-learning-passport-anne-christin-tannhauser-anthony-f-camilleri-and-grainne-conole/?instance_id=

8-9 May 2014: 2nd face-to-face seminar in the frame of the EFQUEL Innovation Forum in Crete

11 June 2015: 3rd face-to-face seminar in the frame of the EDEN Annual Conference in Zagreb

- http://www.eden-online.org/system/files/Annual_2014_Zagreb_BOA.pdf (page 62 and 129)

24 and 26 June 2014: 2nd and 3rd online seminars

- http://webinar.appi.bme.hu/playback/presentation/playback.html?meetingId=e748dada914bd395df158f7561819 ebefc88effd-1403782393114

POLICY

Panorama e-learning PT

Study on PT HEI e-Learning Governance and Practices 2015-2016

Website: http://www.panoramaelearning.pt

Runtime: 01.2013 – 12.2020

Supported / co-funded by: POAT-FSE 2013-2014. NO GRANT 2015-2016

Partners: TecMinho – Minho University Interface; Quaternaire Portugal, Instituto Politécnico do Porto, Universidade de Lisboa, Portugal

Project representative to be contacted for further info: Ana Dias, anadias@tecminho.uminho.pt

The project aims to understand the state of the art – governance and practices – in online education in Portuguese higher education. It puts in common different communities, made of e-learning experts, strategists, policy makers, decision makers and governance. The idea is to build a common understanding of the ways forward in terms of formal and informal education, and in a creative and innovative atmosphere build a Portuguese framework, adapted to local constraints in a global education market. The main results of the study will be a report and a quality framework on online education in higher education to be published until 2016.

Main target groups of the project: e-learning experts, public bodies managing e-learning, decision makers

Significant public results: all on the Portal www.panoramaelearning.pt, a report on governance and practices of e-learning in Portugal 360º 2014, case studies on the website, 1st online learning quality chart in Portuguese; theses, articles, legislation and links to materials and to experts. Connected to a Facebook group www.facebook.com/panoramaelearning with 950 members – focused on debating online education governance and practice issues, project based on open innovation, results validated by the community and with the community, all materials are in Portuguese by now.

RECOGN TECHN

ECVET-STEP

ECVET for Strengthening Training to Employment Pathways

Website: http://www.ecvet-step.eu/

Runtime: 01.2014 – 12.2015

Supported / co-funded by: LLP LEONARDO – Development of innovation

Partners: Technological Educational Institute of Athens (EL); University of Duisburg-Essen (DE); Kmetijsko gozdarska zbornica Slovenije-Chamber of Agriculture and Forestry of Slovenia (SI); AOC Raad (NL); Ústav zemdlsk ekonomiky a informací-Institute of Agricultural Economics and Information (HU); Eummena (BE); Colegio Mayor Menendez Pelayo-Instituto Nevares de Empresarios Agrarios (ES); Universidad de Alcalá (ES).

Project representative to be contacted for further info: Cleo Sgouropoulou (csgouro@teiath.gr)

ECVET STEP aims in making the best value of the ECVET system, facilitating the transfer, accumulation and recognition of credits and learning outcomes or competence acquired otherwise between countries, thus promoting mobility learning in VET. Towards this aim, the main goal of ECVET STEP is to bridge the gap between descriptions of job profiles and training opportunities, while at the same time promoting mobility of people engaging in VET activities. ECVET STEP aspires to support organisations to "take the ECVET STEP" by following a step-wise, quality-controlled approach in adopting ECVET. ECVET STEP aspires to build a harmonization basis, combining ECVET with other leading European instruments and valuable outcomes of European standardization and LLP projects to develop i) an operational and transferable framework for managing the ECVET process, for all VET stakeholders, starting from the agricultural domain but ranging to other domains and sectors ii) design patterns for reusable units of learning outcomes associated with credits and methods for assessment, validation and recognition, covering the perspectives of different stakeholders and different contexts including formal, non-formal, informal VET activities and iii) valuable technology based solutions and services. The expected benefits for European citizens, being life-long learners engaging in VET activities with trans-national mobility are equally important, ranging from enhanced possibilities to expand and enrich their professional competence, to opportunities for individualisation of their learning paths and integration of internationality in their personal study plans, enhanced quality of mobility and easier to validate competence acquired abroad, easier job hunting across Europe and, generally, a more transparent and understandable system for life-long personal development and matching of preferences with existing job opportunities.

Significant public results:

1. Report on national implementation of VET processes
2. Model of European-wide learning mobility in agricultural VET (MoMoVET)
3. Report on ECVET provisions for MoMoVET
4. Quality Management for the ECVET adoption process
5. The ECVET Capability Maturity Framework

SADE ICDE ON

SADE ICDE Operational Network-Nordic and Baltic Countries

Website: http://www.sverd.se

Runtime: 01.2015 – 12.2017

Supported / co-funded by: The International Council for Open and Distance Education (ICDE)

Partners: The Swedish Association Distance Education (SVERD, Eng. SADE) Sweden, Flexible Education Norway, Aarhus University Denmark, Vilniaus Kolegija Lithuania, Riga Technical University Latvia, University of Jyväskylä Finland, Tallinn University Estonia

Project representative to be contacted for further info: Ebba Ossiannilsson (Ebba.Ossiannilsson@gmail.com)

The Swedish Association Distance Education (SADE) is a professional organization for all those involved in distance, online and flexible learning in Sweden. SADE involves and serves all sectors of education – from schools and universities, organizations and companies – in Sweden. SADE was founded in 1984, and is designed to broaden the knowledge of and participate in the development of flexible education and distance learning.

Activities by SADE:

- initiate the exchange of experience and cooperation between our members
- create open communities by including organizing conferences and seminars
- promote international exchanges and cooperation
- stimulate the development of knowledge in the areas of distance learning and flexible learning
- contribute to the development of the area monitored in governing body SADE has since many years, with start (2005), been involved and responsible for the Boldic OER project and Boldic Awards, a project financed by NORDPLUS, by the Nordic Council of Ministries. The general purpose of the "Boldic - open learning resources online" project is to deepen and bring further the co-operation between Nordic and Baltic organizations dealing with distance education, flexible learning and e-learning by opening the community for new partners from both the Baltic and the Nordic countries http://www.boldic.org

During 30 years SVERD has worked with members and authorities in Sweden, but also as mentioned above in the Boldic countries as well as in the Nordic countries, and can thus be serve as a regional node. As an associated member in ICDE, SADE will have an interest to work as a node with ICDE ON, with the activities and responsibilities outlined in the call.

The proposed synergy event during the EDEN Annual conference will gather individuals and organizations mainly from the Nordic and Baltic states. The aim is to discuss concrete events and networking within the ICDE Operational Network. The Synergy event targets the strand on Opening the classroom, to expand education.

Main target groups of the project: Educational organisations and providers in the Nordic and the Boldic countries

Significant public results: Liaise and support ICDE initiatives relevant for the Nordic countries (Denmark, Finland, Iceland, Norway and Sweden) as well as their autonomous regions (the Åland Islands, the Faroe Islands and Greenland) and the Baltic region (Estonia, Latvia and Lithuania) with conferences and events, projects, promotional activities etc.). When appropriate and agreed, organize regional/local networking events for our Nordic and Baltic interest groups and ICDE members. Be in contact with and liaise with regional/local stakeholders relevant for ICDE (regional/local UNESCO offices, cooperating organizations as regional ICDE members associations etc.). Establish good collaboration with relevant regional ODL associations and aim for synergies, mutual achievements and reinforcements. Promote ICDE membership for relevant target groups and institutions. Participate in concrete project and initiatives when agreed. Examples could be to build up contact databases, regional or global surveys, contribute to global or regional webinars. Support the information and communication function of ICDE. Could be tasks as act as multiplier for the newsletter, regional news agent, and media contact point for ICDE, if wanted and agreed – translate parts of the website in another language. Our SADE members, with long experience in the field of distance and online learning can be a rich source in such a national /regional node described in the call.

POLICY METHOD OPEN

OERup!

OER Uptake in Adult Learning Institutions

Website: http://www.oerup.eu

Runtime: 09.2014 – 08.2016

Supported / co-funded by: Erasmus+ Programme of the European Union

Partners: MFG Innovation Agency Media and Creative Industries, Germany (Project manager); SOPHIA Research & Innovation, Italy; Institutul Român de Educaţie a Adulţilor (IREA), Romania; National Institute of Adult Continuing Education (NIACE), UK; Universitat Oberta de Catalunya (UOC), Spain.

Project representative to be contacted for further info: Ines Kreitlein (kreitlein@mfg.de)

The OERup! Project takes up the need to promote and foster the successful implementation of OER (Open Educational Resources) and OEPs (Open Educational Practices) in adult education in Europe in order to widen participation in Open Education.

Addressed are adult learning institutions, and educational professionals as well as decision and policy makers across Europe with the objective to:

- **Identify** the status quo of OER use in adult learning;
- **Raise** awareness around the value of OER & OEP;
- **Foster** quality frameworks of OER & OEP;
- **Improve** digital competences of educational professionals to ensure inclusive approaches to OER;
- **Set in motion** a new culture of Open Education, hence a modern and innovative learning environment
- **Support** education institutions and professionals in developing and implementing sustainable OEPs (including integrative business models)

The project will provide practitioners with a need analysis and training package (training concept and material) in a blended-learning format on the topic of OER, developed by five established European partners throughout the projects lifetime. All project results will be published on our online platform. A Google+ community ensures access to information, advice and guidance, as well as good practice around OER by sharing experiences with actors in other European countries.

Main target groups of the project: adult learning institutions (management and staff), educational professionals, as well as decision and policy makers of adult learning

Significant public results:

By the EDEN conference, the following outcomes will be developed:

- A multiregional need analysis report
- A concept of a blended-learning training package on the topic of OER
- The results of an International Multiplier Event previous to the EDEN conference that will take place in Barcelona
- A Website and a Google+ community (both currently available)

Objective for the participation in the synergy strand:

Our intention is to bring together as many players as possible on this issue – not only education providers, teachers, colleges and universities but also relevant policy makers. Within the framework of the EDEN Conference Synergy Strand we would like to openly discuss (for example in a world café set-up) the results of our need analysis reports as well as the training package concept. Further we are highly interested in exchanging ideas concerning possible synergies with other projects in order to ensure sustainable and broad exploitation of our project results.

ARMAZEG

Developing Tools for Lifelong Learning in the Transcaucasus Region: e-Learning

ARMAZEG
Developing tools for lifelong learning inTranscaucasus region: e-Learning

Website: http://www.armazeg.com/en

Runtime: December 2013 – November 2016

Supported / co-funded by: Tempus

Partners: Katholieke Universiteit Leuven, BE (coordinator); State Engineering University of Armenia, AM; Ministry of Education and Science of the Republic of Armenia, AM; Institute of Informatics & Automation Problems of NAS RA, AM; Orbeli Institute of Physiology of NAS RA, AM; Armenian State Pedagogical University after Kh. Abovian, AM; St. Andrew the First-Called Georgian University, GE; Georgian Technical University, GE; Università degli Studi di Firenze, IT; University of Granada, ES; European Distance and E-Learning Network, UK; Ivane Javakhishvili Tbilisi State University, GE.

Project representative to be contacted for further info: Mariet Vriens (Mariet.Vriens@kuleuven.be)

Financed by the European Commission within the TEMPUS program the ARMAZEG project aims to stimulate educational reform in Armenian and Georgian partner universities by establishing e-Learning centres and training for their staff members – with special attention to lifelong learning methodologies.

The project involves twelve partners from Europe and Transcaucasia with a clear vision to establish new links in the educational sphere between the two regions. With the assistance of four European partners ARMAZEG's Armenian and Georgian institutions will import and adapt e-Learning practices in their educational agenda to realise a flexible organisation of higher and adult education locally. A thorough needs analysis accompanied by study visits to the state of the art European universities will help the Transcaucasian partners improve learning by supporting student-centred methodologies, support research-based higher education and enable the internationalisation of their higher education services.

Amongst the most important outcomes of the project will be the establishment of e-learning centres in 7 partner universities of Armenia and Georgia and the implementation of pilot projects in different disciplines. To ensure the sustainability of the concept in Transcaucasian partner institutions, the project also includes, besides the above mentioned policy makers' study visits, trainings of trainers and regional and national workshops.

Main target groups of the project: Higher education stakeholders (University management, lecturers, administration staff, students)

Significant public results:

- Documents:
  - State-of-the-Art report on Armenian and Georgian e-learning (available)
  - Policy recommendations regarding e-learning and ICT for LLL in Armenia and Georgia
  - Long-term capacity building strategy regarding e-learning competences for staff
  - Quality assurance framework for e-courses
- Established e-learning centres with trained staff and specific business strategy
- Training material for teachers regarding e-learning and ICT for lifelong learning
- Pilot projects (implemented e-courses)

POLICY

UAB System

Open education from distance learning of Brazil

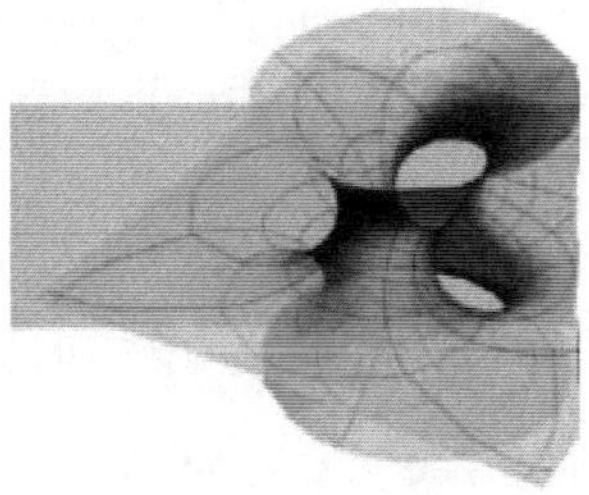

Website: https//:dgp.cnpq.br/dgp/espelhogrupo/9349840891402281

Runtime: 07/2011 – 07/2016

Supported / co-funded by: Euclides da Cunha Foundation/ Brazil

Partners: Universidade Federal Fluminense, Universidade Estadual de Londrina, Universidade Estadual de Campinas (UFF, UEL, UNICAMP)

Project representative to be contacted for further information: Maria Renata da Cruz Duran (mariarenataduran@gmail.com)

The Brazilian Open University system (UAB) was established by Decree 5800 on June 8, 2006. Its objective is to link Public Institutions of Higher Education (IPES), state and local delegates and the federal government, in favour of distance learning modality application on meeting the specified targets by the National Plan for Basic Education Teachers' Formation (Plano Nacional de Formação de Professores da Educação Básica). Today, the system works with approximately 200.000 enrolled students, 92 IPES and 500 active presence support centres.

The distance learning locus of UAB is represented by the presence support centres, which are places equipped with laboratories, libraries, offices, classrooms and conference rooms where distance learning docents and students find their meeting location and mainstay. The basis provided by the presence support centres to the UAB system are a feature of Brazilian distance learning higher education as a whole, whose specificity is the semi-presence regime guaranteed by law.

Some presence support centres could work with the management of local interests, as strategy points of evasion control. Still, articulating the IPES plans, some centres could optimize academic efforts and, in particular cases, potentialize them. At least, the support centres serve as a dynamo of public universities values as they capture new students even for the presence courses. In face of these points of view, our objective is to verify how UAB system presence support centres could be improved in this new scenario of distance learning education in Brazil?

In order to answer this question, our starting point was to verify the type of these centres. This study was made between 2011 and 2013 and it was based on research, which was already presented at EDEN (DURAN, 2013), concerning north, south and northeast regions. According to the previously mentioned classification into types, the presence support centres that have profile A work with from10 to 15 courses of initial and continued training, in cities with from 20 to 30 thousand inhabitants, 186 miles far from state capital, just with Federal IPES, more than 3 IPES, 3 to 5 people at multidisciplinary team. These courses coordinators are women whose age range from 31 to 50 years old. They are graduate students coming from state or municipal education departments with no previous experience in distance education. These centres are always open (morning, afternoon and night) and frequently have a lack of contact with the IPES.

Profile B works with from 05 to 10 courses with initial teacher training in cities with until 20 thousand inhabitants which are more than 300 miles far from state capitals. In these places state IPES are the majority, but the number of institutions does not exceed 3 institutions per centre. The centres are open for students all nights and weekends, with 3 to 5 people as part of a multidisciplinary team. There is a dialogue involving the centres and the IES, but very few centres use IES's facilities. Without previous experience in distance education, the coordinators of these centres are graduated women, who are from 51 to 65 years old. They come from state and municipal education departments, and had no academic continuing formation from state or federal public polices.

Profile C has more than 20 courses. Continuing teacher training, federal IPES and technological institutes are the majority in these spaces, which articulate more than 3 IPES with 10 people forming a multidisciplinary team which works all nights and Saturdays at UAB system. The team develops a lot of parallel projects with the local, state and federal government, as well as university projects. These courses are 50 miles distant from the state capitals, with a population around 70 thousand inhabitants and are coordinated by women, who are from 31 to 50 years old who have a master degree and previous experience with distance learning education.

This classification into types of the presence support centres helps us to better understand the position of each centre coordinator regarding the potential and the limits of this centre as a space for the production and dissemination of scientific knowledge. The most direct result of this action-research was to promote a kind of professional consciousness with these coordinators that involves their knowledge of official evaluation systems, the extension of their work in terms of the UAB synergy system, and finally, their role as a “solution-makers”.

Currently, what we are doing is to establish research contacts to study how the best presence support centres (according to the IPES) from southeast and centre regions (pioneers at distance learning education in Brazil) could create peer-to-peer dynamics to improve their spaces into regional scientific knowledge producers.

Main target groups of the project: To present 3 groups of successful cases for presence support centres management both to reformulate official evaluation processes, and to develop scientific/digital culture in terms of production at these centres.

Significant public results: https://universidadeestadualdelondrina.academia.edu/MariaRenataDuran

METHOD TECHN ASSESS OPEN COMM INFORM

UDLnet

Universal Design for Learning: A Framework for Addressing Learner Variability– UDLnet

Website: http://www.udlnet-project.eu

Runtime: 12.2013 – 11.2016

Supported / co-funded by: Lifelong Learning Programme, COMENIUS Multilateral networks

Partners: Ellinogermaniki Agogi (Greece); Universal Learning Systems (Ireland); National and Kapodistrian University of Athens (Greece); Pan Cyprian Organization "Angalia Elpidas" (Cyprus); The Finnish Association on Intellectual and Developmental Disabilities (Finland); NHL University of Applied Sciences (Netherlands); Centrum für angewandte Systemlösungen e.V.v (Germany); Spanish Confederation of Education and Training Centres (Spain); Enable Ireland Disability Services Ltd (Ireland).

Project representative to be contacted for further info: Katerina Riviou (kriviou@ea.gr)

Article 24 of the UN Convention on the Rights of Persons with Disabilities states that persons with disabilities should be guaranteed the right to inclusive education at all levels, regardless of age, without discrimination and on the basis of equal opportunity. State Parties should ensure that children with disabilities are not excluded from free and compulsory primary education, or from secondary education. Still, there is a long way ahead before reaching a society where equal opportunities are guaranteed for all.

Inclusive and quality education is a key means to achieve this goal. In many special as well as mainstream schools, however, there is still much uncertainty and a lack of knowledge. Though the policy context supports a shift to inclusion, professionals need more support to develop their practice. In order to bridge the gap between policy and practice the UDLnet network aspires to address this necessity collecting and creating best practices under the framework of Universal Design for Learning (UDL) on the following envisaged themes: inclusive learning environments, accessible resources, teachers' and school leaders' competences, examination of barriers and identification of opportunities. Moreover, current needs related with the use of mobile devices will be investigated, and the proposed network will cater for the delivery of accessible educational resources through wireless and mobile devices along with the application of the UDL framework in real inclusive educational practices.

UDLnet building upon experience of previous and current projects aims at exchanging/creating good practices on inclusive education for students with disabilities, and not only, across Europe, in order to cater for their wholesome development, smooth transition in the next grades and consequently for employability, working inclusion and for active European citizenship.

Main target groups of the project: Teachers (in-service, pre-service), Teacher trainers, School leaders, Curriculum developers, Educational Policy Makers, ICT support/technical staff

Significant public results:

- A summer school on "Teacher Competences Fostering Inclusive Learning" is to be held in Attica, Greece on July 12-17, 2015, organized by Ellinogermaniki Agogi. The aim of the course is to have a positive impact on the development of students' transversal competences, creativity, collaboration, and effective communication skills by promoting the use of real world authentic learning activities by immersing participating teachers in the process of resource based approaches via their interaction with a unique collection of open educational resources (OER). More information: http://udlnet.ea.gr
- UDLnet Inventory (Best Practices, Media Resources), http://udlnet.di.uoa.gr
- Universal Design for Learning: A Framework for Addressing Learner Variability Community (on Open Discovery Space Portal), http://portal.opendiscoveryspace.eu/community/udlnet-universal-design-learning-framework-addressing-learner-variability-669613

METHOD TECHN ASSESS OPEN COMM INFORM

Publications:

- Riviou, K., Kouroupetroglou G., Bruce, A. "UDLnet: A Framework for Addressing Learner Variability", 14th International Conference on Computers Helping People with Special Needs, ULD TRACK, pp. 83-94, Paris, France, 09-11 July , 2014
- Riviou, K., Kouroupetroglou G. "Designing an educational scenario using the Principles of Universal Design for Learning", 14th IEEE International Conference on Advanced Learning Technologies (ICALT 2014), Athens, Greece, IEEE Computer Society, 978-1-4799-4038-7/14, pp.732-733, 7-9 July 2014

POLICY METHOD TECHN OPEN COMM

LeHo

Learning at Home and the Hospital

Website: http://www.lehoproject.eu/

Runtime: January 2014 – December 2016

Supported / co-funded by: LLP-KEY3 Networks / 543184-LLP-I-2013-I-IT-KA3-KA3NW

Partners: FPM: Fondazione Politecnico di Milano, IT (applicant, University of Perugia – Department of Education and Human Sciences, IT, Bednet vzw, B, Staatliche Schule für Kranke München, D, MMB – Institute for Media and Competence Research, D, EDEN: European Distance and E-Learning Network, UK, FUNDITEC, ES, Leicester Children's Hospital School, UK, Children's Cancer Hospital, EG

Project representative to be contacted for further info: Matteo Uggeri (matteo.uggeri@polimi.it), Livia Turzo (turzo@eden-online.org)

LeHo – financed by the Lifelong Learning Programme of the European Commission – is developing an online hub that will provide tools and resources for those engaged or involved in home and hospital-based education for children with medical conditions. The initiative is coordinated by the Fondazione Politecnico di Milano and involves 9 organizations that include universities, hospital schools, IT solution providers and European networks.

In the first phase of this 3-year project, a definition of the key educational factors and highlighting good practice in the field are the initial outcomes that will be used to access further aims, such as providing a Practical Guide and a Toolkit for everybody involved in Home and Hospital Education (HHE) including medical staff, nurses, volunteers, teachers, parents, etc. By the end of the project, the resulting resource will target the policy makers and will conclude the experiences of the participants and contributors of LeHo, highlighting strengths, challenges and weaknesses that may require further development across the partner countries.

The LeHo online hub is already available and open for everybody involved and interested in the topic and includes resources that are being developed or collected by the LeHo team. A Board of Experts was founded in order to support LeHo's work. Members of the BoE include professionals with a high level of experience in the field of HHE who also take on a liaison role between the teachers, medical staff and the decision makers at policy level. Focus group discussions are and will be also presented on the online hub.

Main target groups of the project:

- teachers already involved or potentially involved in HHE;
- other personnel/workers of schools not directly involved in the education process:
  - technicians (IT administrators, usually) in charge of ICT structures (from computers to webcam to printer, scanners or cables...);
  - medical staff (nurses, doctors...);
  - volunteers and volunteers associations;
- students, not only with medical needs but in general: this is because in many cases the students themselves are the main 'engine' and helpers for their classmates with medical need and even for their own teachers, especially in the use of technology;
- schools directors and decision makers (in hospitals and schools): 90% of the times any project of home tuition or in general variations in the normal teaching path has to be evaluated and accepted by the school and hospital decision makers.

Secondary target:

- policy makers;
- representative of institutions related to education (at local, regional and national level);
- parents and parents associations;
- supporting institutes providing ICT solutions (i.e. Bednet (Be), KlasseContact (Nl), PSO (ITA)...;

- high and higher education students representatives;
- students with a disability: even if the focus is not specifically on them, we need to take into account the needs of people suffering from some specific form of disabilities (e.g. special high contrast, bigger letters, audio transcriptions of videos, etc.).

Significant public results:

The LeHo online hub, including international and national communities: http://www.lehoproject.eu

LeHo on Facebook: https://www.facebook.com/groups/677222725654610/

LeHo on Linkedin: http://www.linkedin.com/groups/LeHo-Learning-Home-in-Hospital-4966339

Examples from the LeHo Repository's content:

- LeHo Board of Experts and their report on the state-of-the art of HHE in their country: http://www.lehoproject.eu/en/board-of-experts
- First Focus Group Discussion Report: http://www.lehoproject.eu/en/documents/viewdownload/17-international-community/170-focus-groups-with-hhe-teachers-and-medical-staff-full-report-of-the-first-round-v-6-2
- Glossary of terms in use in the Home and Hospital Education: http://www.lehoproject.eu/en/glossary

INFORM

Intergenerational Game Creation

Intergenerational Game Creation

Website: Silver Gaming working group within the ACT project: http://actproject.ca/working-groups/

Runtime: 2014-2021

Supported / co-funded by: Canada Social Sciences and Humanities Research Council (SSHRC)

Partners:

- Margarida Romero, Université Laval, Canada
- Josep Blat, Pompeu Fabra University, Spain
- Eugène Loos, Utrecht University, the Netherlands

Project representative to be contacted for further info: Margarida Romero (margarida.romero@fse.ulaval.ca)

Engaging elders and secondary level students in intergenerational learning about immigration through participative game design.

Margarida Romero, Université Laval (margarida.romero@fse.ulaval.ca), Eugène Loos, Utrecht University and University of Amsterdam (e.f.loos@uu.nl)

Engaging older people in digital creation activities is required if we aim to design games they really want to play and profit the benefits. Participatory design of digital games should allow them to engage in game creation activities instead of using games that have been designed for them by younger generations. The goal is not the game product but the game creation process. We present an intergenerational game design experience developed last December in Québec engaging an older person to share his life narrative as an immigrant and acts as narrative director during the whole process, eight secondary level students as game designers, and a pre-service secondary teacher acted as an instructional designer helping to link older people's experience with the curricular learning objectives of the Social Universe curriculum in Quebec secondary education system. This pilot was based in an intergenerational participatory design approach to promote an open discussion on the topic of migration and a guided interactive Digital Game Based Learning (DGBL) life narrative construction.. We aim to disseminate the research protocol and learning materials (storyboards templates encouraging the audience to remix and replicate this intergenerational game design experience in their communities. We will discuss the project and positive assessment of both our older person and secondary level students and reflect upon the intergenerational digital game design experience both as a motivating methodology and a way for understanding the complexity of migration through a real life narrative.

Main target groups of the project: Lifelong Learners, Older adults, Secondary Level Students, Pre-service teachers.

Significant public results:

The **intergenerational game creation Summer Camp** (Québec, 20th and 21st August, 2015) aims reunites elders and secondary level students in a creative game creation experience during two days. The Summer Camp will also engage a group of researchers and graduate students working in the area of game based learning and active ageing (silver gaming) and secondary level social universe teachers. The summer camp will engage elders in an intergenerational creative collaborative activity inviting them to create their own life narratives through the use of technology. Secondary level students will collaborate with elders in the creation of their digital life narrative and learn from the elders' experience. Elders will collaborate with the secondary level students in the digital creation of their life narrative. Researchers and graduate students will support the intergenerational game creation experience and discuss the opportunities of intergenerational learning through game creation. Secondary education social universe teachers' will be invited also to discuss the opportunities of the intergenerational game creation experience from the perspective of the curriculum objectives.

EHLSSA

European Home Learning Service for Seniors Association

Website: http://www.ehlssa.odl.org

Runtime: 09.2014 – 08.2017

Supported / co-funded by: Erasmus + KA2 Strategic Partnership

Partners: University of Erlangen Nürnberg – Innovation in Learning Institute, Germany, Universitat Jaume I., Spain, University of Helsinki, Finland, Dublin City University, Ireland, E-SENIORS association, France

Project representative to be contacted for further info: Anne-Marie Lipphardt (Anne-Marie.Lipphardt@ili.fau.de)

The EHLSSA (European Home Learning Service for Seniors Association) project is based on widely accepted and reported Europe-wide analysis about (missing) learning opportunities for elderly and its consequences. All steps to overcome this miserable situation can clearly be derived by logical and empirical evidence.

The first analysis element: European elderly are, in their majority, excluded from continuous learning. Whilst all other citizens, starting from one year of age, have a guaranteed life accompanying education and training offer, the after retirement population does not have this. All reliable offer ends in a moment where people have, in average, to expect some more 20 or 30 years of life. This is known and discussed Europe-wide since many years and no solution was found so far. This proposal claims to enter a new phase of elderly (online) learning and to show a way to overcome the entirely unsatisfying current situation.

The second element of analysis concerns learning of elderly: It is evident that, in a rapidly changing world, life without learning leads to a couple of unpleasant effects for the individual and for the society, just to name some: reduced autonomy, increasing dependency from others, less integration, social isolation, segregation of generations, reduced satisfaction of life, more fragile health... Every reported effect could be underlined with empirical data, is on the other hand self-evident.

The consortium will compile all elements which are needed to provide in principle every elderly in Europe, independent of her/his geographical situation, mobility, availability of time and daily rhythm, with a reliable learning offer with courses which are relevant for them and where they contribute according to their competences, within ten years' time. EHLSSA will model and empirically validate this risky promise.

The partnership consists of five experienced elderly learning institutions from France, Finland, Germany, Ireland, Spain, countries with very scarcely populated regions. They will be ideal test beds for the EHLSSA Service to be established.

The impact is very clear. Elderly in Europe will have, on the long run, a reliable learning offer equivalent to the other ages, not based on their random living conditions but based on a sustainable service. This will lead to a more participating, involved, included, and healthy generation of elderly.

Main target groups of the project:

- Senior learners, that will be able to take advantage of the on-line courses
- Trainers and adult education institutions (as managers, educational facilitators, designers, etc.), that can (re)use the material and also adopt the methodology used in EHLSSA for developing the training units.
- Researchers, interested on adult education pedagogies, and on the potentialities on the technology enhanced learning to senior learners.
- Other stakeholders and decision-makers when proposing ICT blended educational activities for senior citizens.

Significant public results:

- 3 completely virtual courses (prototype) specifically designed to senior citizens (based on user need analysis)
- Pedagogical guide (for the training) and methodological guide (for the content production)
- Course test and impact analysis

TECHN

SenApp

Seniors Learning with APPs

Website: http://www.senapp.eu

Runtime: 01.2014 – 12.2015

Supported / co-funded by: Lifelong learning programme – Grundtvig multilateral project

Partners: University of Erlangen Nürnberg – Innovation in Learning Institute, Germany, E-SENIORS association, France, Universitat Jaume I., Spain, Grupul pentru Integrare Europeana, Romania.

Project representative to be contacted for further info: Sonia Hetzner (Sonia.Hetzner@ili.fau.de)

The project SenApp – Seniors Learning with APPs – aims at developing a Training App for seniors in four European countries (France, Spain, Romania and Germany) to support them effectively and individually to become competent ICT (Information and Communication Technologies) users.

This project focuses on the need for eInclusion of senior citizens in Europe, the latter still being very much under-represented when it comes to competent and self-directed use of ICT. The digital divide still concerns, to a major extent, the older population. Using a mobile learning training Approach for easy to handle tablet-computers SenAPP will support seniors optimally in the process of accessing and becoming involved in the information and knowledge society, by applying the well-proven formula of using ICT as a learning medium as well as a learning content (eLearning environment). SenApp will utilize the potentials of ICT for the older generation by developing a non-formal, flexible and accessible App-based ICT qualification course that matches the very specific needs of this heterogeneous target group. Special focus will be given to multimedia-enriched didactic elements (demonstrations, audio-visual elements, interactive exercises), in order to cope with the diverse impairments, fears and disabilities of seniors. The modular course concept makes it possible to choose and aggregate a variable number of learning units into one course in the training App environment, to respect prior knowledge, demands and preferences. The effective and flexible App-Training Approach will be designed and developed in a way that makes it possible to localize the training system to every country and language interested in using it. The project expects to highly contribute towards the digital society and the Europe 2020 goals.

Objectives

- Develop a mobile learning environment dedicated to Tablet-PCs, adapted to the requirements of seniors and mobile learning and offered to the senior citizens
- Develop 25 learning units conceived and tailored to the learning needs of seniors in four European countries
- Contribute in an innovative way to the eInclusion (digital inclusion) of Seniors
- Research and Innovation on innovative technology-based training concepts for heterogeneous target groups.

Main target groups of the project:

- Senior learners, that will be able to take advantage of the course
- Trainers and adult education institutions (as managers, educational facilitators, designers, etc), that can (re)use the material and also adopt the methodology used in SenApp for developing the training units.
- Researchers, interested on adult education pedagogies, and on the potentialities on the technology enhanced learning to senior learners.
- Other stakeholders and decision-makers when proposing ICT educational activities for senior citizens.

Significant public results:

- 25 learning units
- Pedagogical guide (for the training) and methodological guide (for the content production)
- Course test and impact analysis

RECOGN TECHN ASSESS INFORM

PRONURSING

Website: http://www.pro-nursing.eu

Runtime: 09.2014 – 09.2016

Supported / co-funded by: EU-Funded Erasmus +

Partners:

- Coordinator: University of Siegen, Institute of Knowledge Based Systems, Germany
- Full partners: Universiteit van Amsterdam – Amsterdam Business School, The Netherlands; Beta Klinik GmbH, Bonn, Germany; Netpositive Ltd.

Project representative to be contacted for further info: **Dr. Gábor Kismihók** (g.kismihok@uva.nl)

Challenges:

Across Europe, the demand of the health sector for highly qualified nurses is great and growing. According to the German Federal Statistical Office of Germany (DESTATIS), care dependency across Germany is projected to increase by up to 50% in the 2007-2030 period. As employers, Medical institutions,, are looking to recruit nurses (job applicants) who have acquired the required skill set. Specifically, they need knowledgeable employees who are eligible to reliably perform certain tasks in over time.

Obtaining the required skills is not only achieved by means of curricular coursework. Nurses need to practice and implement the learning material, and develop their level of proficiency by providing care in various situations over time. The key challenges that the Pro-Nursing project aims to investigate:

- How nurses apply skills and skill prerequisite knowledge in various task situations
- How nursing tasks are embedded in nursing processes
- How nurses may acquire that knowledge which is required for successful job performance.

Work-based education and training has a considerable impact on improving nurses' job performance, and therefore detecting and compensating existing lacks in the nursing knowledge domain is critical. In this project, nurses, medical supervisors (employers), educators, and researchers from the knowledge management and HRM disciplines, are collaborating to create solutions to the aforementioned challenges.

Figure 1.

Objectives:

Within the German nursing context, PRO-NURSING aims at bridging between tasks, knowledge domains and nursing curricula, the result of which could serve as a benchmark for other European states. The triple attributes of nursing will be considered dynamically by incorporating evidence of change with respect to standards and protocols of nursing. The dedicated system will be developed as a web-based application with an ontological back-end. This is innovative, especially in supporting nursing educators and supervisors to sustain the quality of nursing care in both clinics and hospitals. Pro-Nursing is the descendant project of Med-Assess.

Main target groups of the project: Academia, Industry, Policy

METHOD TECHN

P4G

Play4Guidance: A European Business Game to Train and Guide Students and Young Unemployed on Entrepreneurial, Transversal and Mathematical Skills

Website: http://play4guidance.eu

Runtime: 01/09/2014 – 31/08/2017

Supported / co-funded by: Erasmus Plus

Partners: Coordinator: Fondazione Politecnico di Milano (FPM), Italy; National and Kapodistrian University of Athens (NKUA), Greece; Science View, Hellenic Association of Science Journalists, Science Writers and Science Communicators (Science View), Greece; Universita Carlo Cattaneo LIUC, Italy; Tekkekoy Ilce Milli Egitim Mudurlugu (MEM), Turkey; Bulgarian Industrial Association – Union of the Bulgarian Business (BIA), Bulgaria; Dublin City University (DCU), Ireland; Hochschule Ruhr West (HRW), Germany.

Project representative to be contacted for further info: Stefano Menon (stefano.menon@fondazione.polimi.it)

One of the greatest challenges that Europe faces is upgrading, adapting and widening the skills portfolio of individuals to create and fill the jobs of tomorrow. Currently, the challenge in education and training is to find new ways of engaging people in learning processes. Play4Guidance (P4G) is an EU funded project that introduces an innovative Business Game with the aim to train and guide students and young unemployed on entrepreneurial, transversal and mathematical skills.

Why Business Games? Business Games are an innovative learning method that reinforces managerial, entrepreneurial, digital and collaborative competences, and promotes critical thinking, problem solving and leadership. Business Games encourage people to learn and update their skills, beyond simply using ICT. The participants assume the role of decision makers by operating within a model that simulates the evolution of an economic reality, micro-economic (enterprise) or macro-economic (market). Business simulation games are used by numerous schools, universities and companies worldwide and are a valuable companion tool for business classes, social studies, and financial literacy programs. They supplement the core curriculum, reinforce key concepts, and provide an interactive educational approach to business, economics, and entrepreneurship.

P4G main objectives:

- To bring the world of education and training in close contact with the job market, in order to match school and university curricula to the market's real needs.
- To boost entrepreneurial culture in young Europeans and help young Europeans acquire the skills needed to create new businesses. This will potentially contribute to a reduction in EU unemployment.
- To identify essential business skills among target groups and target countries and collect them in the Great Common Denominator Skills Matrix.
- To produce an effective European tool able to:
  - support students and unemployed in developing basic math, economic, digital and entrepreneurial transversal skills with a strong focus on problem solving and leadership,
  - allow students and unemployed to self-evaluate their skills, understand what being an entrepreneur means and realise what skills they need to improve on,
  - support various institutions such as guidance centres, job centres, SMEs, companies and universities in evaluating participant skills and guiding them through training and skill-building.

Main target groups of the project: Direct target groups – high school students, university students, young unemployed. Indirect target groups: teachers, employment centres, training and guidance centres, SME

METHOD **TECHN**

Significant public results:

- P4G Business Game available for free on the project educational platform
- P4G Greatest Common Denominator Skills Matrix (GCDS Matrix) on math, economic, transversal entrepreneurial and digital skills among target groups and target countries. The matrix will be used in order to create the P4G tool for evaluation and guidance
- Training system through the Business Game
- P4G toolkit and training materials
- P4G syllabus (achieved)
- P4G initial assessment report – 1000 surveys and 15 focus groups run in 5 different Countries (expected for end of April)
- P4G Pedagogical framework & Model: P4G for self-evaluation, evaluation and guidance
- P4G Educational platform (expected for end of April)

METHOD TECHN LANAL ASSESS INFORM

EDUWORKS

Crossing Borders in the Comprehensive Investigation of Labour Market matching Processes: An EU-Wide, Trans-Disciplinary, Multilevel and Science-Practice-Bridging Training

Website: http://www.eduworks-network.eu

Runtime: 10.2013 – 09.2017

Supported / co-funded by: EU-Funded FP7 Marie Curie Initial Training Network

Partners: Coordinator: University of Amsterdam, Netherlands; Full partners: Central European University, Hungary; Corvinno Technology Transfer Center, Hungary; University of Salamanca, Spain; University of Siegen, Germany; Trinity College of Dublin, Ireland. Associated partners: http://eduworks-network.eu/pages/associated-partners

Project representative to be contacted for further info: **Dr. Gábor Kismihók** (g.kismihok@uva.nl)

The objective of EDUWORKS is to train talented early-stage researchers in the socioeconomic and psychological dynamics of the labour supply and demand matching processes at aggregated and disaggregated levels. EDUWORKS brings together researchers from several academic disciplines, namely: Labour Economics, Sociology of Occupations, HRM, Lifelong Learning, and Knowledge Management.

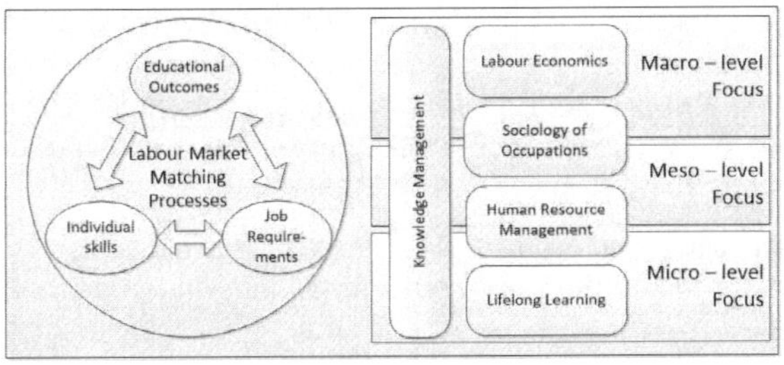

Figure 1.

EDUWORKS focuses on matching processes at three levels and on one overarching topic:

- Individual level fit between job demands – persons' abilities
- Meso-level employers' demands for occupational skills versus occupational dynamics
- European and national level labour supply and demand matches and mismatches
- Knowledge Management for supply and demand matches

The specific research training aims of the research in the ITN are to develop expertise in:

1. Investigating demands - abilities fit, that is the extent to which individual skills and abilities match the demands (tasks) and requirements of organizations, and the ways in which organisations allocate tasks to jobs.
2. Investigating the mechanism concerning the division of work reflected in task sets of occupations and the shaping of occupational boundaries, the skill sets related to these occupations and the ways in which organisations define their skills need.
3. Investigating the wide range of mechanisms causing skills mismatches in national and European labour markets, including the impact of the 2008 crisis on skills-occupation mismatch in Europe, and workers' responsiveness to labour market shortages concerning gender, age, and ethnicity.
4. The establishment of a common language on the basis of which future investigations on the topics may draw to further facilitate training and knowledge exchange.
5. The strengthening of interdisciplinary research cooperation so as to advance our understanding of the matching mechanisms and the interactions between different levels of aggregation, including research cooperation with private and academic organisations.

Main target groups of the project: Academia, Industry, Policy

POLICY METHOD TECHN LANAL OPEN INFORM

RIPE NCC Academy

Réseaux IP Européens Network Coordination Centre Academy

Website: https://academy.ripe.net

Runtime: Started in November 2014. Available 24/7

Supported / co-funded by: Funded by the RIPE NCC membership as part of the organisation's activity plan

Partners: There are no partners in this project

Project representative to be contacted for further info: Sandra Brás, email: sbras@ripe.net

Following the project of the Master's thesis, presented at EDEN 2014 "The importance of eLearning in transforming organisational strategies: the case study of the RIPE NCC", we spent 2014 developing the RIPE NCC Academy based on that research. The RIPE NCC Academy is an integrated learning system that uses a Virtual Learning Environment (Moodle) to facilitate learning journeys to anyone who would like to learn about how the Internet works and RIPE NCC-related topics. Our goal is to offer free and open courses that can help Network Engineers, Network Administrators, ISP's Customer Services Representatives and Management to do their job, although anyone can join our courses free of charge.

The RIPE NCC Academy is focused on providing the tools to help our students to perform certain tasks at work and solve problems in an easier way. Given that there was a gap in our industry, our courses offer short sections focused on what people need to learn and always having in mind that our students are full-time employees who want to learn something very quickly to move on with their job. Our pedagogy is learner-centred, and it is based on interactive content and personalised tutor support, which is one of our highest values.

Currently, we offer one open and self-paced course (RIPE Database Expert Course). We are already working on two more courses of this type on topics such as IPv6 and Local Internet Registry, which we are planning to launch in April 2015.

In the summer of 2015 we will launch an Online Summer School that is going to make the offering in the Academy much more diverse and that also aims to have courses related to the Internet but on a more political and leadership level, e.g., Internet Governance course.

During the development of our courses we make sure that the content is easily accessible on any device and that it follows the same structure in every course provided.

Main target groups of the project: Anyone who wants to learn more about the Internet and RIPE NCC-related services, more specifically, Network Engineers, Network Administrators, Internet Provider's Customer Services and ISP's Management and Internet Leaders.

Significant public results: In 2014, the RIPE NCC delivered 112 face-t-face training courses in more than 39 different countries to more than 2290 participants. We had 699 participants in the 51 webinars we delivered also last year. As one of the Regional Internet Registries whose main function is the distribution of Internet Number Resources (IPv4 and IPv6 addresses and AS Numbers) to our more than 11000 member organisations located in 76 different countries (Europe, Middle East and Central Asia), the RIPE NCC also needs to train its members on the tools and procedures they need to master to be able to do their job. Although we try to reach as many people in as many countries as we can, it is quite difficult for us to travel to some countries with political instability: currently Iraq, Syria, Yemen, Lebanon and Gaza.

In the training courses we have also noticed that people like certificates, especially our members in South and Easter Europe. It is based on these two premises that the RIPE NCC exists: We offer online learning possibilities to our members who cannot travel to attend our training courses and we also make sure that they are certified for the skills they acquire.

The RIPE NCC Academy exists since early November 2014 and it has been an extremely successful service. All the feedback we have received is highly positive. Currently we have 737 registered users, 422 enrolled in the RIPE Database Expert course and 117 students have already obtained their certificate.

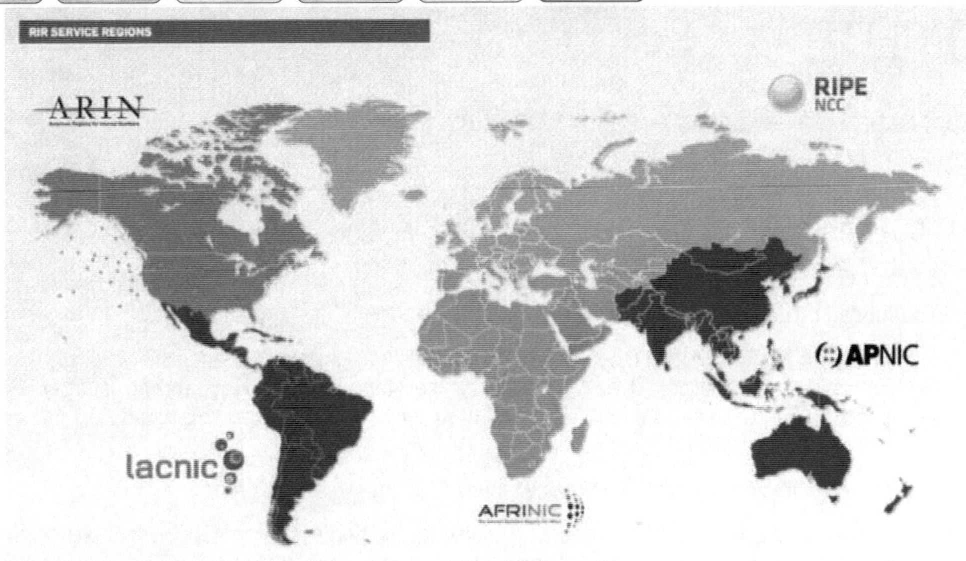

Figure 1. The services regions of the five Regional Internet Registries
The RIPE NCC's region is represented in yellow

In the future we are hoping to collaborate with the other Regional Internet Registries and other organisations, such as Universities or Governments to promote the integration of our courses with Computer Science degrees or any degree related to the Internet and Network Engineering. Our aim is to promote this knowledge to all interested parties and to form healthy partnerships to carry on the growth and the development of the Internet.

METHOD TECHN COMM

CCD FLITE

Concurrent Design Framework for eLearning in IT Entrepreneurship

FLITE

Website: http://www.ccdflite.eu

Runtime: 10.2013 – 09.2015

Supported / co-funded by: Lifelong Learning, Erasmus Multilateral projects

Partners: Mid Sweden University, Sweden (coordinator); Sør-Trøndelag University College, HiST, Norway; University of Greenwich, UK; CENFIM – Vocational Training Centre for the Metallurgy and Metalworking Industry, Portugal; Alexander Technological Educational Institute (ATEI) of Thessaloniki, Greece; Anne Fox ApS, Denmark; XLAB, Slovenia; TISIP, Norway.

Project representative to be contacted for further info: Anne Fox (annef@annefox.eu)

Aims: The FLITE-project is creating an entrepreneurship course focused on best practice tools for collaborative work for bringing ideas to market (including innovation, business planning, reach-out, etc.) in a distributed environment. The course aims to bring together students/graduates from higher education and employees from the IT-sector, allowing them to create innovative solutions. ConCurrent Design (CCD) is a process method focusing on how to collaborate in a more effective way. Originally developed by NASA, CCD has been further developed by several of our partners. We will also produce a reusable framework, that others interested in setting up a similar course can use, and a free app containing information on the framework, collaboration tools and processes, and how to set up a similar course. Our most important goal is to connect students and the labour market, facilitating the two-way knowledge transfer between academia and industry and generating opportunities for innovation. This provides the possibility for students to connect to and get insight in their future work and creating a network cross Europe. One of the main planks of the course is training participants in group collaboration processes such as ConCurrent Design which is a way of rapid prototyping by making use of all the expertise of the group in a series of planned, structured synchronous meetings rather than by dividing up tasks and hoping that they will fit together at the end.

Pilot courses:

In a globalised world online collaboration is becoming routine, therefore the proposed training:

- is offered online
- comprises a mixture of HE and industry-based learners
- focuses first on personal development plans
- requires small groups of learners to become familiar with their respective institutions' innovations
- progresses to a business development plan
- includes an internal dissemination plan
- ends with a peer-reviewed online presentation

The course consists of theoretical input on entrepreneurship as well as support for using tools such as the Business Model You, Business Model Generator and ConCurrent Design. The end product of the course is a business plan summarised in a video elevator pitch which is peer reviewed by the other groups. Intangible results include the connections made within and across the participant groups as a result of intense collaboration.

Challenges: The course is not tied to a specific platform; we are trialling two during the project. The main challenges we face are how to better promote structured self-directed learning (SSDL) and how to manage the formation of groups. We offered a small-scale pilot to test the structure of the course and our second pilot will be on a larger scale, tending towards MOOC proportions, where we can stress test and evaluate the scalability of the SSDL pedagogy and group formation and collaboration processes.

Outcomes: Course students meet in a mixed setup with other participants from different countries, with different business cultures and backgrounds. They then have to work together in groups choosing an idea of their own to be developed into a business model. To that end, they will have access to basic knowledge in entrepreneurship, training in collaboration and tools for business modelling.

METHOD TECHN COMM

Main target groups of the project: IT students close to completion of their bachelors or in the course of a Masters or PhD as well as employees in an IT company or department wishing to explore intrapreneurship and/or entrepreneurship.

Universities and businesses (initially IT departments or companies) wanting to promote more links across sectors and borders

Significant public results:

Open Seminar – ONLINE ENTREPRENEURIAL COURSE,

Conference "**Entrepreneurship in a new Training context**" organized by CENFIM and FLITE consortium, in **Lisbon 7th October 2014**,

Global Education Online conference, 18th November 2014 "Promoting Collaboration across borders: Two approaches" Anne Fox.

TECHN OPEN

StartUP

Intelligent Training Needs Assessment and Open Educational Resources to Foster Entrepreneurship

Website: http://www.startupproject.eu

Runtime: 01.2013 – 08.2015

Supported / co-funded by: Lifelong Learning Programme – KA3 – ICT Multilateral Projects

Partners: SOPHIA Research & Innovation, Italy (coordinator); BEST Institut für berufsbezogene Weiterbildung und Personaltraining GmbH, Austria; UPM, Universidad Politécnica de Madrid, Spain; FWE, Foundation for Women Entrepreneurs, Malta; CECE, Confederation of Education and Training Centres, Spain; Inova Consultancy, United Kingdom; Profesia, Italy

Project representative to be contacted for further info: Cristina Stefanelli, SOPHIA R&I (cristina.stefanelli@gmail.com)

Linkage with Open Educational Resources and the entrepreneurial sector is in an early stage of investigation. StartUP aims to fill the blank spot for where no open and flexible entrepreneurial training opportunities are in place for reaching the lifelong learner.

The project developed an innovative pedagogy and assessment approach, based on Open Educational Resources (OER), to support the diverse individual learning pathways and to better assess all types of learning outcomes and future learning needs related to entrepreneurship competences (entrepreneurial mindset and sense of initiative), a key competence for the lifelong learner. The project challenges the matching process between available OER and individual training needs, with the aim to promote the use and re-use of OER in a pedagogically-rich context, increasing the number of OER users and foster the effectiveness of OER for entrepreneurial educational purposes.

Main target groups of the project: StartUP addresses a wide target audience, composed by secondary school, higher education teachers and students, VET trainers and trainees, adult learners and professionals.

Significant public results:

OER Gateway: It is the online tool developed by the project. It is based on the concept that "one size doesn't fit all", in particular when it comes to the development of an entrepreneurial mind-set. Within the OER Gateway, learning needs of individual learners match selected relevant contents, retrieved from available OER repositories worldwide. The OER Gateway is an open learning architecture that provides users with personalized training sets based on their specific needs, using the most effective contents openly available online. The OER Gateway is composed by the following components: a Virtual Expert, an Authoring System, a Rating function and a Recommender (http://www.startupproject.eu/?q=oer-academy).

The OER Gateway offer training sets in relevant entrepreneurial-relates clusters: Business, Management, Communication and Self-development competences.

POLICY RECOGN TECHN LANAL COMM INFORM

iPro

The iProfessional

Website: http://www.ipro-project.eu

Runtime: 10.2013 – 10.2015

Supported / co-funded by: Lifelong Learning Programme; Education Audiovisual and Culture Executive Agency; Erasmus]

Partners: Nine (9) Partners' in eight (8) countries – Coordinator: Institute for training of personnel on international organisation (ITPIO) http://www.itpio.eu. List of partners at: http://ipro-project.eu/project/partners

Project representative to be contacted for further info: Philip Penny (philip.penny@iadt.ie)

The aim of the iPro project is to set up a pilot collaboration between HEIs and VET providers in 8 European countries to investigate the potential for a closer collaboration between the world of the interactive media and arts design business and the higher and further education institutions for Media and Arts Design Studies. The collaboration will focus on detection of possible skills and competences mismatches between education and the professional world and will consequently put in place a pilot mechanism to address this mismatch by designing and piloting a curriculum design framework for use in this specific sector. We are currently in month 15 of a 24 month project and have recently compiled the results and analysis of the iPro survey. Ultimately the project also aims to build, test and then distribute a research based model framework that will assist the Education sector and especially VET and the Higher Education Institutions to match, in a digital way, the curriculum of their students in Media and Arts Studies with the professional requirements expressed by the international community of media and arts businesses. This framework will demonstrate its effectiveness and quality in a series of pilots projects in the participating HEIs, as well as in other institutions that express their interest.

iProfessional survey results and analysis

The iProfessional survey collected data about the skills and competences of professionals working in digital media and arts in 8 European countries. The rich and complex data that are the result of the survey investigates the impact of education on the worker in his or her professional environment including the effect of internship.

This is the first comprehensive survey of this type in Europe within this professional category. The survey has allowed us to make a quantitative and qualitative analysis of the profiles of media workers with regard to the competences, skills and attitudes they possess related to media businesses, such as artistic skills, technical skills, business processes knowledge, communication, project management, structuring of content, team work, problem solving, time management, etc. The survey resulted in a comprehensive list of transversal skills and competences that are required by the professional digital media and arts worker set against those acquired in formal education as well as on the job.

Main target groups of the project:

1. Higher education institutions;
2. University students;
3. SMEs;
4. Corporations;
5. VET institutions;
6. VET students.

Significant public results:

The main public result or output will be a research based model framework that will assist the Education sector and especially VET and the Higher Education Institutions to match, in a digital way, the curriculum of their students in Media and Arts Studies with the professional requirements expressed by the international community of media and arts businesses. The results from the survey can be found:
http://ipro-project.eu/sites/default/files/outcomes/iPro_Deliverable_D3_3_FINAL.pdf

TECHN

m-commerce

m-commerce

Website: https://www.m-commerce.enterprises/

Runtime: 09.2014 – 09.2016

Supported / co-funded by: Erasmus+ Strategic partnership KA2

Partners: FH Joanneum Graz (Austria), University of Alcala (Spain), Politehnica University of Timisoara (Romania), Center for Knowledge (Macedonia)

Project representative to be contacted for further info: prof. Radu Vasiu (radu.vasiu@upt.ro)

The project m-commerce focuses on the training of staff and employees of Small- and Medium-sized Enterprises (SMEs) in order to develop the further development and expansion of m-commerce activities.

The project is divided into different phases that build up on each other. The first phase includes a state-of-the-art analysis of m-commerce activities and its demands, which is based on online surveys, controlled interviews and the evaluation of secondary data. The results, which are unified due to the country-dependent findings, are the basis for the development of the training course m-commerce. Another result of this phase is a best-practice database, in which already existing as well as successful m-commerce solutions are displayed.

In phase 2, the training course as such is developed on the lessons learned in phase 1. The training course is developed by the project partners: FH Joanneum Graz (Austria), University of Alcala (Spain), Politehnica University of Timisoara (Romania), Center for Knowledge (Macedonia). Phase 3 is characterized by the implementation of the training curse. The training course is conducted in all partner countries. In this context, the choice of participating companies is taking into consideration in order to achieve a balanced mix of trades and industry.

In the project m-commerce, the following activities are conducted:

- Survey of the current status quo of m-commerce in different European regions
- Collecting best practice examples from different regions
- Development of teaching and learning materials for the training course m-commerce
- Implementation of the training course in all seven partner countries, having a minimum of 10 participating employees of SMEs each training cycle
- Participating SMEs of each training cycle are equipped with m-commerce strategies and first possible solutions for m-commerce implementation

Main target groups of the project: SMEs employees

Significant public results: The **m-commerce training course**, a holistic approach, includes economic, legal and technical topics that are necessary for the switch to m-commerce. The course consists of three blocks, having duration of two days. The blocks are arranged in such a way that they can be attended individually. Each block focuses on one major topic.

Block 1 aims at familiarizing the participants with the topic m-commerce. In this context, e-business models and business processes are addressed. The second part of this block deals with country specific legal and safety-related issues of online businesses. A basic understanding of the processes and procedures in e-commerce and m-commerce is the basis for customer satisfaction as well as an increased turnover.

Block 2 deals with the aspects of online marketing in the first place. Further, possibilities of social media marketing are discussed. Not only the usage of different marketing channels, but also the critical reflections concerning the results of these activities, as well as the personalization of offers enlarge the range of customers of the participating enterprises.

Block 3 deals with the technical aspects of m-commerce. In this context, usability, responsive design and mobile first approaches are considered for already existing e-commerce applications. The goal of this block is it to optimize current e-commerce tenders for mobile devices. In this context, we can speak of a holistic system tuning, ranging from the representation, to performance and storing of data.

POLICY OPEN

HOME

Higher Education Online: MOOCs the European Way

Website: http://home.eadtu.eu/

Runtime: 01.2014 – 06.2016

Supported / co-funded by: Life Long Learning programme, KA3. Project number: 543516-LLP-1-2013-1-NL-KA3-KA3NW

Partners: Coordinated by EADTU, Netherlands. In total 23 full list available at http://home.eadtu.eu/partners

Project representative to be contacted for further info: Darco Jansen, darco.jansen@eadtu.eu

Short description of HOME: The HOME project develops and strengthens an open network for European cooperation on open education, in general, and MOOCs, in particular.

The specific objectives of this project of HOME are to:

- determine the opportunities and characteristics for a European cooperation on MOOCs and to further develop these characteristics based on European values like openness, equity, quality and diversity;
- explicate and develop the didactic and pedagogic models for MOOCs on a European scale;
- develop the conditions for shared educational services in offering and monitoring European MOOCs;
- develop sustainable business models for joint efforts on these European MOOCs at a global, European, national and institutional level;
- build up a sustainable open knowledge network for these types of MOOCs which is open to the whole world;
- initiate activities in different learning communities to enhance European-wide competence development on main topics related to developing and offering MOOCs;
- create guidelines and the policy incentives on a local, national and European level for an open knowledge network in MOOC offerings.

Main target groups of the project: The main target group are European experts (and those that want to become experts) in the field of open education and MOOCs. Those experts are facilitated by the HOME project to work on issues together with the HOME partners.

Significant public results:

- definition of what's a MOOC and what isn't in collaboration those EU-funded MOOC projects (http://home.eadtu.eu/images/Results/Definition_Massive_Open_Online_Courses.pdf);
- open call for position papers on the opportunities and characteristics for European cooperation on MOOCs (http://home.eadtu.eu/images/News/Open_Call_Position_paper_MOOCs_Update_8Sept.pdf). In total 19 experts submitted their papers. After review of the papers 12 were selected to present their views at a conference organised by HOME. After revision the total 15 papers were accepted for publication in a separate report (http://home.eadtu.eu/images/Position_papers_for_European_cooperation_on_MOOCs.pdf);
- survey to benchmark strategies on MOOC of European institutions and governments. In total 67 institutions responded out of 22 European countries representing in total about 2.8 millions of students (http://home.eadtu.eu/news/88-survey-on-benchmarking-mooc-strategies-in-europe);
- conference titled "Mapping the European MOOC Territory" in Porto. This conference was on invitation only and limited to 80 participants. At the end 74 experts from 22 countries attended the conference (http://home.eadtu.eu/images/News/Home_Conference_Final.pdf);
- after the conference we published a Porto declaration on European MOOCs. During the first three months of 2015 the Porto declaration was amongst the most popular items on the portal Open Education Europa. Until March 2015, 72 institutions, projects and associations supported this declaration (http://home.eadtu.eu/images/News/Porto_Declaration_on_European_MOOCs_Final.pdf);
- published the survey results in a report titled "Institutional MOOC strategies in Europe". Although published in February 2015, we already received many positive reactions. On request four quest blogs were published about the outcomes of this report (http://www.eadtu.eu/documents/Publications/OEenM/Institutional_MOOC_strategies_in_Europe.pdf).

POLICY

D-TRANSFORM

DigiTal Resources As a New Strategical Factor fOr a Renovation of Modernization in Higher Education

Website: http://www.dtransform.eu/

Runtime: 01 September 2014 – 31 August 2017

Supported / co-funded by: Erasmus+

Partners: Fondation Maison Des Sciences De L'Homme, FR (coordinator); Université de Lorraine, FR; Sero Consulting Ltd, UK; Fundacio per a la Universitat Oberta de Catalunya, ES; Politecnico di Milano – METID, IT; European Distance and E-Learning Network, UK; Budapest University of Technology and Economics, HU.

Project representative to be contacted for further info: Angela Procoli (procoli@msh-paris.fr)

The D-TRANSFORM project is a first attempt to set up a "University Leader Program" at the European level, addressed to university presidents and vice-presidents on the role of e-Education in shaping University strategies. It gathers together specialists of e-Education from various institutions (University, higher education ministries, consultancy in learning innovation, e-Education networks) and primarily considers that digital technologies, like Massive Open Online Courses, (MOOCs) and Open Educational Resources are an essential lever for transforming the higher education systems and adapting them to the new needs of youth and requirements of work-market (lifelong training).

D-TRANSFORM intends to produce recommendations on various aspects of a university strategy on the use of digital tools. Based on these recommendations, D-TRANSFORM will set up two "leadership schools", dedicated, for the 1st time in Europe, to the university governances.

Main target groups of the project: HE Institutions and schools, presidents, vice-presidents and staff involved in management at the highest level

Significant public results:

Publication of **guidelines** of a training program for university leaders on the base of state-of-the art and context analysis of European and national public policies, a business model for online training, rationalising the costs of HE through the use of digital teaching by evidence-based analysis and case studies.

Organisation of **two leadership schools** for university leaders (presidents and vice-presidents) of partner universities, establishing an **online training kit** based on assessment of training outcomes

Integration of the leadership school program and **the online training kit** into the lifelong training programs of the partner universities and national and European associations of university presidents.

3 multiplier events, organised yearly.

TECHN ASSESS

TALOE

Time to Assess Learning Outcomes in e-Learning

Website: http://taloe.up.pt

Runtime: January 2014 – December 2015

Supported / co-funded by: Lifelong Learning Programme – Key Activity 3 – ICT; Multilateral projects

Partners: University of Porto, Portugal (Co-ordinator); Dennis Gabor College, Hungary; University of Zagreb University Computing Centre – SRCE, Croatia; Innovate4Future – Center for Advanced Educational Solutions, Romania; Universidad Nacional de Educación a Distancia – UNED, Spain; University of Padua, Italy; European Distance and E-Learning Network – EDEN, UK; European University Continuing Education Network – EUCEN, Spain

Project representative to be contacted for further info: Éva Szalma, EDEN, United Kingdom (szalma@eden-online.org), Jüri Lõssenko, Information Technology Foundation for Education, Estonia (Jyri.Lossenko@hitsa.ee)

The TALOE project approached the e-assessment concept by using technology for assessing students' learning. The main purpose of TALOE is to develop a web based e-assessment platform to help teachers and trainers decide on the e-assessment strategies to use in their online courses.

The TALOE web tool is developed to help teachers and trainers decide on the assessment strategies to use in their online courses. The tool is envisaged to be used by teachers either to check if the existing assessment methods of their course or module are in line with the stated learning outcomes or to be advised on the most appropriate assessment methods for a new course or module. The decision engine is based on the ALOA model and consists in the estimation of a score as a measure of the best matching between the cognitive processes submitted by the user and the specific ones of a given assessment method.

The web platform also provides support and guidance to teachers to formulate the learning outcomes in accordance to Bloom taxonomy increasing this way the accuracy of the outcome received from the tool.

The TALOE web tool will be freely available to different stakeholders. These include Higher and Continuing Education institutions as well as vocational training organizations. It is also available for stakeholders associated with processes of recognition and accreditation. The tools of TALOE and user guides will be developed in English and will be translated into German and French to facilitate its use by different audiences.

Main target groups of the project:

- Teachers and trainers from all levels of education: they may use the TALOE tool to define e-assessment strategies for their courses or modules

Secondary target groups include:

- Researchers dealing with Learning Outcomes and e-assessment
- Recognition and accreditation staff may use TALOE to verify the validity of assessment methods of prior learning or to provide evidence for accreditation of programmes
- Programme developers may use TALOE to define e-assessment strategies recommendations for new online programmes
- Decision makers may use TALOE to define valid e-assessment strategies for their institutions
- Networks and initiatives operating in the fields of LOs, assessment, vocational training, higher education, continuing education and recognition and accreditation

Significant public results:

Web based e-assessment platform (available).

Series of webinars: Talks on E-Assessment and Learning Outcomes (available and still on-going).

POLICY TECHN LANAL OPEN

EDUOPEN

Federated Platform MOOCs

Runtime: March 2015 – February 2016

Supported / co-funded by: presented to MIUR (Italian Ministry for University and Research)

Partners: EDUOPEN is coordinated by Prof. Pierpaolo Limone, Delegato alla didattica e all'e-learning dell'Università di Foggia and Prof. Tommaso Minerva, Delegato all'e-learning dell'Università di Modena e Reggio Emilia, Direttore del Centro Interuniversitario EDUNOVA e Presidente della Società Italiana di e-learning Siel.

The University of Genoa is represented by Prof.ssa Marina Rui – marina@chimica.unige.it

Project representative to be contacted for further info: Giuliana MERAVIGLIA CANU – meraviglia@unige.it

The Conference theme referred is: The intersection between higher education and MOOCs

The project is aimed to realize a national network for the innovation of university teaching in a perspective of open access and open knowledge.

The project is focused on the following issues:

- shaping an action of educational innovation through the creation of an Italian ecosystem of MOOCs allowing the acquisition of ECTS through the participation of several universities already active in the field of distance education;
- build an internationalization strategy based on offering MOOCs in English, on the interchange of ECTS and the participation in the major international consortia MOOCs;
- promote an extensive educational and teaching research useful for developing "evidence-based" strategy for the dissemination of Italian open educational resources. We will investigate, by means of learning analytics, particularly: formats, patterns of interaction, teaching approaches and students' best practices.
- develop proper training for teachers and administrative staff of the involved universities to foster the use of technology in education.

Outcomes of the project to be realized:

1. guidance courses to face the shift from the high school to the university education(Bridging The Gaps);
2. courses intended for the upper university education (graduate schools, master or specialization courses).

At this stage the aim is to set up an inter-university Working Group to draft a proposal concerning the formal accreditation of CFU / ECTS related to potential curricular courses.

Main target groups of the project: the Italian University system.

EDEN Barcelona Conference seems to be the best forum for collecting suggestions and ideas from colleagues of all over Europe and beyond and to compare the various experiences already running elsewhere.

TECHN

Flexible Toolbox Project

Student Success Toolbox for Flexible Learners: Supporting Transitions from Thinking about Study to the First Few Weeks

Website: http://www.studentsuccess.ie

Runtime: February 2015 – January 2016

Supported / Co-funded by: National Forum for the Enhancement of Teaching and Learning / Fund for Building Digital Capacity – €254K

Partners: Leader partner: National Institute for Digital Learning, Dublin City University. Supporting partners: Dundalk Institute of Technology, Maynooth University, Silgo Institute of Technology, Ireland

Project representative to be contacted for further info: Dr James Brunton (james.brunton@dcu.ie)

Short description of the initiative:

This Synergy Paper reports on an externally funded research and development project currently in progress in the Republic of Ireland. The project seeks to address the problem of effective transitions and the foundations for student success during the initial stages of the study lifecycle with a specific focus on flexible learners. In the context of this study a broad definition is adopted of flexible learners, which includes adult, part-time and online/distance students. Enhancing retention and completion rates of this group of flexible learners is a significant problem both globally and within the Irish context. Although the number of flexible learners in Ireland is relatively low in comparison to many other countries, around 17% of all undergraduates (HEA 2012), there are increasing concerns about their ability to progress towards successful completion. Set against this backdrop and with support from the National Forum for the Enhancement of Teaching and Learning in Higher Education (http://teachingandlearning.ie), the project involves an initiative to address this problem by four partner institutions.

The particular focus of this project is on supporting flexible learners through key transitions in the early stages of the study lifecycle: from thinking about study, making choices, the registration process and through to the first few weeks. A basic premise of the project is the foundations for student success start early in the study lifecycle and insufficient attention has been given in the literature and within institutions to the importance of the period before flexible learners formally commence their study. A related underlying assumption is that this crucial transition period may be enhanced by the availability of appropriately designed digital readiness and preparation tools, which help to scaffold both prospective students and those about to embark on online/distance study for the first time.

There are five phases to this project.

- Phase One involves the project establishment, including formalising the project team, partner agreements and scope of the work packages.
- Phase Two involves an analysis of relevant literature and current digital readiness tools available internationally to support successful transitions during initial stages of the study lifecycle for flexible learners. The main deliverable of this phase is an analysis of the digital tools adopted internationally to enhance transitions to study for this unique sub population of learners.
- Phase Three involves building on the above synthesis to develop a strategically targeted suite of research-informed digital readiness tools. While they will have wider application across the sector, the tools will focus on facilitating adult learners who are transitioning to part-time undergraduate study. The major deliverable from this phase will be the development of a toolbox of a minimum of eight digital tools that can be used and/or adapted by other institutions in the Higher Education sector to support student success at this crucial period of the study lifecycle. The final selection, design and appropriateness of the digital readiness tools will be informed by the literature review and institutional analysis completed in Phase Two.
- Phase Four involves piloting and evaluating the digital tools across the partner institutions. Based on feedback gather during this evaluation phase, the digital tools will be adapted/augmented to ensure that they are fit for purpose.

- Phase Five will produce a Digital Guide for Supporting Flexible Learners, which will provide guidance for institutions and discipline teams on how to effectively deploy the suite of digital readiness tools. Another key deliverable of this phase is a series of workshops delivered in different higher education institutions on how to support transitions for flexible learners.

Main target groups of the project: Flexible learners in the early stages of the study lifecycle

Significant public results: Eight digital tools will be produced as OERs that the Higher Education sector can use to enhance the readiness and success of flexible learners; a Digital Guide for Supporting Flexible Learners will be published to support these tools; a series of workshops will be offered to assist other institutions to adapt and implement the digital readiness and preparation tools; a comprehensive report will be published with a literature review on supports and interventions that can be developed to enhance the success of flexible learners.

TECHN

MMSQC

A Multi-Platform Mobile Learning System for More Qualified Courses in the ICT Era

Website: http://www.marketingenius.org

Runtime: 04.2012 – 04.2014

Supported / co-funded by: British Council UK-Turkey HE Partnership Programme / TR/012012/KP18; Anadolu University Scientific Research Projects, 1209E146

Partners: Anadolu University, Turkey, University of Wolverhampton, UK, Okan University, Enocta, Turkey

Project representative to be contacted for further info: Nilgün Özdamar Keskin, nozdamar@anadolu.edu.tr

Anadolu University and Okan University collaborated with the University of Wolverhampton and Enocta, the Turkish commercial partner in order to improve their mobile learning vision, to develop advanced mobile learning applications, and to follow the latest developments in education and technology innovations for increasing the delivery of accredited courses in higher education in Turkey and Britain. In accordance with this goal, we organized four meetings between Turkey and Britain in the first year of the project and also conducted an extended workshop in the second year of the project.

Year 1 of the project has seen the successful development of a prototype university-level marketing studies multi-platform app. a multi-platform mobile learning system including marketing education was built by a team of Anadolu University. The Mobile learning system named as Marketing Genius Application is being published Google Play and Apple Market now. In 2014-2015 Fall semester, the application tested on students taking Marketing Course in Business Faculty in Anadolu University.

The workshop was conducted on 12 June 2013, Wednesday at Tuzla Campus of Okan University. The participants of the workshop include representatives from major operators of Turkey, faculty members of universities, companies working on mobile learning, specialists from distance learning centers of universities, Ministry of Education Fatih Project Formatters, YEGITEK (General Directorate of Innovation and Education) representatives, public and private primary and secondary education organizations, teachers and administrators, and representatives from various companies interested in this field. And it has enabled the assessment and consideration of the subject on a wide spectrum.

Main target groups of the project: This project let the Turkish trainers and companies understand the concept of mobile learning and need more qualified courses on that. It also enabled more precise approach to the subject.

Significant public results: Owing to our project and workshop Turkish learning sector had given more importance to mobile learning. Especially firm representatives who joined the workshop began advocating the importance of mobile learning. Enocta as a partner were influenced by us to make more qualified mobile learning products for the market. Dynamism of mobile learning affects the implications. There is now a tendency to have more mobile learning materials and easiness of using mobile learning had been understood.

There were several people working with each other during the project, more than 8 university representatives. More than 35 researchers come along together and had discussed mobile learning (e.g. quality; implementations; how to do etc) also K12 teacher and managers had faced the new opportunities for their educational settings. Industry representatives faced with this new approach.

It really helped for the cultural learning opportunity for both sides. Everyone appreciated the partners' work and approaches on the subjects. Industry has newly started to have this kind of products and concepts. Therefore there is some way to come. However this is kind of a leadership for the education industry. Enocta has accelerated their work on this issue. Some teachers commenced on this subject and want to launch into these kinds of products. But they need more guidance from academia.

- http://www.okan.edu.tr/haber/a-multiplatform-m-learning-system-for-more-qualified-courses-in-the-ict-era-2
- http://blog.britishcouncil.org/turkey/2013/02/20/projects-constructing-our-future-thoughts-on-m-learning-in-the-ict-era/
- http://www.britishcouncil.org.tr/sites/britishcouncil.tr2/files/knowledge-partnerships-for-an-innovative-future.pdf

TECHN

- https://tojde.anadolu.edu.tr/tojde55/articles/article_14.htm
- http://ab.org.tr/ab13/bildiri/274.pdf
- http://www.enocta.com/enocta/web/kurumportal/Content/okan-universitesi-mobil-ogrenme calistayi/1036/
- http://www.cedtech.net/articles/61/615.pdf

RECOGN OPEN

BEU

Badge Europe!

Website: http://www.openbadges.eu

Runtime: October 2014 – September 2017

Supported / co-funded by: Erasmus+

Partners: Beuth-Hochschule fuer Technik Berlin (Germany); Cambridge Professional Development (UK); ADPIOS (France), EDEN – European Distance and E-Learning Network (UK); Discendum Oy (Finland); Dienst Uitvoering Onderwijs (The Netherlands); Institute for Sustainable Technologies – National Research Institute (Poland); Digitalme (UK), ARTES – Applied Research into Training and Education Systems (Italy)

Project representative to be contacted for further info: Serge Ravet (serge.ravet@gmail.com), Livia Turzo (turzo@eden-online.org)

Get recognition for learning that happens anywhere. Then share it on the places that matter.

The Badge Europe! initiative (acronym BEU!, pronounced "Be You") reaches out to learners, citizens, educators, employers, public authorities and policy makers with the overall aim to create the conditions for:

- Providing systematic access to the recognition of all learning, whether non-formal, informal and formal.
- Increasing the transparency, trustworthiness and quality of the recognition of learning achievements.
- Empowering individuals for more balanced relationships with institutions and authorities.
- Creating new opportunities for employment, social inclusion and learning for all.

Main target groups of the project:

- Educational and human resource professionals.
- Employers and self-employed professionals and organisations.
- Organisations and learning communities where educational practitioners and leaders operate (educational institutions, businesses, public and private, small and large).
- Local, regional and national authorities, policy makers.
- Citizens at different stages of their education and life in a perspective of lifelong and life-wide learning.
- Professionals working with disadvantaged groups (learners with special needs, school push/drop out, women back to work, unemployed, migrants, etc.).
- Sister initiatives / projects (e.g. ODS, LeHo, VM-PASS, OpenPROF, etc.)
- Institutions, organisations who have influence and/or commitment in the recognition of informal learning and in-demand workplace skills.

Significant public results:

- Creation of an Open Badges European professional network.
- Open Badges MOOC (Massive Open Online Course).
- Open Badges initiatives to support learning regions and cities.
- Open Badges infrastructure.
- Integration of Open Badges at policy level, in particular with the Europass initiative.

TECHN

eLene4work

Learning to Learn for New Digital Soft Skills for Employability

Website: http://www.eLene4work.eu

Runtime: 12.2014 – 10.2017

Supported / co-funded by: Erasmus+ Cooperation for innovation and the exchange of good practices, Strategic Partnerships addressing more than one field

Partners: Fondazione Politecnico Di Milano, IT; EDEN, UK; Universite Paris Ouest Nanterre La Defense, FR; SEN / Junior Achievement Greece, GR; Maria Curie Sklodowska University, PL; University of Helsinki, FI; European University College Association, BE; Universität Bremen, DE; University of Dundee, UK; Fundacio per a la Universitat Oberta de Catalunya, ES; Politecnico Di Milano, IT

Project representative to be contacted for further info: Matteo Uggeri (info-eL4w@eden-online.org)

eLene4work strives to help students and new entrepreneurs develop soft skills (such us the capacity to deal with a problem in a creative way, learning to learn, the ability to work in team, to communicate clearly and effectively, to adapt to different cultural contexts, to solve problems, to manage conflicts, to show endurance in complicated or stressful situations, etc.) often required by companies of all sizes. The eLene4work outputs and services, therefore, will also help companies exploit the digital talents of young employees. The project proposes a strategic partnership whose goal is to test and monitor the possibility offered by MOOCs and OER to address the demand for digital soft skills (like e-collaboration, digital communication, social network participation, social media management and web 2.0 activities in general) formally not taught at universities but desirable by most employers on the labour market.

The aim of the eLene4work project is to allow students to:

- autonomously identify their own:
  - gaps in soft skills and competences, in order to develop or improve them;
  - potential in digital soft skills, to increase their professional attractiveness on the labour market.
- autonomously learn how to:
  - fill their skill gap using MOOCs (and other OERs);
  - include in their CV their soft skills and digital soft skills in order to enhance the opportunity to enter the labour market.

Students will learn to learn how to use and exploit their own digital competences and soft skills on the labour market.

Main target groups of the project: The various project outputs are being developed to bridge a clearly identifiable gap between what employers seek and job seekers can offer in terms of today's essential digital skills. From the educational point of view both VET institutions and universities (deans, presidents, rectors, teachers as well as students) will benefit from the eLene4work services, while on the other hand managers, HRs, entrepreneurs, chambers of commerce and company associations are also primary target stakeholders. The project's secondary target audiences include instructional designers, e-learning experts, researchers and policy makers.

Significant public results:

The *eLene4work self-evaluation tool* is an online questionnaire for students' self-assessment of soft skills and digital soft skills with a final "Personal development plan" included in order to indicate which actions will be undertaken and which courses will be followed to fill the perceived 'gap'.

The *Orientation tool for students and young workers* is a coordination tool specifically developed for the students, who will approach their personal development in soft skills and soft skills 2.0, drawn on the results produced within the project (primarily the Comparative analysis on state of the art of soft skills and soft skills 2.0, the 2 rounds of Focus groups) and a set of resources where the students can refer to their personal development.

The *Personal Journal* is a template to give a method to students about how to learn autonomously and further develop themselves and to evaluate the whole learning path held through the MOOCs.

Finally, the *Lesson learned kit* is a set of recommendations targeted at different groups, with a collection of all the experience developed within the project, with a particular attention to the filled evaluation of the students' learning experience and the tutoring and monitoring of the students' path.

TECHN OPEN COMM

MERIT – Manufacturing Education and Research with Information Technology

UNIVERSITY WEST

Work-Integrated Learning and Technology Enhanced Competence Development for Experts in the Manufacturing Industry

Website: http://www.ptw.hv.se/en/projects/ongoing-projects/technology-enhanced-learning-at-advanced-level-for-engineers-merit

Runtime: 04.2013 – 12.2015, further applications are submitted for more funding.

Supported / co-funded by: In partnership with the Swedish Knowledge Foundation.

Partners: Swedish partners; University West in collaboration with GKN Aerospace Sweden, VBG Group Truck Equipment, Combitech, Siemens Industrial Turbomachinery, Spicer Nordiska Kardan (Dana Holding Corporation), Industrial Development Centre, Innovatum development foundation and Swerea IVF.

Project representative to be contacted for further info: Monika Hattinger (monika.hattinger@hv.se), Kristina Eriksson (kristina.eriksson@hv.se)

The manufacturing industry is challenged by increasing global competition, high level of customer needs, shorter product cycles and reduced production time and therefore require expert knowledge for an effective production. A prerequisite is to continuously plan for advancement of skilled employees to achieve high performance in everyday work. Learning through work can be combined with formal education outside the company to meet knowledge requirements, but as time and place is limited there is a need for flexible and digital learning. Thus we argue for competence development through work-integrated learning (WIL) supported by e-learning in collaboration with higher education.

In this action research project the aim is to design and offer e-learning courses with engineering content that is co-created between the Production Technology Centre (PTC) at University West together with collaborating manufacturing companies in Sweden. WIL is described as an umbrella term including different approaches concerning learning through integration of theory with practice of work within a purposefully designed curriculum. Our definition of e-learning includes: *interaction and learning technologies* for distribution and communication of learning content as LMS, web-meeting systems etc. and, *digital learning content* as instructional video, tutorial guides, wikis etc.

Over a period of 24 months the PTC project group of 15 engineering and informatics researchers collaborated in a network with about 15 industry stakeholders. Initial project focuses were competence mapping and collaborative relations between industries and higher education (i.e. PTC) to explore companies' e-learning readiness. Initially, we conducted 16 semi-structured interviews with 27 HR managers and manufacturing managers that resulted in a broad variation of awareness, e-learning maturity, dynamic capability and co-creativity. Continual research actions were and still are, company seminars for competence mapping and discussions of courses, resulting in design principles for e-learning courses. Also, to assist engineering teachers in their design and course content development, regular ICT-seminars with pedagogical and technical issues were offered. Following the challenging teaching situation to digitalize engineering knowledge content, we explored five teachers' experiences and ideas of e-learning through an interview study.

The first three courses in industrial automation, machining and negotiation skills (2.5 ECTS each), were completed during spring and autumn 2014. In total 36 industry employees participated in courses with only four drop outs. Through formative assessment actions we followed up the courses and concluded with a focus group workshop (respectively). Discussions from these sessions show diverse perspectives on design and use of digital learning material as instructional video, digital assessment and web-meeting systems. Some participants emphasize the importance of on-line chat and discussion forums for learning and encourage teachers to use such applications. In a recent submitted conference paper to American Conference of Information Systems (AMCIS), we summarize these results which show a broad interpretation and usefulness of realized actions in the e-learning artifact and in the project collaborations. Different learning levels and learning fields are interrogated and negotiated through new types of technological artifacts and e-learning IT-facts as boundary objects can give opportunities for new learning. Still there is a continual need to design and develop more digital learning content as well as deepen the use of communication technologies. During 2015 we continue the design work of additional courses through competence mapping actions to develop design knowledge and experiences of e-WIL courses in collaboration with manufacturing companies. We recommend further research on how learning actions are integrated and transformed in the workplaces that will strengthen co-constructive actions leading to transformative learning in the workplace.

Emerging challenges within the engineering field where we seek collaboration and knowledge sharing are; virtual labs, digital course content (in English) as creative commons, digital project cases, tutoring and sharing of 3D-applications on-line, successful on-line didactics and work-integrated learning experiences.

Main target groups of the project: Employees, mainly engineers within manufacturing industry

Significant public results:

Hattinger, M.; Eriksson, K.; Malmsköld, L.; Svensson, L. (2014). E-learning Readiness and Absorptive Capacity in the Manufacturing Industry. In *International Journal of Advanced Corporate Learning (iJAC), 7(3),* (pp. 33-40).

Hattinger, M.; Spante, M.; Ruijan, D. (2014). Mediated and Situated Engineering Education. In *Proceedings of World Conference on E-Learning in Corporate, Government, Healthcare, and Higher Education 2014,* Chesapeake, VA: AACE.

POLICY RECOGN OPEN INFORM

ADOERUP

Adult Education and Open Educational Resources

Website: http://poerup.referata.com/wiki/ADOERUP

Runtime: 12.2014-03.2015

Supported by: European Parliament, Culture and Education Committee

Partners: Sero Consulting Ltd (UK); experts from Sweden, Hungary and Latvia

Project representative to be contacted for further info: Paul Bacsich (paul.bacsich@sero.co.uk)

In 2013 the European Commission published a communication on OER and MOOCs. This was the subject of a report in the European Parliament's Culture and Education Committee. The EP pointed out that "OERs geared towards the needs of adult learners should be developed so as to ensure greater lifelong learning opportunities for low-skilled European citizens, bearing in mind... that many learners have low ICT skills".

The goal of this study is to highlight the possibilities offered by OER with the overall aim to: a) Review the availability and feasibility of OER in adult learning, and b) Make suggestions for possible action to be taken.

Specific questions will be addressed, as well:

1. How can OER be integrated into certified courses provided to adult learners? What is their sustainability (in terms of work and funding)?
2. What quality aspects may be considered in the use of OER in adult learning? How OER can improve the quality and efficiency of training and education in adult learning?
3. Is management of Creative Commons licenses specific and in what respect?
4. Do OER improve the knowledge base on adult learning and contribute to a better monitoring of the adult learning sector? If yes, how?
5. How OER can contribute to raising participation rates in adult education?
6. What are the implications for educational planners and decision-makers of use of OER in adult learning? In particular what issues of accreditation/validation could be considered?
7. How existing policy tools to support adult learning can best be used for the inclusion of OER?
8. What is the role of educational establishments to design/plan/implement education based on OER?

Countries studied in detail were:

1. United Kingdom – large population, north, world language also an official language in one other Member State (Ireland); but with minority languages (Welsh, Gaelic) and very different traditions of adult education in the home nations; very active in OER though mostly in England
2. Spain – large population, south, world language; but also with minority languages (Catalan, Basque) and strongly autonomous communities
3. France – large population, west, world language spoken in one other Member State (Belgium) and in other nearby countries (Switzerland, Monaco etc)
4. Sweden – medium population, north, Scandinavia, regional language spoken in one other Member State (Finland)
5. Latvia – small population, east, Baltic States, less used language, and a Russian-speaking minority
6. Hungary – medium population, central, regional language spoken in several other Member States (Romania, Slovakia, Austria) and other nearby countries (Ukraine, Serbia)
7. Romania – large population, east, Romance language spoken also in several nearby countries
8. Germany – large population, central, regional/world language spoken in several other Member States (Austria, Italy, Belgium etc) and nearby countries (Switzerland, Liechtenstein)

Four other EU countries were studied in less detail, as well as Norway, US and Canada.

Main target groups of the project: Adult education staff planning sustainable use of Open Educational Resources in their institutions; policy experts; institutional strategists.

Significant public results: none yet, but there will be a final report to be published in summer 2015 with an Annex on the country studies.

RECOGN TECHN ASSESS INFORM

OntoTechnology

OntoTech

Website: http://ontotech.eu

Runtime: 11.2013 – 02.2016

Supported / co-funded by: EU-Funded Lifelong Learning Programme (LLP)

Partners:

- Coordinator: CVO Antwerp, Belgium
- Full partners: University of Amsterdam, Netherlands; Netpositive, Hungary

Project representative to be contacted for further info: **Dr. Gábor Kismihók** (g.kismihok@uva.nl)

The OntoTechnology approach believes in utilizing job knowledge as a predictor of future job performance. Job knowledge, as opposed to disposition, has the major advantage of being malleable, thus allowing a person a centered approach to personnel selection. The main aims and objectives of this project are to provide detailed personalized assessment and training of essential technical competencies and related job knowledge elements that are required for a certain position. Characteristics of the consortium: Center of Job Knowledge Research (University of Amsterdam), CVO Antwerpen, Netpositive Ltd.. A general description of outcomes includes: – a customizable, adaptive job knowledge test – a general mental ability test – an applicant ranking based on integrated job knowledge and GMA test performance – an automatic and tailored e-Learning content delivery on the basis of test results – a cutting-edge semantic technology for job knowledge structuring, testing and evaluation.

Main target groups of the project: Academia, Industry, Policy

TECHN **OPEN**

ICARD

Individual CAReer Development

Website: http://www.icard-project.eu

Runtime: 09.2014 – 08.2016

Supported / co-funded by: Erasmus+, Strategic Partnership in Higher Education

Partners:

- University of Padova, Italy
- Melius Srl, Italy
- University Alexandru Ioan Cruza, Romania
- University of Maastricht, the Netherlands
- University of Salamanca, Spain
- KU Leuven, Belgium
- Militos Emerging Technologies and Services, Greece
- Queensland University of Technology, Australia

Project representative to be contacted for further info: Gilda Rota, gilda.rota@unipd.it

Drawing from the existing best practice of the Queensland University of Technology (QLD QUT), the ICARD project develops a transversal, transdisciplinary European Career Development Programme (ECDP), a learning programme, covering the entire study cycle. The ECDP aims to provide University students with personalized and systematic guidance and individual support, helping them realise their potential, abilities, competencies, skills and ambitions and build their career path.

Main results of ICARD are:

- Compilation and analysis of the state-of-the-art of available programmes, modules or practices within HEIs promoting self-awareness, self-development and career management of University students;
- Development of the European Career Development Programme, a transversal learning programme aimed at fostering acquisition of professional awareness and career management skills by University students, composed by modules, learning materials, evaluation and assessment tools;
- Piloting of the material in four countries in Europe;
- Preparation of guidelines and recommendations for the adoption of the programme by further universities;
- Raised awareness on the need of a more aware and skilled young workforce.

Main target groups of the project: higher education students

Significant public results: (by June 2015)

- Practices repertoire on approaches and tools to promote acquisition of career development skills;
- Draft of the learning architecture for the ECDP.

LACE

Learning Analytics Community Exchange

Website: http://www.laceproject.eu/

Runtime: January 2014 – June 2016

Supported / co-funded by: FP7

Partners: Open Universiteit Nederland, NL; Cetis, the Centre for Educational Technology and Interoperability Standards at the University of Bolton, UK; Institute for Educational Technology at the Open University, UK; Infinity Technology Solutions, IT; Skolverket, the Swedish National Agency for Education, SE; Kennisnet, NL; Høgskolen i Oslo og Akershus, NO; ATiT, Audiovisual Technologies, Informatics and Telecommunications, BE; EDEN, European Distance Education Network, UK.

Project representative to be contacted for further info: Sally Reynolds (sally.reynolds@atit.be).

LACE partners are passionate about the opportunities afforded by current and future views of learning analytics (LA) and educational data mining (EDM) but we are concerned about missed opportunities, undesirable consequences of mis-application, investment funding failing to realize value, market failure, etc. LACE is our response, a project to reduce risk and to increase benefit through an approach that accounts for the necessary unity of research, policy and practice.

- Organise a range of activities designed to actively and passively integrate communities that are conducting LA/EDM research, early practitioner adopters, and those who are building first-generation commercial or open-source software. This integration is to be used to stimulate creativity and accelerate the identification of viable and effective solutions to real problems, and hence to drive both current research and technology transfer.
- Create and curate a knowledge base of evidence. This will capture evidence for the effectiveness and the relative desirability of the outcomes resulting from use of various tools and techniques.
- Actively participate in the exploration of plausible futures for learning analytics and EDM by combining the creation of imaginative scenarios with participatory workshops and structured methods including a Policy Delphi to assess differences of opinion about the feasibility and desirability of possible future states, thus informing future research and policy agendas.
- The LACE project brings together existing key European players in the field of learning analytics & EDM who are committed to build communities of practice and share emerging best practice in order to make progress towards four objectives.

Objectives: (i) Promote knowledge creation and exchange; (ii) Objective 2 – Increase the evidence base; (iii) Objective 3 – Contribute to the definition of future directions; (iv) Objective 4 – Build consensus on interoperability and data sharing.

Main target groups of the project: Researchers, practitioners and stakeholders interested in learning analytics and how learning analytics can be used to enhance ICT-supported learning in particular. LACE targets schools, higher education and workplace learning separately while helping to support cross-sector learning and exchange where relevant in the area of learning analytics.

Significant public results:

Conference and event presentations

Workshops and learning opportunities both on and off-line

Community and network support

Evidence hub that aims to gather the evidence about learning analytics, and relate it to a group of propositions

INFORM

Digiskills – Network for the Enhancement of Digital Competence Skills

Sharing Best Practices in Teachers' Professional Development

Website: http://digiskills-project.ea.gr **Good Practices**: http://www.digiskills-project.eu

Runtime: 1 December 2012 – 30 November 2015

Supported / co-funded by: Lifelong Learning Programme – Erasmus; Multilateral projects

Partners: Ellinogermaniki Agogi (EA), GR; Maria Curie Sklodowska University – University Centre for Distance Learning (MCSU), PL; Computer Technology Institute and Press "Diophantus" (CTI); GR; European Federation for quality in e-learning (EFQUEL), BE; European Distance and E-Learning Network (EDEN), UK; Bundesministerium für Unterricht, Kunst und Kultur (BMUKK), A; Fondation Ynternet.org (Ynternet.org), CH; Confederación Española de Centros de Enseñanza (CECE), SP; University of Split, Faculty of Science (USP), CRO

Project representative to be contacted for further info: Eva Suba, suba@eden-online.org

This 3 years long project offers and online platform to share the resources, events and contests for teachers and trainers to meet and discuss their practices. A growing repository of best practices invites teachers and trainers to upload and download, use and test good practices from various educational background. The project also invites teachers from various communities to network and discuss problems and solutions enriching thus their won and each other palette of educational tools and competences

Teachers have been, over the years, constant promoters of innovation in schools. However, when considering the integration of ICT, many do not possess the necessary competences for the pedagogic use of ICT. According to the Opening Up Education Initiative introduced by the European Commission in 2013 only seven countries have 30 to 50% of students at grade 4 and/or grade 8 taught by digitally confident and supportive teachers, with high access to ICT and who face low obstacles to their use at school. Studies also show that 70% of teachers in the EU would like to have professional development on ICT skills. A joint EC-OECD survey shows that six teachers out of ten have not received any training on how to use ICT in the classroom. An urgent emphasis on digital pedagogic competences is also needed during continuing professional development to keep teachers updated. Addressing this challenge is at the heart of interests of several stakeholders who, in the context of the Grand Coalition for Digital Jobs, have already pledged to develop European initiatives at large scale to train teachers in specific skills so as to contribute to boost their digital skills.

Digital competence development for teachers and trainers is the focus of the DigiSkills project. The DigiSkills project funded by the European Commission's Lifelong Learning Programme presents a series of professional development opportunities, and provides a platform for teachers and trainers to show their own scenarios of use of learning tools and methodologies tested in their own classrooms. Teachers and trainers are invited to show their working educational solutions with ICTs in all levels of education and in various settings. Numerous best practices are openly available, downloadable, shareable and are open for everyone to use and see if it works in their own settings.

In the framework of DigiSkills project the consolidation of best practice will be achieved by:

1. **Bringing into the classroom a unique collection of digital resources and tools that are based on real-world problems**. The resources involve students in finding their own problems, testing ideas, receiving feedback, and working collaboratively with other students or practitioners beyond the school classroom. A series of eLearning tools provide scaffolds that enhance learning, support thinking and problem solving, model activities and guide practice, represent data in different ways, and form part of a coherent and systemic educational approach.
2. **Giving students and teachers more opportunities to evaluate the quality of their own thinking and products for feedback, reflection, and revision**.
3. Building local and global communities where teachers, teacher trainers, education policy makers, parents, students, practicing scientists and other interested members of society are included in order to expand the

learning environment beyond the school walls and expand opportunities for teachers' professional development. This includes helping teachers to think differently about students and learning, reduces barriers between students and teachers as learners and creates new partnerships among teachers, students and parents.

The main outcome of the project is the Digital Competence Academy that aims to deliver large scale online professional development courses for teachers in specific areas such as maths, science, technology, rural education, environmental education, use of mobile devices in school practice as well as will support a network of organisations involved in in-service training for teachers. Currently more that 1000 teachers are participating in the Digiskills activities in different European countries.

Participating teachers are asked to provide information for their competence profile according to UNESCO ICT Competency Framework for Teachers (United Nations, 2011). The modules of the DigiSkills Academy are organized in different levels of teachers' competence. Specific modules or courses are proposed to them according to their level. These modules include a series of practical implementations that in the framework of the project are named DigiSkills Best Practices. These are applications that have proven their efficiency in developing teachers' digital competencies and more specifically supporting teachers to become developers of educational content and authors of their own technology enhanced educational scenarios (3rd level of the UNESCO ICT Competency Framework for Teachers). The Digiskills Academy is hosted at the Open Discovery Space Academies Infrastructure that is supporting different aspects of school Innovation (http://portal.opendiscoveryspace.eu/training-academies).

According to our interim evaluation 78% of the 600 registered DigiSkills users agree or fully agree on the proposed Best Practices had significant impact to their professional development; 85% of users agree or fully agree that the DigiSkills Platform is a good environment to exchange Best Practices; 82% of users would recommend the platform to their colleagues and 80% would use the tools provided to develop resources and upload their own lessons and materials to the DigiSkills platform.

METHOD TECHN ASSESS INFORM

SCORE2020

Support Centres for Open education and MOOCS in different Regions of Europe 2020

SCORE2020

Website: http://score2020.eadtu.eu

Runtime: 10.2014 – 09.2016

Supported / co-funded by: Erasmus+ programme, strategic partnerships. Project number: 543516-LLP-1-2013-1-NL-KA3-KA3NW

Partners: Coordinated by EADTU, Netherlands. Other partners are

- Open Universiteit Nederland
- Universidad Nacional de Educación a Distancia
- UNIVERSITETET I TROMSOE
- Univerza v Ljubljana
- Dublin City University
- International Telematic University UNINETTUNO
- Fédération Interuniversitaire de l'Enseignement à Distance

Project representative to be contacted for further info: Darco Jansen, darco.jansen@eadtu.eu

Short description of SCORE2020: SCORE2020 is building on a consortium of regional players in the field of open, online and flexible education. The partnership will set up regional expertise centres for the development and use of MOOCs and open education.

1. The regional expertise centres will promote, stimulate and activate the development and the delivery of MOOCs and other modes of open education as well as use of MOOCs in their region.
2. The regional expertise centres constitute together a European strategic partnership, which is supported by the European OpenupEd MOOCs platform. This will valorise the MOOCs developed in different regions in a broader European and global context. It also will strengthen each of the regional centres by sharing and developing transnational expertise of which each can benefit.

The partnership of SCORE2020 is based on selected partners that already have started with some form of regional structure / governmental support to MOOCs and Open Education. The added value of this partnership is that it represents institutions that already have a structural position in their respective regions in open and online education, and as an institution are strongly connected to the supportive infrastructure in their country. SCORE2020 aims to enhance the collaboration between these national initiatives.

Main target groups of the project: staff and stakeholders of regional support centres for the development and use of MOOCs and open education

Significant public results so far: Need analysis for support in MOOCs and Open Education and Overview existing training and awareness materials

ASSESS

SAILS

Strategies for Assessment of Inquiry Learning in Science

Website: http://www.sails-project.eu

Runtime: 01.2012 – 12.2015

Supported / co-funded by: FP7 Science in Society

Partners: SAILS Coordinator Dublin City University (DCU), see more at http://www.sails-project.eu/portal/partners

Project representative to be contacted for further info: Sally Reynolds (sally.reynolds@atit.be)

Crucial to the development of key competencies in young people is their engagement in the education process. Methodologies such as inquiry based science education (IBSE) have been highlighted as having the potential to increase student engagement in science at primary and second level and provide such development opportunities.

The aim of SAILS is to support teachers in adopting an inquiry approach in teaching science at second level (students aged 12-18 years) across Europe. This is being achieved by utilising existing resources and models for teacher education in IBSE, both pre-service and in-service. In addition to SAILS partners adopting IBSE curricula and implementing teacher education in their countries, the SAILS project is developing appropriate strategies and frameworks for the assessment of IBSE skills and competences and preparing teachers not only to be able to teach through IBSE, but also to be confident and competent in the assessment of their students' learning. Through this unified approach of implementing all the necessary components for transforming classroom practice, i.e. teacher education, curriculum and assessment around an IBSE pedagogy, a sustainable model for IBSE will be achieved. SAILS provides teacher education workshops in IBSE across the twelve participating countries and promotes a self-sustaining model encouraging teachers to share experiences and practice of inquiry approaches to teaching, learning and assessment by building a community of practice.

The SAILS consortium consists of thirteen partner organisations, including universities, SMEs and a multi-national organisation, from across twelve European countries. By using a pan-European approach, SAILS is ensuring that the diverse practices built up in each country can be analysed and shared, resulting in the development of models of best practice. These are being used not only in all the consortium countries but are also being made available for other countries to adopt.

Main target groups of the project: Science teacher educators and trainers in Chemistry, Physics and Biology along with practicing science teachers. The target group also includes stakeholders concerned with innovative science teaching practices and the promotion in particular of inquiry based science teaching.

Significant public results: The main outcomes of SAILS are a series of Teacher Education Programmes developed in the 12 participating countries focussed on effective assessment strategies for Inquiry Based Learning. These programmes are being delivered for both in-service and pre-service teachers.

A second significant outcome of the project is the series of 20 teaching and assessment units which provide an extensive learning scenario and pedagogical guide for each of the 20 topics along with detailed case studies of how these units have been used in different countries. They also include a synthesis of each unit based in the experience of those who used them in the classroom providing examples of evidence tracked, materials used and teaching resources.

OPEN

ODS

Open Discovery Space

Website: http://www.opendiscoveryspace.eu

Runtime: 04.2012 – 09.2015

Supported / co-funded by: The European Union's Information and Communications Technologies (ICT) Policy Support Programme (PSP)

Partners: http://opendiscoveryspace.eu/consortium

Project representative to be contacted for further info: Evangelos Argyzoudis (contact_ods@intrasoft-intl.com)

Open Discovery Space is an innovative, socially powered and multilingual open learning infrastructure and community hub aiming to boost the adoption of eLearning resources.

ODS empowers stakeholders through a single, integrated access point for eLearning resources. The project engages stakeholders in the production of meaningful educational scenarios and activities by using a social-network style multilingual portal, offering eLearning resources as well as services, such as trainings and webinars, for the production of educational activities. ODS also assesses the impact of the new educational activities, which could serve as a prototype to be adopted by stakeholders in school education.

The project contributes to the modernisation of school education, the acquisition of digital competences and the demand for eLearning resources. It also engages teachers and pupils in the development of innovative educational practices, bestowing them with 21st century skills and competences. Most importantly, the project strengthens European integration by increasing state cooperation, bringing together different cultures and supporting multilingual practices.

By becoming ODS members, schools can create digital communities and resource libraries and connect to a vibrant European Network. Teachers can create, share and access lesson plans and scenarios, participate in online training academies as well as summer and winter schools and use self-assessment and professional development tools.

Main target groups of the project: ODS provides helpful solutions for addressing potential digital barriers through networking and further collaboration among K-12 stakeholders (teachers, learners, parents, content and technology providers, and policy makers).

Significant public results:

In March 2015 the ODS professional community consists of 2,756 schools, connecting 7,535 teachers from all over Europe.

Over the past 3 years ODS established an open collection of 807,000+ Open Educational Resources, thousands of which have been created and/or repurposed by the portal's registered members.

The various interrelated project activities facilitated the creation of 530 Learning Communities of teachers for different cognitive interests.

ODS offers online training academies, webinars, summer and winter schools to teachers, content and technology providers, as well as parents.

The project collaborates with a growing number of meaningful educational initiatives (http://opendiscoveryspace.eu/friends-ods). It organises/attends national and European conferences, seminars and workshops to raise awareness and receive feedback and advice from targeted stakeholders, i.e. educational practitioners, school leaders, regional, national and EU policy and decision makers.

In 2014 and 2015 ODS organised a series of two national and Pan-European Contests, where teachers of all kinds of subjects, from science through languages to sports, designed their innovative open learning scenarios. These learning resources were first reviewed by experts from the participating countries, and then the national winners were subjected to open popular votes by their peers and the greater public.

OPEN

The **ODS Final Conference**, organised in connection with the next EDEN Open Classroom Conference, will take place on **18-21 September 2015** in Athens:

- http://www.eden-online.org/eden-events/open-classroom-conferences/athens2015.html
- Community portal: http://www.opendiscoveryspace.eu/
- Facebook page: https://www.facebook.com/opendiscoveryspace.eu?fref=ts
- LinkedIn Group: https://www.linkedin.com/grp/home?gid=8186100
- YouTube channel: https://www.youtube.com/user/OpenDiscoverySpace

METHOD TECHN ASSESS OPEN COMM INFORM

Hands-On ICT

Hands-On ICT: Learn, Practice, Teach Creativity and ICT

Website: http://handsonict.eu/

Runtime: 01.2013 – 04.2015

Supported / co-funded by: Lifelong Learning Programme, KA3 Multilateral projects

Partners:

- Fundació per a la Universitat Oberta de Catalunya, Spain (Coordinator)
- Ellinogermaniki Agogi, Greece
- Open University of the Netherlands, Netherlands
- Euro-Mediterranean University, Slovenia
- MirandaNet Ltd., United Kingdom

Project representative to be contacted for further info: Katerina Riviou (kriviou@ea.gr)

The Hands-On ICT (HANDSON) project aims at facilitating the integration of ICT tools in teaching and learning by developing a learning-by-doing environment to be explored by themselves or with the guidance of a mentor. The environment offers teachers a set of learning activities complemented with 1) the competences it addresses, 2) the lesson plan, 3) the open source ICT tool, 4) the open content, 5) a sandbox for the tool. In addition, teachers find a ready-to-use online space to bring students over to carry out the activities with the appropriate ICT.

In sum, HANDSON is a holistic environment that provides teachers everything they need to learn in relation to the choice making and use of the most suitable ICT tools for a given pedagogical activity while also providing the cloud arena for putting into practice these activities with students.

The initial activities will be based on creativity techniques. By addressing transversal competences in today's knowledge society we reach out to teachers across a wide variety of sectors and subject contents. The HANDSON environment allows for the practice required to really learn a creativity method.

Main target groups of the project: The HANDSON environment main targets are SE and VET teachers and HE faculty members. Teacher trainers are also main users of the project outputs.

Significant public results:

- http://handsonict.eu/
- https://twitter.com/handson_ict
- http://www.youtube.com/watch?v=kjfCy-YEQF8&feature=youtu.be
- Riviou, K., Barrera C.F. and Domingo M.G. "Design Principles for the online Continuous Professional Development of Teachers", 14th IEEE International Conference on Advanced Learning Technologies (ICALT 2014), Athens, Greece, IEEE Computer Society, 978-1-4799-4038-7/14, DOI 10.1109/ICALT.2014.212, pp. 727-731, 7-9 July 2014.

METHOD TECHN

INUITEL

Intelligent Tutoring Interface for Technology Enhanced Learning

Website: http://www.intuitel.eu

Runtime: 10.2012 – 06.2015

Supported / co-funded by: FP7/318496

Partners: http://intuitel.de/partners/

Project representative to be contacted for further info: Christian Swertz (christian.swertz@univie.ac.at), Eran Gal (erang@hit.ac.il), Dan Kohen-Vacs (mrkohen@hit.ac.il)

The objective of INTUITEL is to enhance state-of-the-art Learning Management Systems with individualized recommendations for navigation and feedback on learning strategy. To do so, learner behaviour is monitored and combined with ontologies created by pedagogical experts. Recommendations and feedback are deduced by automatic reasoning.

The educational starting points are the freedom of the individual learner, the open future of the learner and the temporality of teaching and learning processes. The educational objective is to create an environment where the dynamic of the connection between the pedagogical ideas of the teacher and the interests of the learner is increased. To reach this, the metadata system and vocabulary of Web Didactic are used. Web Didactic provides a simple metadata system that differentiates between concept containers (topics) and knowledge objects (content). Concept containers and knowledge objects are both connected by typed relations, where the relation type expresses a specific learning pathway.

With INTUITEL, teachers use the typed relations to express their recommendations for learning pathways. Different learning pathways, like deductive or historically forward between concept containers and multi stage learning and inquiry based learning among knowledge objects, can be suggested in the same course. Learners can pick one of these pathways. Suggestions of the teacher, selections of the learner, log data and profile data are combined to calculate recommendations and feedback. In order to enhance LMSs with the INTUITEL system, interfaces were specified and developed for four example LMSs (ILIAS, MOODLE, CLIX, EXACT). These interfaces provide connectivity for the INTUITEL system and a window were recommendations and feedback for the learner are presented. These interfaces can also be added to an existing course without adding metadata. In that case, only log data and learner profiles are used to calculate recommendations and feedback. To express learning pathways, an external editor has been developed that connects to the LMS through the LMS interface. Additionally, content can be described by attributes like "suitable for blind" or "estimated learning time". If provided, these attributes will be considered to calculate recommendations and feedback.

In INTUITEL, an ontology based approach is used. The system is based on an enhanced OWL framework and an OWL 2 DL reasoning framework. A layered set of ontologies has been developed. The first layer is a pedagogical ontology which instantiates concept containers, knowledge objects and offers a vocabulary for knowledge and media types. The second layer is cognitive maps for knowledge domains where typed links between topics are expressed. The third layer is cognitive content maps where learning content is related to cognitive maps. The fourth layer is a learning model ontology where automatically calculated didactic factors (like repeated calls of one knowledge object by a learner) are expressed. The fifth layer is a learner state ontology where the cognitive position of a learner is represented. Additionally, a ranking system to calculate the next recommendable knowledge objects and to calculate the selection of feedback messages has been developed. To ensure validity of the approach tests with real students were conducted using an INTUITEL mock-up in April 2014. The experiment was focused on real learners' reactions to the INTUITEL recommendations as received by means of an INTUITEL-enabled LMS. 19 students participated in a two phase testing procedure in order to analyze the learners' behaviour INTUITEL, the influence of the tutoring system, and the usefulness of the system in online learning courses as perceived by learners. Results show that students with INTUITEL follow more suitable learning pathways. Besides, the general satisfaction level of participants is increased. Most learners appreciate INTUITEL, would follow its recommendations and consider the messages shown by INTUITEL as useful and caring.

Main target groups of the project: content developers, eLearning providers

Significant public results: http://intuitel.de/resources/

TECHN

CAMELOT

CreAting Machinima to Empower Live Online language Teaching and learning

Website: http://www.camelotproject.eu

Runtime: December 2013 – November 2015

Supported / co-funded by: Lifelong Learning Programme

Partners: University of Central Lancashire, UK; Istanbul University, TR; University of Western Bohemia, CZ; Polish ADL Partnership lab of National Defence University, PL; ICC the international language association, DE; let's talk online sprl, BE; LinguaTV, DE; EduActive, PL; TELL Consult, NL (http://camelotproject.eu/project-consortium/).

Project representative to be contacted for further info: Michael Thomas (Project Coordinator) (mthomas4@uclan.ac.uk), Christel Schneider (Research Assistant for the CAMELOT Project, CSchneider@uclan.ac.uk)

Moving pictures, sound and stories are becoming one of the most powerful ways of communicating learning content in the digital age. An increasing number of learners today across all educational sectors use digital video as the favoured means of communication. YouTube has become the second most popular online community after Facebook and the second largest search engine after Google – not only as a tool of self-expression but also as a tool for learning. CAMELOT derives from the shared interest of the partners in the use of a new generation of cost effective digital video tools and applications to enhance the student experience in an EU language learning context.

The distinctive foci of CAMELOT are evident in four main development areas:

- Language learning in authentic virtual environments with a task-based approach
- Real-time animation video production
- Field testing *machinima* across four educational sectors (school, HE, adult education, and vocational)
- Teacher training course and pilot test

In the CAMELOT Project partners are investigating the use of machinima in task based learning situations. The consortium are making machinima, field testing, researching results of all stages of the project and developing a teacher training to be carried out which will help teachers to be able to make and use their own machinima.

Main target groups of the project: Language educators who wish to learn how to create videos (machinima) in virtual worlds and integrate them into their language teaching.

Significant public results:

- Monthly Webinars: http://camelotproject.eu/webinars/
- Monthly Interviews: http://camelotproject.eu/spot-on-2/
- Monthly Newsletter: http://camelotproject.eu/newsletters/
- Facebook: https://www.facebook.com/camelotprojecteu;
- YouTube Channel: www.youtube.com/camelotprojecteu
- Twitter: www.twitter.com/camelotprojeu
- Information media for download: http://camelotproject.eu/information-media/
  Poster: http://camelotproject.eu/wp-content/uploads/2014/01/CAMELOT_poster_A3.pdf
  Flyer: http://camelotproject.eu/wp-content/uploads/2014/12/FlyerCAMELOT-final-approved.pdf
- Increasing list of Network Partners: http://camelotproject.eu/network-partners/
- Machinima Open Online Training course (MOOT) as stand alone and as facilitated course.
  http://camelotproject.eu/moot-entry-form/
- Sample Training Session: https://youtu.be/ZwYbQ72tyhc

- Report: http://camelotproject.eu/wp-content/uploads/2015/02/2013_3752_PR_CAMELOT_pub.pdf
- CAMELOT AWARDS 2014 http://camelotproject.eu/camelot-award
- CAMELOT AWARDS 2015 http://camelotproject.eu/the-camelot-2015-award/
- CAMELOT received the LinguaTV AWARD in the competition for the best video looking for the funniest German word. https://www.youtube.com/watch?v=A7J3sbH9q08
- Guidelines for teachers using machinima; Templates for scripting
- Training videos for getting involved with creating machinima
- Selection of Videos of Dissemination:
- CAMELOT Presentations: 23 October 2014 in Greece: https://www.youtube.com/watch?v=6gpkQenb0BY&list=UUJhrRl2BKvTEe65ZQ_VAJNg
- International Conference Manchester March 2014: http://youtu.be/1annOiZNFpU
- Eurocall August in Groningen 2014 machinima training session: https://www.youtube.com/watch?v=iNoTinG2Tl8&list=UUJhrRl2BKvTEe65ZQ_VAJNg
- Case Study: Using machinima in a German lesson: https://youtu.be/HA4YzzGG6ck

TECHN INFORM

JamToday

The European Game Jam Learning Hub

Website: http://www.jamtoday.eu/

Runtime: 01.2014 – 12.2016

Supported / co-funded by: CIP – This project is partially funded under the ICT Policy Support Programme (ICT PSP) as part of the Competitiveness and Innovation Framework Programme by the European Community.

Partners: University of the Arts Utrecht (HKU) (Applicant – NL), Dutch Game Garden (Coordinator - NL), MFG Medien-Un Filmgesellschaft Baden-Wuerttemberg MBH (GER), European Network of Living Labs (BE), Clicks and Links Ltd (UK), Innovazione Nelle ICT S.C.A.R.L. (IT), FH Joanneum Gesellschaft M.B.H. (AU), Zürcher Hochschule der Künste (CH), Centro Europeo de Empresas e Innovacion del Principado de Asturias (ES), Conservatoire National des Arts et Métiers (FR), The Glasgow Caledonian University (UK), Fondazione Politecnico di Milano (IT), College of New Technologies (ES), Gemeente Utrecht (NL), Universitaet Linz (AU), ARC Consulting EOOD (BL), Vandejong BV (NL), AGE Platform Europe AISBL (BE), Mathema S.R.L. (IT), Macromedia Hochschule für Median und Kommunikation (GER), Katholieke Hogeschool Limburg VZM (BE), Fundació Privada pel Foment de la Societat del Coneixement (ES), ATiT BVBA (BE), Stockport Metropolitan Borough Council (UK), Eurokleis S.R.L. (IT).

Project representative to be contacted for further info: Coordinator: Pierre Mersch (HKU) – pierre.mersch@hku.nl; presenter here at EDEN: Matteo Uggeri (FPM) – matteo.uggeri@polimi.it

Game-based learning is becoming more and more popular, with many 'serious games' now being developed. But not enough attention is given to how to implement these games in learning environments and how to make sure there are significant learning outcomes. With the JamToday network, we want to use the principles of applied game design not just to create useful and meaningful games, but also to explicate and design the context (such as the classroom or curriculum) in which games can be most effectively implemented and used. In this sense, our task is to help turn learning professionals into educational designers with the help of game design knowledge and practice. Equally, we can help to turn learners into gamebased thinkers and from only being technology users to becoming ICT practitioners, with a corresponding ability to express themselves in videogames as a medium.

Each year, JamToday provides opportunities to collaborate at local, regional, national and European levels by establishing a series of game jams around different themes:

- Improving ICT skills (such as learning coding skills or creating games) – 2014, done.
- Adopting healthier lifestyles (such as healthy eating or changing antisocial behaviour) – 2015
- Supporting learning of mathematics (such as sustaining engagement) – 2016

We aim to provide a bridge between different sectors to guarantee the successful uptake of the next generation of educational games across Europe. And we can offer you the necessary structure, guidance, tools and support to get involved.

Main target groups of the project: students from university and school level, teachers

Significant public results:

- The website: http://www.jamtoday.eu/
- The first year (2014) **'serious game jams' (jamtoday's) all around Europe** and the planned ones for 2015: http://www.jamtoday.eu/game-jams/
- The **games done during the first year jams,** all downloadable for free: http://www.jamtoday.eu/games/
- The **toolkit on how to design and make a 'serious gam jam'**: http://www.jamtoday.eu/toolkit-introduction/ (for registered users only)
- The **JamToday fair** done in Brussels in February 2015: http://www.jamtoday.eu/jamtoday-fair/ (and the following one that will be in Barcelona)
- The Game Scope, which is a tool to allow the structured validation/evaluation of the potential of game prototypes (as an app for Android/IOS and as paper cards): http://www.jamtoday.eu/game-scope/

POLICY OPEN

SharedOER

A Scoping Study on the Potential of Shared, Cross-Border OER and Syllabi in Europe

Website: http://poerup.referata.com/wiki/SharedOER

Runtime: 07.2014-03.2015

Supported by: European Union Joint Research Centre

Partners: Sero Consulting Ltd (UK); IPTS (Spain)

Project representative to be contacted for further info: Paul Bacsich (paul.bacsich@sero.co.uk)

SharedOER is a scoping study on the potential of shared, cross-border OER and syllabi in Europe. It is being carried out for IPTS (Institute for Prospective Technological Studies), part of the Joint Research Centre, the European Commission's in-house science service.

The aim of the SharedOER study is to make an inventory of the existing cases within the context of formal education (focussing on later years in the school sector and early years of higher education) where a core curriculum or syllabus is shared across borders (e.g. state, national, linguistic and cultural). It concentrates on the EU but provides relevant information from the wider global context.

The first part of the study located initiatives and organisations deemed relevant to this domain. It briefly describes what those entities are working on and what have they achieved and published; then summarises the situation.

Secondly, the study focuses on one of the most recent cases, which is the **Common Core State Standards** initiative in the US, providing a case study on it. For the case study, the main focus was to understand the impact that the CCSS initiative is having on the production, reuse and dissemination of OER.

Finally, the study concludes by 'mapping' the domain to identify potential gaps but also innovative approaches and opportunities that may lie undiscovered, in order to better understand the drivers and hurdles that a common syllabi/core curriculum could have on the uptake of OER with the policy context of the European Union.

Main target groups of the project: Educational staff planning sustainable use of Open Educational Resources in their institutions; policy experts; institutional strategists

Significant public results:

1. Deliverable 1: Towards a world tour for Shared OER: Scoping cross-border syllabi/curriculum initiatives in the context of formal education), http://poerup.referata.com/wiki/Towards_a_world_tour_for_Shared_OER, March 2015
2. Deliverable 2: The Common Core State Standards Initiative and its impact on OER, http://poerup.referata.com/wiki/The_Common_Core_State_Standards_Initiative_and_its_impact_on_OER, March 2015
3. Final report (Areas of further investigation focusing on synergies between cross-border syllabi/curriculum and OER in the context of formal education in the EU), to be published by IPTS Summer 2015

OPEN

OEI2

Open Educational Ideas

Open Educational Ideas and Innovations – Towards Open Idea and Innovations Sharing for Learning, Education and Training

Website: http://idea-space.eu

Runtime: 10.2013 – 12.2015

Supported / co-funded by: Lifelong Learning Programme – ERASMUS multilateral projects

Partners: University of Jyväskylä, Finland (coordination); Duale Hochschule Baden-Württemberg, Germany, ESCP Europe Business School Berlin, Germany; National Centre for Scientific Research Demokritos, Greece; Vytautas Magnus University, Lithuania

Project representative to be contacted for further info: Henri Pirkkalainen (henri.j.pirkkalainen@jyu.fi)

The project aims at enabling Open Education at an early stage: instead of sharing complete Open Educational Resources (OER), we aim at sharing ideas in the early design process. This process will create a fundamentally different uptake of OER by creating Emotional Ownership for the resources in progress.

Our approach tackles the main barriers of OER: the not-invented-her syndrome, curricula differences and lack of motivation. In simple words: we bring educators together sharing ideas and early stage developments, so that they can collaborate on open education. This brings a variety of benefits

1. Boosting OER uptake by involving educators at an early stage
2. Creating collaborations between educators across borders
3. Increasing cultural and curricula understanding between educators
4. Creating collaborations and virtual mobility activities

The project is organized as following:

- **Engagement and requirements**: we ran workshops across Europe to create awareness on Open Education – we created future scenarios (how to implement the OEI approach) and gather requirements. The main outcome was an understanding of the needs as well as initial awareness.
- **Idea Sharing Space** allows educators to share/post ideas, find collaborators and – based on OEI – create OER together using our creativity, authoring and collaboration tools.
- **Good practices** are being created in initial trials and larger scale validations, leading to future recommendations.

Main target groups of the project: Educators, learners, educational authorities, and technology providers.

Significant public results:

An online idea space

Publications:

- A theoretical overview on "Emotional Ownership" and "Idea Sharing"
- A good practice guide how to embed to embed Open Educational Ideas into learning and teaching (programmes)

OPEN COMM

OpenPROF

Open Professional Collaboration for Innovation

Website: http://www.openprof.eu

Runtime: September 2014 – August 2016

Supported / co-funded by: Erasmus + KA2

Partners: Lithuanian Association of Distance and E. Learning, Siauliai Vocational Education and Training Centre, Lithuania, The European Distance and E-Learning Network, United Kingdom, Fondo Formación Euskadi, Spain, Auxilium pro Regionibus Europae in Rebus Culturalibus, Austria, Universidade Aberta (UAb), Portugal

Project representative to be contacted for further info: Airina Volungeviciene, LieDM (info@liedm.net)

Designing innovative and sustainable curriculum is a new challenge for the majority of teachers, trainers and adult educators. Professionals supporting innovative services at institutions contribute substantially to developing professional identify, self-esteem, and self-potential. Online learning and open educational resources meet these needs and suggests solutions for innovative, quality work – based learning curriculum designing.

The project addresses key innovations in training of teachers and trainers, as well as adult educators: open educational resource and open curriculum development and licensing, open collaboration, as well as designing curriculum for diverse target groups including the mode of work - based learning. The project aim is to foster open and international professional collaboration for innovation by training them to openly collaborate in the development of online innovative curriculum designing using open educational resources. The requirements raised in this project for the innovation of curriculum will allow creating learning services suitable for diverse learners and target groups, including work - based learning.

Main target groups of the project:

1. Institutional level: teachers and trainers, as well as adult educators at partner institutions'
2. Local and national level: VET / CVET organizations, adult training organizations, companies, higher education institutions
3. International level: European adult learning community consisting of organisations/institutions listed above, Professional networks

Significant public results:

We have recently published the training material on ICT tools:
http://openprof.eu/training-material/Training_material_on_ICT_tools

ECO

ECO Elearning Communication Open-Data

Website: http://www.ecolearning.eu

Runtime: 02.2014 – 01.2017

Supported / co-funded by: CIP Programme / Programme under grant agreement n° 21127

Partners: Coordinator: UNED – Universidad Nacional de Educación a Distancia. The full list of partners is available here: http://ecolearning.eu/partners/

Project representative to be contacted for further info: Stefano Menon (stefano.menon@fondazione.polimi.it)

Open Educational Resources (OER) have the potential to broaden access to education and to improve the quality and cost-effectiveness of teaching and learning in Europe. The best way to put OERs into practice is through Massive Open Online Courses (MOOCs). MOOCs are large-scale courses that represent one of the latest developments in open education, an initiative that is always trying to improve quality, access and equality in education and training.

MOOCs can be implemented in formal, informal and non-formal learning, and make learning ubiquitous. ECO will focus on expanding the most successful experiences with MOOCs in Europe into a pan-European scale. This will be achieved through pilots and demonstrations of the best practices implemented in regional hubs of excellence all over Europe, and also through evaluations of outcomes, results and lessons learnt from them in an open and mobile learning context.

ECO will use leading-edge technology to create a combined MOOC platform – based on individual platforms and resources provided by project partners – making it possible to combine and transfer pilot activities in all the hubs involved.

The expected impact of ECO will be increased by training certified teachers who will be able to create their own online courses and other educational resources and distribute them through the learning platform that comprises all pilots.

Main target groups of the project: teachers and trainers, anybody interested in innovative didactics and the general public

Significant public results:

After the first year of the project 17 new MOOCs have been published and tested in the first of 3 sessions planned. The second session is going to be delivered in April 2015 with some revisions based on feedbacks.

They have been produced in several languages: Italian, French, Spanish, English, Portuguese, Germany.

This is the list of titles:

1. E-Learning-Projektmanagement an Schulen
2. Competências digitais para professores
3. Introdução aos Sistemas de Informação Geográfica
4. Necessidades Educativas Especiais. Como ensinar, como aprender
5. DIY Education aux médias et à l'information
6. MPSW : "Ma pédagogie à la sauce web 2.0"
7. Flipped Classroom
8. Alfabetización Digital para Personas en Riesgo de Exclusión: Estrategias para la Intervención Socioeducativa
9. Comunicación y aprendizaje móvil
10. Sexualidad Amigable y Responsable
11. Innovación Educativa y Desarrollo Profesional. Posibilidades y límites
12. Competencias creativas para el profesorado (Creativity MOOC Camp)
13. Videos for teaching, learning and communication

14. Artes y tecnologías para educar
15. M'appare il mondo: dalle carte alla Terra digitale partecipata
16. Recursos Educativos Abiertos. Aplicaciones pedagógicas y comunicativas
17. Pre-calculus: introduzione alla matematica

The last MOOC published (18) titled "sMOOC Step by Step" is of particular interest because it has been translated in all the 6 languages of the project and it has been designed to support teachers that wish to become active agents in the production of sMOOCs.